GROUND WATER

GROUND WATER

ROBERT BOWEN
Ph.D., B.Sc.

Exploration Consultants Limited
Harleyford, Marlow, Buckinghamshire, UK

APPLIED SCIENCE PUBLISHERS LTD, LONDON

HALSTED PRESS DIVISION
JOHN WILEY & SONS, NEW YORK

First published in 1980 in Great Britain by
Applied Science Publishers Ltd

British Library Cataloguing in Publication Data

Bowen, Robert
    Ground water.
    1. Water, Underground
    I. Title $TD\ 403$. $B8$
    551.4'9   ~~GB1003.2~~   79-41727

ISBN 0-85334-864-2 (APPLIED SCIENCE PUBLISHERS)
ISBN 0-470-26940-5 (WILEY)

WITH 19 TABLES AND 25 ILLUSTRATIONS

© APPLIED SCIENCE PUBLISHERS LTD 1980

Published in the U.S.A. by
Halsted Press, a Division of
John Wiley & Sons, Inc.,
New York

Printed in Great Britain by Galliard (Printers) Ltd, Great Yarmouth

Contents

Introduction

Next to air, water is the most essential of Man's requirements for life and most fresh water is located underground. Its place in the planetary water balance is indicated in Table I.1 which is derived from R. L. Nace and H. W. Menard.[1,2] The global water balance will be considered later in Chapter 13.

GROUNDWATER p. 1

The amount of water necessary to society has increased as populations and urbanisation have, hence the development of subterranean water supplies has received a stimulus. The resolution of accompanying problems becomes ever more significant therefore and many new techniques have been devised and are discussed. These relate to such matters as the occurrence and movement of ground water, the improvement of extraction methodology, conservation, and the value of heat which originates in the crust and mantle of the Earth and produces geothermal water which can be employed in such diverse activities as electrical power production and space and process heating. There is no doubt that the demand for ground water for a variety of purposes will continue to grow, so that probably knowledge of its hydrology will also continue to augment.

On a point of semantics, it might be as well to clear the air immediately. Subterranean water from the saturated strata is sometimes referred to as *ground water* and sometimes as *groundwater*, and in fact there has been much discussion as to which version is more acceptable. The author prefers the former. If groundwater is to be utilised, why not riverwater or lakewater or, for that matter, soilmoisture or geothermalwater? Such a degradation of the English language appears to be most undesirable. Consequently, *ground water* will be retained.

The plan of the book is to begin with some basic considerations regarding voids (openings) in rocks since without these, water could not be stored in or

1

GROUND WATER

TABLE I.1

THE DISTRIBUTION AND RESIDENCE TIME OF VARIOUS CONSTITUENTS OF THE PLANETARY
WATER BALANCE

Item	Volume (km^3)	Percentage of total	Residence time (years)
Supply			
Oceans	$1·37 \times 10^9$	97·2	40 000
Icecaps, glaciers	$29·2 \times 10^6$	2·13	10 000
Ground water down to 4 000 m	$8·35 \times 10^6$	0·59	5 000
Fresh water lakes	125×10^3	0·008 9	100
Saline lakes, inland seas	104×10^3	0·007 4	100
Soil moisture and vadose water	67×10^3	0·004 75	1
Atmosphere	13×10^3	0·000 92	0·1
Rivers (average instantaneous volume)	$1·25 \times 10^3$	0·000 09	1
Total	$1·41 \times 10^9$	100	
Budget			
Annual evaporation from oceans	350×10^3	0·026	
Annual evaporation from land	70×10^3	0·005	
Total annual evaporation	420×10^3	0·031	
Annual precipitation on oceans	320×10^3	0·024	
Annual precipitation on land	100×10^3	0·007	
Total annual precipitation	420×10^3	0·031	
Annual runoff to oceans	32×10^3	0·003	
Annual ground water outflow to oceans	$1·6 \times 10^3$	0·000 1	
Total annual runoff and outflow	$33·6 \times 10^3$	0·003 1	

transmitted through them. The fundamental aspects of aquifers, subterranean water-bearing reservoir beds, and the employment of nuclear techniques in relation to them are described and the actual chemical quality of the water concerned is examined. Ground water basins are described. The artificial recharge of aquifers and sea water intrusion into them are discussed and the role of ground water in construction is assessed. Then, surficial and subsurface investigational methods are examined. The interrelationship of ground water and heat to produce geothermal energy is analysed. Ground water and the law is a matter of great importance and it is referred to in the last part of the book. This also contains a part devoted to ground water modelling and one concerning water balances. The Appendix comprises a set of sections on such matters as a dictionary of water terms, an index of relevant organisations and some representative porosities and permeabilities for some geologic materials.

The book is primarily concerned with ground water, but other parts of the hydrologic cycle are referred to because they have a bearing on this subject. In fact, it is permissible to think of water in general as being divisible into two categories, namely water in the atmosphere and water in the lithosphere and circulation in these regions is an interconnected process, one of dynamic nature as opposed to static phenomena such as storage of moisture in the air and moisture transfer at the surface.

Water circulation in the atmosphere is very important because it involves the transport of moisture and this is a determinant of climatic differentiation. Comparisons of annual average precipitation and evaporation totals for latitude zones demonstrates that in low to middle latitudes, precipitation exceeds evaporation, the reverse being the case in the subtropics. The consequent regional imbalance is maintained by net moisture transport into (convergence) and out of (divergence) the respective zones (ΔD, where divergence is positive) so that, if E is evaporation and P precipitation, then

$$E - P = \Delta D$$

Water circulation in the lithosphere commences with the deposition of precipitation on the ground. This is then distributed in three ways, namely by re-evaporation or by running off to the oceans or by percolation into the soil. The last two stages may be delayed for days, weeks or even months where the precipitation falls in the form of snow. It is relevant to mention that, according to season, snow accumulation occurs on 14–24% of the surface of the Earth (about two-thirds on land and one-third on sea ice). The global detention of water on land, i.e. as snow accumulation, stream runoff and soil moisture, attains its maximum value in the period March–April. The seasonal variation in this detention is paralleled by an inverse pattern of oceanic storage so that in October, for instance, the oceans are estimated to possess $7 \cdot 5 \times 10^{18} \, cm^3$ more water than in spring, equivalent to a sea level change of only 1 or 2 cm.

In this situation, the residence time of water on land is short, about 10 to 100 days although glaciers and ice caps have storage times of the order of years. Similarly, ground water is a stable component of the hydrologic cycle. Most of it represents precipitation which has percolated through the soil layers into a saturated region where all openings in rocks are filled. On average, ground water contributes about a third of total runoff.

All of these matters reflect the significance of the hydrologic cycle which is discussed in the first chapter and later and which is definable as a series of transformations taking place in the circulation of surface waters to atmospheric to ground (as precipitation) and back to surface and subsurface waters. The hydrologic cycle is a vast natural system of water interchange, therefore, but it is also one with a tremendous impact upon society and has a technological significance which is almost impossible to over-estimate. For instance, in the USA, it is believed that about *one-tenth* of the national wealth is located in capital structures designed to *alter* the hydrologic cycle; to collect, divert and place in storage about 25% of the available surface water, distribute it where it is required, transport it and return it to the natural system.[3] Associated technical structures are everywhere and include dams and reservoirs, canals and sewers and some especially orientated towards ground water exploitation. As regards this latter, many authorities may become involved, for instance again in the USA, there are over 18 000 municipal water supply systems and around 8000 industrial water supply systems. Then too, there are geothermal waters which are utilised on a large scale in California and elsewhere. Of these, the writer has described a number, including The Geysers, in *Geothermal Resources* also published by Applied Science Publishers Ltd, London, but some reference to them is also made in this book, see Chapter 10.

Water, particularly ground water, is a resource of first importance, therefore, truly what Pliny in his *Olympian Odes* referred to as 'the best of all things' and it is hoped that the present book will be of use to as wide a spectrum of those interested as possible.

REFERENCES

1. NACE, R. L., 1967. Water resources: a global problem with local roots. *Environmental Sci. Tech.*, **1**, 550–560.
2. MENARD, H. W. and SMITH, S. M., 1966. Hypsometry of ocean basin provinces. *J. Geophys. Res.*, **71** (18), 4305–4325.
3. CHORLEY, R. J. and KATES, R. W., 1976. *Introduction to Physical Hydrology*, ed. Richard J. Chorley. Methuen, p. 3.

CHAPTER 1

The Significance of Interstitial Openings in Rocks

Hydrologists and hydrogeologists are interested in rocks because of their voids, i.e. their interstitial openings, spaces which act, potentially or in fact, as conduits for water movement and/or as places for water storage. These two aspects constitute very important factors in ground water studies and are defined as permeability and porosity. Of course, the mineralogical, structural and other characteristics of rocks are also highly significant in that, collectively, they delimit the geological framework of any hydrological system, particularly an aquifer. Hence, geological analyses provide basic data essential to water studies in rocks.

Some fundamental considerations may be examined at this point. Firstly, the concept of 'rocks' ought to be looked at, because the term has somewhat differing connotations for different people. To a geologist, a rock comprises a mass of mineral material, an assemblage of mineral grains, consolidated or not. A piece of granite, therefore, is thought of as a rock, but so is a handful of sand. While the latter may be composed sometimes entirely of, say, quartz, the former is more complex. Rocks comprising only one mineral species are said to be monomineralic in contrast to those consisting of several, for instance the granite alluded to above. In civil engineering practice, however, rocks are thought of as hard, consolidated and able to bear a load. Thus, something like a granite, which has to be blasted or at the very least drilled in order to remove it, may be taken properly to be a rock. Handfuls of sand or silt clearly fall outside the category on this view. Here, the geological definition will be used, since it fits the purpose of the book better.

1.1. PERMEABILITY AND POROSITY

Passing on to permeability and porosity, the former may be considered as having a meaning often coinciding with that of perviousness. A rock is said to be permeable if water or any other liquid contacting its upper surface can pass through to its lower surface. In nature, this is usually effected primarily in a semi-horizontal direction (except for loess† in which movement is predominantly sub-vertical). Perviousness is a special case of permeability whereby the water or other liquid travels through mechanical discontinuities such as joints, faults or other fractures (occasionally including bedding planes). Porosity is quite different in that it refers to water content and not to water movement. A rock is said to be porous if it contains holes between mineral grains, i.e. voids, capable of containing water or some other liquid. This void space is defined by the porosity and also by another concept, the void ratio. This latter may be defined as the ratio of the space not occupied by solid particles to the volume of solid particles. It may be added that there is a quantity relating permeability to unit conditions of control and this, normally written K, is called the coefficient of permeability. The relation is:

$$K = \frac{Q}{A}\frac{L}{h} = \frac{v}{i} \quad \text{(Darcy's law)}$$

where Q is the amount of water per unit time, A the gross cross-sectional area through which flow occurs, h the pressure head loss, L the distance through which head is lost, v the discharge velocity, i the hydraulic gradient, i.e. ratio between head lost and distance in which it is lost. Incidentally, the state of water movement on which permeability depends is termed percolation.

As regards porosity and void ratio, these may be expressed as follows:

$$n = \frac{V_v}{V_t} = \frac{e}{1+e}$$

$$e = \frac{V_v}{V_s} = \frac{n}{1-n}$$

---

† Loess is a word used to describe accumulations of wind-blown dust which is mainly siliceous and derived from arid regions or vegetation-free zones around ice sheets. Loess is well graded and possesses a particle size range normally of from $\frac{1}{16}$ to $\frac{1}{32}$ mm. It does not show stratification as a rule, but does have well-developed vertical jointing.

where n is the porosity, e the void ratio, V_t the total volume, V_v the v
voids, V_s the volume of solids.

It is apparent that the above-mentioned index properties of soils and rocks are basic to the study of ground water. Permeability is especially important because it is the fluid conductivity, the capacity of the particular rock to transmit water under the influence of a pressure gradient. This movement occurs as a result of the presence of holes in rocks. However, only some of these contribute significantly to permeability and it has been shown that in a large body of near-homogeneous rock, permeability is statistically related to porosity.[1] Nevertheless, the magnitude of storage and flow is usually estimated without reference to porosity. In such an isotropic, porous mass, the nature and number of openings will probably be rather similar throughout the rock. They may be classified with regard to the time and origin of their enclosing rock as primary, e.g. intergrain pores in loose sands or gas vesicles in basalt, or secondary, e.g. systematic joint systems in limestones or openings in fault zones. Of course, all such openings are subject to later modification as a result of erosional and sometimes tectonic forces. Consequently, for instance, joints may become infilled with clay or they may be widened by solution. Clearly, interconnections are extremely important, facilitating, as they do, water movement. In the field, homogeneous rock masses are rather rare and differences between the porosities of adjacent rock masses common. Such porosity boundaries should be considered as just as important in hydrology as lithological boundaries between different rock types are to the geologist.

Two hydrological rock types exist, therefore, namely porous homo-geneous ones and porous heterogeneous ones. Of course, this is really a simplification and intergrading between them is to be expected and does occur. Sand, silt and other such loose materials together with some consolidated rocks such as sandstones, are quite homogeneous as regards porosity. Heterogeneous rocks, on the other hand, usually possess less openings and these are normally rather variable, both in size and shape. Crystalline rocks such as granite, totally lack intergrain porosity as a rule and can transmit water only when jointed or faulted. A similar state of affairs exists in carbonate rocks and here fracturation may expand through solutional effects.

Probably it is best to regard rocks as forming a continuous series in respect of porosity.

It is relevant here to point out that samples having similar grain packing patterns have the same porosity irrespective of the diameters of these grains. In the following discussion, spherical grains are postulated for simplicity and their volumes may then be computed from

$$V = \tfrac{1}{6}d^3$$

where d is the diameter of the sphere.

To illustrate, two samples may be taken, both with cubic packing. One has grains of 0·5 mm diameter and the second has grains of 1 mm diameter. It may be assumed that the grain centres lie at the intersections of a cubic network with cell dimensions equalling the grain diameters. The respective grain volumes will be, therefore, in the first case

$$V = \tfrac{1}{6}0·5^3 = 0·021\,\text{mm}^3$$

and in the second case

$$V = \tfrac{1}{6}1^3 = 0·166\,\text{mm}^3$$

The respective cell volumes will be computed from the respective sides which are 0·5 mm and 1 mm, so that they turn out to be in the first case

$$0·125\,\text{mm}^3$$

and in the second case

$$1\,\text{mm}^3$$

Thereafter, taking, say, 100 such cells and grains, porosities may be derived as follows, where n_1 is the porosity of the first case and n_2 the porosity of the second case

$$n_1 = (100 \times 0·125) - (100 \times 0·021)$$
$$= 12·5 - 2·1 = 10·4 \quad \text{i.e. } 83·2\%$$
$$n_2 = (100 \times 1) - (100 \times 0·166)$$
$$= 100 - 16·6 = 83·4\%$$

and are seen, in fact, to be practically the same. This, despite the different grain diameters.

In practice, the determination of the porosity of granular materials is made by saturating a dry sample with water in order to find out the volume of the pores. Here

$$n = 100\frac{W}{V}$$

where n is the porosity (in percentage by volume), W the volume of pore space (in fact, the volume of water taken up by the dry sample) and V the bulk volume of the sample.

Appropriately, an instance may be given. If a sandstone specimen weighed 80·4 g in air and 84·08 g after immersion in water and its volume is 32 ml, then

$$n = 100\frac{3·68}{32} = 11·5\%$$

1.2. SOIL CLASSIFICATION

Classification of soils is important because of their variability in performance characteristics and these include not only porosity and permeability, but also shearing strength and compressibility. Various approaches to the problem have been made. In 1952, the U.S. Department of the Interior, the Corps of Engineers and A. Casagrande of Harvard modified the latter's Airfield Classification to produce the Unified Soil Classification. From this are excluded gains exceeding 3 in diameter and this category includes both cobbles (from 3 to 12 in diameter) and boulders (more than 12 in diameter).

In the scheme, there are two divisions, namely coarse and fine grains. The dividing line is No. 200 sieve size, i.e. 0·074 mm, and further subdivision gives

G (Gravel)	3 in to No. 4 sieve,($\frac{3}{16}$ in)
Coarse	3 in to $\frac{3}{4}$ in
Fine	$\frac{3}{4}$ in to No. 4 sieve ,
S (Sand)	No. 4 sieve to No. 200 sieve
Coarse	No. 4 sieve to No. 10 sieve
Medium	No. 10 sieve to No. 40 sieve
Fine	No. 40 sieve to No. 200 sieve
M (Silt)	
C (Clay)	

Silts may be separated from clay on the basis of grain size and this has been fixed by some at 5 μm (0·005 mm) and by others at 2 μm (0·002 mm). However, engineering properties do not seem to depend upon particular grain sizes. Hence, there is not a real size distinction in the Unified Soil Classification system, the two materials being rather distinguished by their behaviour. Clays are cohesive and complex, acidic alumino-silicic in nature with a structure reflecting layerings of various thicknesses. They act like Bingham bodies and are thixotropic.

Soils may be well graded (W) or poorly graded (P). As well as the grains and air, they often contain water and the quantity of this produces three main consistencies. These are as follows:

(i)   Liquid: the soil is either in suspension or behaves as a viscous fluid.
(ii) Plastic: the soil is deformable without elastic rebound.
(iii) Solid: the soil cracks on deformation or elastically rebounds.

These three primary states of soil consistency are normally described with reference to the fraction of a soil smaller than the No. 40 sieve size, i.e. the upper limit of the fine sand component. For this particular soil fraction, the water content, as a percentage of dry weight, at which the soil passes from the liquid into the plastic state is termed the liquid limit. Likewise, the water content of the soil at the boundary between the plastic and the solid state is called the plastic limit. The difference between liquid and plastic limits constitutes the plasticity index and this corresponds to the range of water contents within which the soil is plastic. The above-mentioned limits comprise the famous Atterberg limits and they are used to distinguish between clays (plastic) and silts (non-plastic or only slightly plastic).

It may be useful now to examine two specific aspects of porosity. These are the factors controlling this property in a granular rock and the additional concept that only a fraction of the water actually stored within a porous rock is able to move under gravity and, therefore, to drain from or in some way to be extracted from the said rock.

The type, number, shape, total volume and degree of interconnection of voids in any porous granular rock clearly determine its water-bearing and water-transmitting capacities. The difficulty is that to measure all of these characteristics is not always a straightforward matter. It is not surprising to find that many studies have been made on artificial aggregates (usually with spherical grains) and samples of natural materials such as sands.

Specific yield may be examined. Obviously, the volume of water stored in a saturated porous rock expressed as a percentage of the total volume of the rock, equals the porosity of the rock. As regards recoverable water, of course, a volume less than that of porosity is involved as a result of the fact that only a fraction of the water in voids is free to move under gravity. The balance of the water is held in voids in opposition to this force. Molecular and surface tensional forces are responsible. Specific yield, S_y, constitutes the water which can be drained and is a definite fraction of the porosity of a body of saturated rock or an aquifer. Its complement is specific retention, S_r, the ratio given as a percentage of the volume of water which a porous rock will retain after saturation and in opposition to gravity. If the volumes of water retained and drained are given by V_r and V_y, then

$$S_r = \frac{100V_r}{V} \quad \text{and} \quad S_y = \frac{100V_y}{V}$$

Specific yield in aquifer rocks may be determined by a variety of methods, both in the laboratory and in the field. Thus, a sample may be collected, saturated and drained or the volume of sediments drained by pumping a known amount of water from a well may be determined. It may be useful at this point to consider permeability in greater detail, since it is a parameter intimately related to voids, openings, pores and cavities in rocks and soils.

1.3. DARCY'S LAW

The significant empirically derived statement of the phenomenon is given by Darcy's law and the writer has indicated in a previous book that there are certain limitations to this.[2] One statement of the law is given above on p. 6. Another is

$$K = \frac{Q}{A(\mathrm{d}h/\mathrm{d}L)}$$

where Q is the flow rate, A the cross-sectional area of flow and $\mathrm{d}h/\mathrm{d}L$ the hydraulic gradient, K the coefficient of permeability. Rearrangement of this gives

$$Q = KA\frac{\mathrm{d}h}{\mathrm{d}L}$$

and from this

$$\frac{Q}{A} = K\frac{\mathrm{d}h}{\mathrm{d}L}$$

and

$$\frac{Q}{A} = V$$

V being the discharge per unit area, termed a volume flux. Although V has the dimensions of velocity, it must not be confused with the velocity of ground water movement. As V is really a measure of discharge per unit area, the flow velocity is equal to V only in the case where the cross sectional area

A is completely open to flow. The fluid will pass through the open spaces between grains and the open spaces, i.e. the porosity, comprise normally from one-quarter to half of the total volume of a granular, porous material. Hence for unconsolidated sediments, the velocity of flow is about two to four times the volume flux. Representing the porosity by n, the velocity of ground water movement through a sediment is given by

$$v = \frac{K \, dh}{n \, dL}$$

See also Chapter 2, section 2.15.

Henri Darcy was a French hydraulic engineer who looked into the flow of water through horizontal beds of sand intended for water filtration.

In 1856, he proposed his law, based upon the observation that the volume of water flowing through such a bed of sand is proportional to the pressure and inversely proportional to the bed's thickness. Essentially, the law is one of percolation and flow of this type is laminar in nature. Laminar flow is placid and is referred to as viscous flow. In pipes, it takes place when the Reynolds number, N_R, i.e. velocity times diameter divided by viscosity, is less than 2000. As has been indicated, cigar smoke may be taken to illustrate both laminar flow and also turbulent flow. Initially, it is smooth, later swirling.

In regard to permeability studies, clearly the water flows in strata not in pipes and here the relation

$$N_R = \frac{\rho v d}{\mu}$$

is used. Here, N_R is the Reynolds number, ρ the fluid density (which may be ignored), v the velocity, d the average grain diameter and μ the viscosity (unity).

As might be imagined from the preceding discussion, there is no lower limit for Darcy's law because laminar flow can take place at extremely small velocities. However, there is an upper limit. This is determined by plotting a dimensionless Fanning friction factor, f, against N_R.

$$f = \frac{d \, \Delta p}{2 \rho L v^2}$$

where d, ρ, v have the same meaning as above, p is the pressure so that Δp is the pressure difference over a given length of porous media L. Practically, the upper limit is governed by the onset of turbulent flow which by some is thought to commence at a Reynolds number of at least 700.

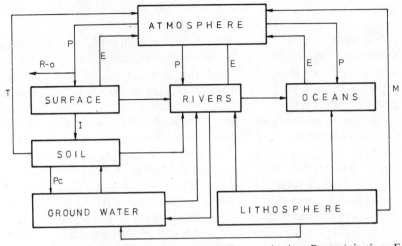

FIG. 1.1.   The hydrologic cycle. R-o, runoff; T, transpiration; P, precipitation; E, evaporation; I, infiltration; Pc, percolation; M, volcanic or magmatic water.

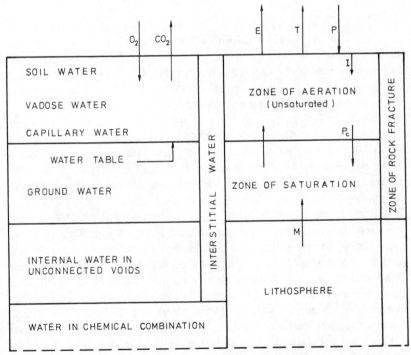

FIG. 1.2.   Ground water in relation to the subsurface water profile. E, T, P, I, Pc and M have the same meanings as in Fig. 1.1.

A defect in Darcy's approach is that his experiments were carried out under isothermal conditions. A method has been proposed, actually by S. Schweitzer in 1974, to extend the law and obtain a first order approximation to the equations governing the motion of flow through a porous medium under non-isothermal conditions.[3]

Reverting now to water in pores and voids of soils and rocks, ground water is that portion of this which occurs in the saturated zone, i.e. it fills all spaces in a geologic stratum. This zone must be distinguished from an overlying unsaturated zone of aeration in which air as well as water occurs in voids. Ground water is an integral part of the hydrologic cycle which, of course, includes atmospheric (meteoric) and surface water as well. The basic elements of the hydrologic cycle are shown in Fig. 1.1. The ground water system and the profile of subterranean water are shown in Fig. 1.2. From this latter, it may be observed that ground water or phreatic water is underlain by water in unconnected voids and this, together with overlying components, constitutes interstitial water.

1.4.   GROUND WATER

Ground water is enormously important to Man. For this reason, it has been developed and used from antiquity. Hence, its utilisation is mentioned in the Bible and kanats, subterranean water tunnels, were used in Egypt and Persia as early as 800 B.C. Springs, which are simply concentrated discharges of ground water at the surface, were also used. For instance, at Nineveh about 700 B.C., King Sennacherib ordered fresh spring water to be conveyed to his palace along an 80 km long waterproofed canal because the Tigris waters were too muddy. Ground water was obtained from wells and tunnels to supply Athens in the fifth century B.C. Water use continually increased. The Romans managed to consume, it is thought, possibly 100 million gallons daily. This is based upon an assumed usage of about 100 gallons per diem per capita and a presumed population of a million or so. However, despite all this, there is no doubt that the mechanics and other aspects of flow were only in part understood by one man, Archimedes. Other ancients had curious ideas. Thus, Aristotle believed that springs result from condensation of air into water in cold, subterranean caverns. However, the Roman architect Vitruvius understood infiltration of precipitation and its subsequent percolation and frequent emergence at mountain bases as streams. The earlier idea that rainfall was insufficient to account for springs was refuted by Pierre Perrault in 1674 as a result of his measurements in the upper Seine drainage basin. A contemporary physicist, Edme Mariotte, confirmed this finding and O. E. Meinzer has said of him that he might well be regarded as the founder of ground water hydrology.[4] Edmund Halley later demonstrated that marine evaporation can easily account for all spring and river flow. In the nineteenth century, of course, came Darcy and his law and important contributions were made by J. Boussinesq, J. Dupuit and others. In the twentieth century, the names of G. Thiem, C. V. Theis, O. E. Meinzer are significant—of course, among a multitude of others. Much of the preceding historical material was derived from D. K. Todd and H. R. Valentine.[5,6]

Ground water derives primarily from surface and meteoric water, but contributions are also received from mantle sources, i.e. magmatic waters. Also, connate water may mingle with it and it is this water which was present in sediments when they were originally deposited and retained after their conversion into sedimentary rock.

1.5.   THE ZONE OF AERATION

As was seen above, ground water is found in permeable, usually granular, geologic formations possessing structural characteristics allowing water movement under normal field conditions. Such water-bearing formations act as ground water reservoirs, aquifers, and these will be examined later in great detail. Investigations both by conventional and isotopic methods will then be described.

Prior to this, it is desirable to analyse vadose water in the zone of aeration. Obviously, the amount of this present in interstitial pores depends upon the soil cover in many cases. Earlier, soil classification was discussed and from this, it is apparent that water will infiltrate successfully through cohesionless materials. Clays and organic matter may arrest the process and much of the original precipitation penetrating the soil layer will be retained and/or remitted back to the atmosphere as a result of evapotranspiration.

That water lying between the surface of the ground and the water table is called vadose (see Fig. 1.2). It underlies soil water proper and, unlike ground water which is entirely free or gravitational, vadose water is in part held in films by rock particles. The rest is also gravitational in nature.

As regards the water table (see Fig. 1.2), this is a plane often reflecting the topography and forming the upper surface of the zone of saturation, therefore constituting the upper surface of ground water. Elevation of the water table, say as a result of unusually high precipitation, may cause it to intersect the land. Springs may result. Clearly, the water table represents the bottom of the capillary zone (see Fig. 1.2).

The capillary zone is a very interesting region of the zone of aeration and perhaps should be regarded as a sub-zone of the latter. It results from rising capillary moisture and it is apparent that the degree of saturation will

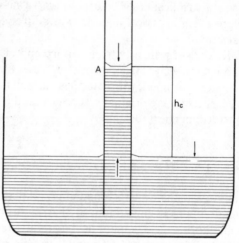

FIG. 1.3. Capillary rise of water in a glass tube. Arrow points mark positions of equal (atmospheric) pressure. h_c is the height to which water rises. Point A below upper arrow tip in tube will be below atmospheric pressure by a quantity equal to the weight of water column above lower arrow tip.

diminish upwards. Where the water table approaches the surface of the ground, saturation of the soil will occur and a swamp may arise.

Above the capillary zone or sub-zone, soil grains will attract water vapour from the atmosphere and hence acquire a film of hygroscopic water vapour. Sometimes, this can be detrimental, for instance in permafrost regions.

Considering a void in the capillary portion of the zone of aeration, if this is treated as a capillary tube, water will rise in it as shown in Fig. 1.3. If the rise is h_c as therein stated, the amount of this will depend upon an equilibrium between the weight of water raised and the surface tension:

$$h_c = \frac{2v}{r\gamma}\cos\lambda$$

where v is the surface tension, γ the specific weight of water, r the radius of the hypothetical tube, and λ the angle of contact between the meniscus and the tube wall, i.e. an angle different from $90°$, clearly.

If v is taken as $0.074\,\mathrm{g/cm}$ at $10°C$, $\gamma = 1\,\mathrm{g/cm^3}$, then

$$h_c = \frac{0.15}{r}\cos\lambda$$

Capillary and hygroscopic forces are responsible for holding non-mobile water in the part of the zone of aeration between the soil and capillary parts in place. Such intermediate water is often referred to as pellicular water.

Naturally, the angle λ is practically nil for pure water on glass and, if this is assumed, water rises of up to several feet in clay may be anticipated. In gravels, rises will be much smaller—a fraction of an inch or so. This variability depends upon the fact that the height of capillary rise is inversely proportional to the diameter of passage. Hence, greater capillary rises will occur in fine-grained materials than in coarse-grained ones.

F. T. Mavis and T. P. Tsui in 1939 gave the maximum capillary rise in inches as approximately determinable by

$$h_c = \frac{2 \cdot 2}{d_{\mathrm{H}}}\frac{(1-n)^{\frac{2}{3}}}{(n)}$$

where d_{H} is the harmonic mean grain diameter in millimetres and n the porosity.[7]

Clearly, the capillary part of the zone of aeration will have an irregular upper surface varying with facies changes and consequent alterations in soil and rock textures.

From the discussion so far, it may be noted that capillarity basically results from the ability of water to wet surfaces with which it comes into contact and also from its surface tension.

However, it must be stressed that theory cannot be extrapolated too far in nature. All that may safely be said is that the upward movement of water from the zone of saturation depends upon grain size expressed as a variable diameter of passage. The maximal diameter is the significant one, but it is almost impossible to assess this under field conditions. Referring to the downward (percolatory) movement of water, the opposite situation is encountered in that it is the minimal passage diameter which is important.

An account of capillary rise in terms of free energy shows that, as soil moisture moves quite spontaneously from saturated to unsaturated regions, the quantity of this in wet soils probably exceeds that of dry soils.

In tubes, the free energy of water below the meniscus at height h above the free water surface is given by

$$\Delta F = -h\gamma_w$$

in which negativity reflects a tensional condition, i.e. a negative hydrostatic pressure with respect to datum. The water is pure with zero free energy.

The factors of porosity and permeability will affect the zone of aeration as well as that of saturation and hence Darcy's law will be equally significant in both.

1.6. K, THE COEFFICIENT OF PERMEABILITY

Some additional information on the factor K, the coefficient of permeability, is now apposite.

It has been shown above that a quantity of water Q flowing in unit time through a cross sectional area A normal to the flow direction is directly proportional to the head loss H associated with the flow and inversely proportional to the thickness of the permeable stratum L so that

$$Q = \frac{KHA}{L}$$

K may be expressed alternatively as follows:

It may be regarded as pertaining solely to the medium, so that

$$k = Cd^2$$

where d is the grain or pore size, C summarising geometric characteristics of the porous medium. Here, permeability refers to length.[2]

Or, it may be regarded as inclusive of both medium and fluid, so that

$$K = k\frac{\rho g}{\eta}$$

where ρ is the fluid density, g the acceleration due to gravity, and η the fluid viscosity.

K, the coefficient of permeability, is sometimes called the coefficient of seepage or, modified from the fluid conductivity alluded to above (see p. 7), the coefficient of hydraulic conductivity. Essentially, K refers to length divided by time, i.e. velocity.

The unit of K is named after Meinzer and is expressed as gallons per day per square foot. A standard temperature of $60\,°F$ ($15\cdot6\,°C$) is used. Of course, in metric countries, the CGS system is used and the coefficient of permeability is given in centimetres per day or metres per day at the same temperature. However, pedologists express it in centimetres per second.

In petroleum work, the darcy is used as a unit depending solely on characteristics of the medium. One darcy (D) refers to a permeability such that 1 ml of fluid with a viscosity of 1 centipoise (cP) flows in 1 second under a pressure differential of 1 atm through a porous material with a cross sectional area of $1 \, cm^2$ and a length of 1 cm.

1.7. PERMEABILITY OF SANDS

This is controlled by the size, shape and degree of interconnection of the voids, factors extremely hard satisfactorily to measure. Nevertheless, they are very important and influence the packing characteristics. It has been demonstrated that permeability may be correlated with the square of a grain size parameter.

M. S. Bedinger in 1961 showed that the field coefficient of permeability (gpd/ft^2) varied from 10–30 for very fine sand to a coarse sand/gravel value of 6000 to 15 000 in alluvial sediments in the Arkansas River valley.[8] (Cf. also section 4 of the Appendix.) Coefficients of transmissibility (i.e. coefficients of permeability times thickness) were also obtained.

Some observations on transmissivity may be made. It is a macroscopic property of an aquifer and refers to the transmission of water throughout the entire thickness. It is defined as the rate of flow of water at the prevailing temperature through a vertical strip of aquifer one unit wide extending the full saturated thickness of the aquifer under a unit hydraulic gradient.[9]

1.8. AQUIFERS

Some amplification on the subject of aquifers will be useful. They are lithologic units or sets of units from which water can be derived in pumped wells or springs. Mostly, they comprise unconsolidated rocks. They may coextend in coincidence with a geological formation or part of one or a group of several. Alternatively, they may transgress formations. Low permeability boundary layers or even inter-stratified beds constitute confining aquicludes. The word aquifuge is occasionally utilised for impermeable formations incapable of either storing or transmitting water, e.g. a solid granite.

Many classifications have been proposed for aquifers. For instance, an approach made by O. E. Meinzer was to arrange them chronologically and following twenty-one physiographic provinces in the USA.[10]

Another way of tackling the problem is to recognise a tripartite aspect, namely into replenishment matters, movement questions and water course complications resulting from hydraulic connection between ground water and surface water.[11] R. G. Kazmann proposed grouping aquifers in accordance with their primary function and recognised the filter plant type, the reservoir type and the mine type.[12] In the first, water intake is critical, in the second recharge–discharge relations are very important and in the third replenishment is small in relation to pumpage.

Of course, aquifers are not just water sources, but also store water and they require extremely careful handling in order to obtain optimal results. Following Kazmann, it may be stated that a practical taxonomic scheme would comprise those:

(i)   maintaining a sustained yield, i.e. where inflow = outflow;
(ii)   mined, i.e. destined for exhaustion;
(iii) transmitting, i.e. to replace canals or surface pipelines;
(iv)   artificially supplied for storage, i.e. by Man.

Obviously, emphasis on discharge of ground water by wells is a highly significant point in classifying aquifers. In the USA, for instance, in the late 1950s, about 15% of the country's water demand was satisfied by such discharge. In 1968, about 20% of national needs was provided by ground water.[13]

1.9. TYPES OF AQUIFER

Many aquifers extend over vast areas and are sometimes subject to recharge, sometimes not. Radioisotope methods to be dealt with later in detail, enable the hydrologist and hydrogeologist to distinguish between the two. In the former case, natural or artificial recharge may be meant. Either way, water enters the ground water system and leaves primarily by pumping through wells or by gravity or by a combination of both. Clearly,

$$I = O \pm \Delta S$$

where I is the input, O the output, and ΔS the change in storage.

The principal source of natural recharge is precipitation and surface water, but there may be a small magmatic contribution as well. Output arises as surface discharge to rivers, pumpage through wells, springs, subsurface outflow and evapotranspiration.

If an aquifer is to have an effective life, the annual volume of water removed must represent a very minute fraction of the total storage capacity. Thus, the safe yield may be defined as the quantity of water which can be withdrawn annually from an aquifer without producing an undesirable result; any excess is termed an overdraft. In practice, particularly in the USA, overdrafts are common and H. E. Thomas pointed out that areas suffering from these constitute by far the greatest ground water problem there.[11]

Two major kinds of aquifer may be mentioned, depending on whether a water table exists or not, and these are:

1. Unconfined aquifers, in which a water table functions as the upper surface of the zone of saturation, rises and falls in accordance with storage changes.

2. Confined aquifers, in which ground water is confined under pressure exceeding atmospheric by an overlying impermeable, confining bed. Confined aquifers may also be called pressure or artesian aquifers. If a well penetrates one, the water level rises above the base of the confining bed and water may flow out at the surface.

In the first case water enters by normal infiltrational processes, but in the second case, recharge occurs only in areas of outcrop of the confining bed or where this terminates underground and the aquifer becomes unconfined in consequence.

Rises and falls of water levels in wells penetrating confined aquifers depend on pressure changes and not upon storage changes as in unconfined aquifers. Thus, confined aquifers are agents of throughput, transmitting water from recharge areas to areas of discharge.

The concept of the potentiometric or piezometric surface is applicable. Meinzer defined the latter as an imaginary surface everywhere coinciding with the hydrostatic pressure level of water in the aquifer.[14] The actual water level in a well which penetrates a confined aquifer indicates the elevation of the piezometric surface at that place (see Fig. 1.4). If the latter lies above the ground surface, then a flowing well will occur. In the event that the piezometric surface falls below the level of the confining layer, then the confined aquifer will become unconfined. Figure 1.4 shows both confined and unconfined aquifers.

A rather unusual instance of an unconfined aquifer is afforded by the perched aquifer found wherever a ground water body is separated from the principal ground water system by a relatively impermeable bed of small areal extent. This latter may be diverse in nature, but clay is a common

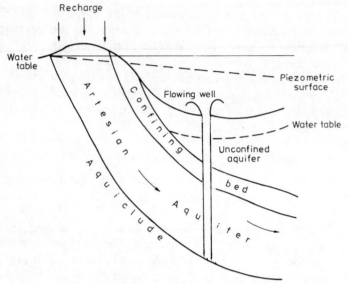

FIG. 1.4.   Cross section of a confined ground water basin showing an artesian well.

example, lenses of this soil in sedimentary deposits often impounding small perched water bodies (see Fig. 1.5). It should be noted that some aquifers are partly confined and partly unconfined, for instance the Lincolnshire limestone of eastern England. For such aquifers, a numerical analysis procedure was considered in the following paper: RUSHTON, K. R. and TOMLINSON, LUCY M., 1975. Numerical analysis of confined–unconfined aquifers. *J. Hydrol.*, **25**, 259–274.

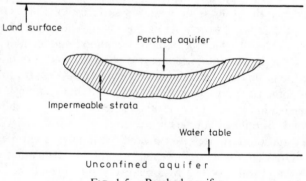

FIG. 1.5.   Perched aquifer.

It has been noted above that recharge of water to or discharge of water from an aquifer implies an alteration in the latter's storage volume. In the case of unconfined aquifers, this can be obtained by considering the product of the change in volume over a specific time and the average specific yield. However, in unconfined aquifers, a different state of affairs exists. If the aquifer remains saturated, then alterations in pressure will hardly affect the storage volume. The hydrostatic pressure within the aquifer partly carries the overburden load, the residual support coming from the solidity of the aquifer. When pumping takes place, the hydrostatic pressure goes down and the load increases with resultant compression of the aquifer. This in turn causes water to be forced out. Lowering of the pressure will cause a minute expansion and later release of water. Hence, the water giving capacity of an aquifer of this kind can be given in terms of the storage coefficient.

Storage coefficient may be defined as the volume of water which an aquifer releases from or takes up into storage per unit of surface area of aquifer per unit alteration in the component of head normal to that surface.[5] Considering a vertical column of square section of 1 ft by 1 ft passing through a confined aquifer, the storage coefficient will be the quantity of water (in ft^3) released from the aquifer when the piezometric surface goes down by 1 ft. Usually, values fall into a range $0.00005 \leq S \leq 0.005$, where S = storage coefficient. This shows that large pressure changes over huge areas are necessary in order to give water yields of any consequence.

The specific yield of an unconfined aquifer corresponds to its storage coefficient.

1.10. ROCKS AS AQUIFERS

Of course, many types of rock and soil are ruled out as aquifers, either because they are practically impermeable even if porous or because they are both impermeable and non-porous.

As noted earlier, most, perhaps 90 % or more, comprise unconsolidated materials such as sands and gravels. Todd divided such aquifers into four categories based on their mode of occurrence.[5] They are:

1. Water courses.
2. Abandoned or buried valleys.
3. Plains.
4. Intermontane valleys.

Water courses are made up of alluvium formed in and underlying stream channels as well as in the neighbouring flood plains. The proximity to rivers means that wells excavated adjacent to them will produce a lot of water, if permeability is very high. This results from the contribution of the streams which augments the ground water itself.

Abandoned valleys are a special case comprising old stream courses now left dry and, as might be expected, they are not so prolific in water production. Plains underlain by unconsolidated materials such as are frequently found in the USA may be very low in water, but sometimes there are good aquifers present.

Intermontane valleys are again underlain by unconsolidated rocks in large amounts and these are derived from the erosion of peripheral mountains. As well as sand and gravels, limestones, highly variable in density, porosity and permeability, may be excellent aquifers. For instance, the Asmari Limestone of the Middle East Miocene is such a one and so is the Chalk (Upper Cretaceous). The latter frequently gives high water yields and J. Ineson found the hydraulic conductivity of it, when unfissured, varied over the range 0·1 to 1·5 millidarcys.[15] Clearly, a widespread network of interconnected fractures is responsible. Solutioning is highly significant in limestones and ultimately, a karst region develops. Here, the subterranean drainage through the limestone creates large aquifers. Gypsum is also soluble and is known to provide aquifer facilities from time to time.

Some volcanic rocks are permeable, especially basalts. Many of the biggest springs in the USA are associated with basalts. Of course, crystalline rocks and metamorphics are practically impermeable and, therefore, do not rate as aquifers. Clearly, ground water occurrences are heavily dependent on geology.

1.11. FLUCTUATIONS IN GROUND WATER LEVELS

These result from changes in pressure on the ground water. It must be remembered that any ground water level shows the elevation of atmospheric pressure of the aquifer. Later, the subject will be examined in greater detail. Here, it is only necessary to mention that both seasonal and secular variations are known to occur. These differ from short-term fluctuations due, for example, to pumpage from a well. Figure 1.6 illustrates the drawdown and recovery of water in the saturated zone near such a well.

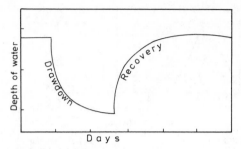

FIG. 1.6. Typical drawdown and recovery of ground water levels near a discharging well.

Other causes of such changes may be wind and seismic shocks. As to long-term changes, these have been verified through many observations. V. C. Fishel has indicated that, in 1956, such were being made on 20 000 or so wells in the USA, some having been monitored for over 60 years and perhaps a majority for 30 years or so.[16]

1.12. HYDROGRAPHS AND NATURAL RECESSION CURVES

Two concepts may now be discussed briefly. These are the hydrograph and the natural recession curve. The first relates to water on the land surface and here runoff, that part of precipitation which does not infiltrate into the ground, is significant. Actually, in flood hydrology, the determination of the distribution of travel times of direct runoff in a basin is the basic problem. Especially interesting to the investigator is the determination of the time of concentration and of basin lag, factors closely related to the mean transit time of the direct runoff. Studies of floods involve the estimation of peak flows from a basin. In Unit Hydrograph (UH) theory, the principle is that every basin produces a characteristic hydrograph, i.e. has a characteristic travel time distribution function in response to a uniform rainfall with a unit depth for a specified period of time. A more rigorous formulation is the instantaneous unit hydrograph (IUH) which corresponds to the impulsive response of a network to a unit impulse introduced into the system. Practically, UH or IUH in a basin are derived by using records of streamflow and precipitation under high flood conditions. More will be said on UH and IUH theory later. It may be stated, however, that nuclear techniques have been applied to the problem.

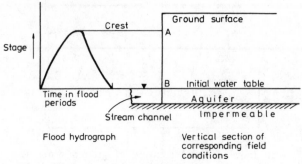

Flood hydrograph   Vertical section of
corresponding field
conditions

FIG. 1.7.

Figure 1.7 shows a typical flood hydrograph and also the effects of a flooding stream in ground water flow.

Floods elevate waters. Decline in the absence of recharge depends on

1. An aquifer's transmissibility (T), i.e. permeability times saturated thickness (usually expressed as Kb),
2. The storage coefficient of the aquifer,
3. The hydraulic gradient.

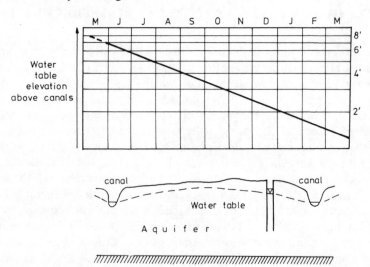

FIG. 1.8. Natural recession curve. Above, Natural recession of water table at well in default of recharge. Below, Section between two canals maintained at a constant level showing well.

After an interval of recharge, water levels decline quickly initially and then more slowly as time goes by because, as storage is depleted, transmissibility and hydraulic gradient both decline. A graphical representation of this situation is termed the natural recession curve (see Fig. 1.8).

In studying recharge, identifying recession curves is very important. In forecasting future ground water levels, this is also true because all aquifers have characteristic recession curves.

Effects of the unsaturated zone on these fluctuations are important.

1.13.   GROUND WATER STORAGE

Ground water storage relates to precipitation and in a very complex manner too, a manner varying geographically and chronologically. In fact, there are two factors which are significant in the matter. One involves the quantity of water actually getting through to the water table and the second relates to the time of arrival. As was noted above, runoff diverts some precipitation where the rate of precipitation exceeds the infiltration capacity of the soil. Evapotranspirative processes also cut off some water from the ground water system. Of course, the losses due to these causes vary seasonally and geographically, but they occur almost everywhere to a greater or lesser extent. Consequently, the water getting to the saturated zone constitutes residual water, i.e. that remaining after the above-mentioned processes have taken place. The time necessary for moisture to percolate down depends upon the depth of the water table and also upon the permeability of materials in the unsaturated zone. If the former is shallow and the latter high, water may reach the water table in a few days. However, it is usual for water to take much longer for this transit—in some cases, years. The actual mechanism of the movement is not as well known as could be wished, despite extensive researches by the USGS and others. Of course, the problem is crucial to an understanding of the water balance, either in the zone of aeration itself or in the underlying zone of saturation. K. O. Münnich has done a lot of interesting work involving isotope tagging.[17] This is another instance of the rather widespread applicability of nuclear techniques to hydrology in general. His and his colleagues' work consisted experimentally of tagging the moisture in a given horizontal plane with an appropriate radioisotope which is thereafter carried down by the moving water. The heaviest hydrogen isotope, tritium, has been used because of its negligible sorption, but it does have disadvantages. The main one is that its relatively long half-life of 12·26 years contributes to environmental pollution over 40 or 50 years. This subject will be analysed later in the book.

1.14. RECHARGE

Sometimes, complications in the recharge process may arise as a result of the fact that, in certain situations, the depth to the water table varies appreciably over quite short distances. Cases like this are found in North America in the northern glaciated areas, e.g. in the western part of Albany, New York state. Here, the land surface comprises many rather steep-sided hills ranging up to 40 ft in height. On the other hand, the water table is quite flat and hence lies either a few feet underground or, when under the hills, up to 45 ft or so underground. Thus, the flow patterns of the water which infiltrates to the ground water system vary from, say, under 5 ft to a maximum of 45 ft or so.

1.15. VOIDS IN ROCKS AND SUBTERRANEAN WATER

The significance of void spaces or interstitial openings, i.e. cavities, in soils and rocks is clearly apparent. Without them, water could not infiltrate underground, nor could it constitute the ground water system. There would be no soil moisture, no zone of aeration, no capillary region, no saturated zone. Such concepts as porosity, permeability, transmissibility, specific yield, specific retention, aquifers, the water table, the piezometric surface, storage coefficient and the recession curve simply would not apply to the lithosphere at all.

As it is, water is present in the rocks of the latter and the above-mentioned factors, discussed in this chapter and owing their significance to the presence of interstitial openings, become important objects of study in order practically and economically to exploit it. It is no exaggeration to say that ground water is the portion of subterranean water of most use to Man and it is, therefore, a primary field of hydrologic investigation both by conventional and nuclear techniques. A past President of the USA received a definition of hydrology from the Ad Hoc Panel on the subject of the Federal Council for Science and Technology.[18] In part, this stated that 'the domain of hydrology embraces the full life history of water on the Earth'. In fact, about 97 % of the world's water is sea water and it is as a consequence of solar distillation (evaporation, condensation and precipitation) that the balance of 3% fresh water originates. This circulation pattern, i.e. the hydrologic cycle, cf. Fig. 1.1, includes evaporation of moisture from the planetary oceans and lakes and its transference as vapour over land masses followed by precipitation as rain, hail or snow, in turn succeeded by runoff, streamflow or infiltration through the ground water system back to the oceans. Of course, the actual picture is more complex because, obviously, only a small part of evaporated oceanic water falls on land since land makes up only a quarter of the Earth's surface. Also, water may be stored for centuries or even millenia as ice around the poles, glaciers and snow and in aquifers also so that return to the oceans is greatly delayed. Polar ice and glaciers represent fresh water stores and, in fact, may take up as much as three-quarters of the 3% balance of fresh water alluded to above. The rest is almost all ground water which, as may be seen, represents a mere 0·75% of the water of the Earth. Of this, perhaps half is within 2500 ft of the ground surface, but it is very irregularly distributed. Only 0·3% of the fresh water exists in lakes, 0·03% in rivers and 0·03% in the atmosphere (as water vapour) and about twice as much is present in soil moisture form in the top few feet of the land mass. The total quantity of ground water is small, but its significance to Man, as was indicated earlier, is enormous. Its recharge depends upon precipitation, mostly rainfall, and the world average of this is approximately 34 in. annually—greater than the average moisture content of the atmosphere over land surfaces at any one time by a factor of 30.[6] Naturally, this rainfall input varies greatly—from less than 10 in. in parts of North Africa, Central Asia, Central Australia and South America to over 100 in. in western India, Assam and Central America.

1.16. THE HYDROLOGIC CYCLE

The vast planetary-wide hydrologic cycle to which ground water belongs is referred to in the Bible and a quotation may be appropriate: 'If ye indeed hearken to My commandments . . . to love the Lord your God . . . then I will give the rain of the land in its season—early rain and latter rain—and thou shalt gather thy corn and thine oil. And I will give grass in thy fields for thy cattle and thou shalt eat and be full' (from Deuteronomy).

That this is a sobering thought may be observed by looking at Fig. 1.9 which shows the terrible drought zones affecting the Earth in 1977. Drought was widespread in the earlier 1970s also, particularly in the Sahel belt of

GROUND WATER

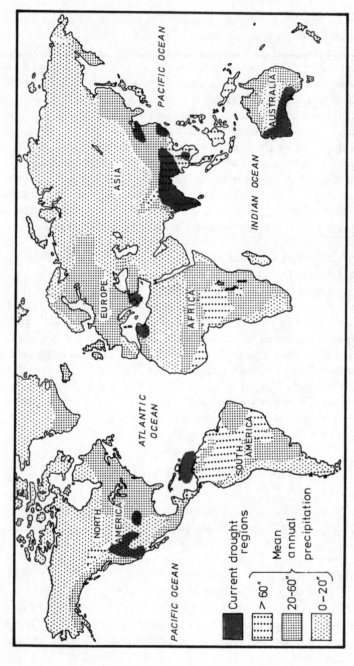

FIG. 1.9. Planetary precipitation and major drought areas, 1977.

West Africa, a region of aridity normally visited by the phenomenon quite often, though unusually badly at that time. In fact, as William A. Hance pointed out, the devastating Sahel drought to which allusion is made really commenced in 1958 and lasted until 1974.[19]

As a consequence of the episode, tens of thousands of people died as well as millions of livestock, the physical environment was severely damaged and socio-political institutions also suffered. The word 'sahel' means 'shore' in Arabic and this was taken over by the French in order to delineate a rather narrow belt of semi-arid climate and vegetation which runs along the northern and southern 'shores' of the Sahara. Those countries which were most affected by what might be termed the Great Drought, the so-called Sahelian Six, were Mauritania, Senegal, Mali, Upper Volta, Niger and Chad and they cover an area 56·5 % that of the USA. In fact, they represent about 19 % of the total area of Africa and, except for the Atlantic states (Mauritania and Senegal), are landlocked. Of course, the Great Drought was not confined to the Six, but also included Gambia and Northern Nigeria, Sudan and, in the later stages, Ethiopia as well. Additionally, much reduced harvests were recorded from Egypt, Kenya, Somalia, Tanzania and Zaire in 1973–74 and from this, it is possible correctly to infer that Africa, as a continent, is number one in the world in terms of dry regions. As well as the regions mentioned, it is only necessary to recall that the Maghreb (Morocco, Algeria and Tunisia), Libya and Botswana are all periodically affected by drought. In fact, Africa includes about one-third of the planet's arid lands so that water constitutes the major factor restricting economic development in over half of the continent. Rainfall in the Sahel amounts at best only to 25 in annually and in the Sahara, the maximum runs to as little as 10 in per year.

During the Great Drought, the hydrology of the entire region was very much affected. The River Niger ran at its lowest level within memory and could actually be forded at Niamey while the River Kano stopped its flow for the first time in history. Lake Chad was reduced to one-third of its normal size. Water table levels fell catastrophically due to lack of recharge; consequently, many wells ran dry. Naturally, as supplies fell in one area, herds concentrated around better wells and thus the surrounding pasture became exhausted. No one knows whether the Sahara is expanding so as to encroach on lands to its north and south. If it is, it is not known whether this is due to Man or to climatic change. Certainly, human misuse of the environment is highly significant. Errors committed include overgrazing, grass burning, overcropping and tree felling. No doubt, increased large scale irrigation would be helpful and several schemes have been proposed, e.g. the Manantali Dam on the Bafing tributary of the Senegal River in Mali. This would allow irrigation of over three-quarters of a million acres and a 100 000 kW hydroelectric station would be installed. There would be a $42 million barrage about a dozen miles above St Louis to prevent the incursion of sea water and facilitate year-round navigation of the river up to Kayes in Mali. Dams ought to be placed in Guinea also, but politics intervene—that country having withdrawn from the Organisation of Senegal River States (OMVS). Some projected developments in the Niger River Basin include headwater dams in Guinea as well as construction of the Sélingué Dam on the Sankarini tributary which would allow irrigation of about 100 000 acres and support a 40 000 kW hydroelectric station.

Other proposals include the $17 million Tiga Dam in Kano State in Nigeria (to irrigate 180 000 acres), the $167 million Bakolori scheme in the Rima Basin in north-western Nigeria to control 75 000 acres and a scheme for Lake Chad.

Clearly, droughts are natural forces encountered as an adverse phenomenon rather too often. Man's needs remain the same, however, although amounts vary. In London, 68 gal per capita daily is the average, for instance, compared with 270 gal in New York and 160 gal in Moscow, to cite some urban centres. As the world population, now over 4 billion, will probably exceed 7 billion by 2000 A.D., the problem grows ever more urgent. A complication is that many aquifers, especially in the USA, are either mined out or soon will be. Farmers in the Texas Panhandle who draw water from the up-to-now abundant Ogallala ground water reservoir believe that their wells will run dry around the turn of the century even without a drought in the meantime. Fortunately, other aquifers are brimful, e.g. a newly discovered one under north-eastern Wyoming is thought to be capable of yielding 1600 gal/min for scores of years.

Some approaches to the problem around the world include desalination (very expensive, hence primarily used by oil-rich Arab states such as Saudi Arabia and Kuwait), deep well sinking (e.g. under the Western Desert in Egypt to depths up to 4000 ft), recycling (e.g. in Japan, where tests are on to see whether water used by Man can later be utilised in industry), and river diversions (e.g. in Australia, where the Snowy River is being rerouted to flow through the Snowy Mountains into farm-land watering systems).

These methods will ease, but cannot fully meet the ever-increasing demand of modern society for water which will become an ever-rarer commodity if present wasteful practices continue.

Clearly, ground water must be studied carefully, used economically and conserved wisely if future requirements are to be served adequately.

REFERENCES

1. ARCHIE, G. E., 1950. Introduction to petrophysics of reservoir rocks. *Am. Ass. Pet. Geol., Bull.*, **34** (5), 943–961.
2. BOWEN, R., 1975. *Grouting in Engineering Practice.* Applied Science Publishers, London and Halsted Press, New York.
3. SCHWEITZER, S., 1974. On a possible extension of Darcy's Law. *J. Hydrol.*, **22**, 29–34.
4. MEINZER, O. E., 1934. The history and development of ground water hydrology. *J. Wash. Acad. Sci.*, **24**, 6–32.
5. TODD, D. K., 1959. *Ground Water Hydrology.* John Wiley, New York and London.
6. VALENTINE, H. R., 1967. *Water in the Service of Man.* Penguin Books, Harmondsworth, Middlesex, England.
7. MAVIS, F. T. and TSUI, T. P., 1939. *Percolation and Capillary Movements of Water through Sand Prisms.* Bull. 18, Univ. of Iowa Studies in Eng., Iowa City.
8. BEDINGER, M. S., 1961. *Relations between Median Grain Size and Permeability in the Arkansas River Valley.* Art. 157 in USGS, Prof. Paper 424-C, C31–C32.
9. DOMENICO, P. A., 1972. *Concepts and Models in Groundwater Hydrology.* McGraw Hill, New York and London.
10. MEINZER, O. E., 1923a. *The Occurrence of Groundwater in the United States with a Discussion of Principles.* USGS, Water Supply Papers 489.
11. THOMAS, H. E., 1951. *The Conservation of Groundwater.* McGraw Hill, New York and London.
12. KAZMANN, R. G., 1965. *Modern Hydrology.* Harper and Row, New York.
13. MURRAY, C. R., 1968. *Estimated Use of Water in the United States.* USGS, Circ. 556.
14. MEINZER, O. E., 1923b. *Outline of Groundwater in Hydrology with Definitions.* USGS, Water Supply Papers 494.
15. INESON, J., 1963. *Ground-water: Geological and Engineering Aspects.* Symposium, Joint Geol. Soc. London and Institution of Water Engineers Meeting, 27 February 1963, *J. Inst. Water Engrs*, **17**, 3, 283.
16. FISHEL, V. C., 1956. Long-term trends of ground-water levels in the United States. *Am. Geophys. Union, Trans.*, **37** (4), 429–435.
17. MÜNNICH, K. O., 1968. Moisture movement. Section IV A3 in: *Guidebook on Nuclear Techniques in Hydrology*, Tech. Repts Ser. No. 91, International Atomic Energy Agency, Vienna, 109–118.
18. AD HOC PANEL ON HYDROLOGY, 1962. Report on Scientific Hydrology, Federal Council for Science and Technology.
19. HANCE, WILLIAM A., 1976. Lessons to be learned from the Sahel drought. Chapter 4, *Africa: from Mystery to Maze*, ed. Helen Kitchen, Lexington Books, D. C. Heath, Lexington, Massachusetts and Toronto, 135–166.

CHAPTER 2

Fundamental Aspects of Aquifers

Aquifers, reservoirs of ground water of great significance to society, may be investigated by means of wells which tap their fresh waters and afford sampling facilities as well as allowing for the introduction of equipment and chemicals for measurement of significant parameters such as the direction and velocity of flow. Some others, together with the general characters pertaining to these bodies, were considered in Chapter 1 in which their classification was discussed.

2.1. COMPRESSIBILITY AND ELASTICITY

In a classic paper published in 1928, O. E. Meinzer[1] considered these properties with reference to artesian aquifers and, basing his remarks on studies of part of the Dakota Sandstone, indicated that these are not rigid and incompressible as had been thought up to that date. That this is indeed the case is seen from the response of water levels in wells to oceanic tides and movements of trains as well as to land surface subsidences. Clearly, as well as hydraulic conductivity, compressibility is a vital factor and refers to the relations at any point between pressure changes caused by superincumbent load or enclosed fluid and corresponding porosity (void) changes. Elasticity is related in that, where it occurs, the effects of such pressure changes may disappear totally after stress relief.

2.2. FLUCTUATIONS IN WATER LEVELS IN WELLS

Those alluded to above are short-term in their nature, reflecting sometimes momentary changes in hydrostatic pressure. For instance, the shallow water table at the Bonneville flats in Utah fluctuates 1·5 to 6 cm daily in summer and 0·5 to 1 cm daily in winter, showing seasonal variation also. (Data from TURK, L. J., 1975. Diurnal fluctuations of water tables induced by atmospheric pressure changes. *J. Hydrol.*, **26**, 1–16.) Other fluctuations may occur which reflect alterations in the quantity of water in storage in an aquifer, ΔS in the hydrologic equation. These are long-term in nature.

Figure 1.6 shows the type of fluctuation resulting from water removal from an aquifer through a pumping well. The shape is the same whatever type of aquifer is being considered and the declining part of the graph represents the period of water withdrawal while the ascending part represents replenishment. Factors promoting short-term fluctuations of water levels in wells have been mentioned above. Other causes include earthquakes and winds. Curiously, in artesian aquifers, i.e. those which are confined, not all wells respond to seismic influences. Nevertheless, others do and, in fact, some aquifers are so sensitive to earthquake waves that fluctuations of level in water wells can be applied to the detection of clandestine thermonuclear explosions. It must be added that, despite this and the intrinsic interest of the phenomenon, such fluctuations are not very important in ground water investigations—with a couple of exceptions with which hydrologists and hydrogeologists are concerned.

2.3. OCEANIC TIDES AND BAROMETRIC PRESSURES

The effects of these may have to be eliminated from water level hydrographs from wells prior to analysing them for the effect of pumping.

Increased barometric pressure will depress the water level in wells and acts directly. A rising oceanic tide inversely results in a rise in such water levels. In order to remove such barometric fluctuations from the hydrograph, the barometric efficiency (BE) of the aquifer must be determined and this is expressed as $BE = S_w/S_b$, where S_w is the net change in water level observed in a well tapping the aquifer and S_b is the corresponding net change in barometric pressure (both given in feet). Most observations yield a BE of between 20 % and 75 %. Barometric efficiency is usually plotted with S_w as ordinate and S_b as abscissa on rectangular coordinate paper. The slope of the linear relationship is BE. A similar concept, tidal efficiency (TE), is expressed as $TE = S_w/S_t$, where S_w is the range of water level fluctuations in feet in a well tapping the aquifer and S_t is the tidal range in feet, if necessary corrected for density. As David K. Todd indicated, C. E. Jacob related BE and TE, equating the sum of both with unity.[2]

2.4. GEOGRAPHIC LOCATION

It is apparent that the above-mentioned factors causing short-term fluctuations in the water levels of wells and classifiable as either meteorological or non-meteorological (tides, earthquakes) relate to a greater or lesser extent to geographic location. Obviously, the sinusoidal fluctuations of ground water levels responding to tides take place in coastal aquifers in contact with the ocean, for example. In piezometric surfaces of confined aquifers located far away from oceans, regular semi-diurnal and small magnitude fluctuations have been observed, for instance in New Mexico. They have been attributed to earth tides caused mainly by lunar, but also by solar, pulls on the terrestrial crust. Probably two daily cycles take place, occurring about 50 min later every day and the average diurnal retardation of cycle agrees closely with that of the lunar transit. Periods of large, regular fluctuations coincide with periods of full and new moon.

2.5. LONG-TERM FLUCTUATIONS

These may be climatic in origin and can encompass years, although some extend only over weeks. Much information is available about them because records exist from tens of thousands of wells in the USA alone, measurements there going back over half a century.

2.6. STORAGE

The amount of water stored in an aquifer, S, responds to two factors, namely recharge and discharge (input and output). Where recharge exceeds discharge, S increases and water levels rise. Where discharge is greater than recharge, on the other hand, the situation is reversed and water levels will drop. Precipitation is the primary source of recharge which, like this atmospheric input, is intermittent. As long as ground water levels anywhere in an aquifer exceed the lowest level at which the aquifer discharges, then discharge is continuous. Consequently, a natural recession curve arises and superimposed upon this will be short-term rises. If recharge is not taking place, water levels just decline continuously according to various factors. One of these is transmissibility, T, expressed as $T = Kb$, where K is the coefficient of permeability and b is the saturated thickness of the aquifer. Another factor is the storage coefficient, S, and a third one is the hydraulic gradient (dh/dL).

2.7.   DECLINE OF WATER TABLE ON A PENINSULA

C. E. Jacob in his study of the correlation of ground water levels and precipitation on Long Island, New York, showed that, in the absence of rainfall, the decline of the water table on a peninsula may be expressed as

$$h = h_0 \exp(-\pi^2 Tt/4a^2 S)$$

where h_0 = initial height of the water table above mean sea level
h = height of the water table after a given time, t
a = half the width of the peninsula
T = product of permeability times thickness.[3]

One of the limiting conditions assumed is that the aquifer thickness is large compared with the height of the water table above sea level.

In fact, the logarithm of h directly increases with time and therefore the plot of log h versus t is a straight line and such plots provide a fund of data very useful in the investigation of changes in ground water storage.

2.8.   PRECIPITATION AND GROUND WATER STORAGE CHANGES

The relations between these, i.e. between recharge and ΔS, are complex and vary both chronologically and geographically. This is in part because most of the precipitation does not enter the ground water system, but is diverted by evapotranspiration, soil moisture replenishment and runoff. Such losses vary seasonally and also from place to place. That which reaches the zone of saturation is essentially residual water and its transit time depends both upon the depth to the water table and the permeability. It may run to many years. The transit phenomenon is infiltration, a discontinuous process reflecting the discontinuous nature of recharge. Clearly, the actual mechanics of movement through the zone of aeration (see Fig. 1.2) is a subject of great significance. Both conventional and nuclear methods may be utilised in studying it (cf. Chapter 1, p. 27, ref. 17).

It is also important to understand the effects of ground water withdrawal on an aquifer in order to predict the results of future withdrawals.

2.9. AN AQUIFER AS A PIPELINE

Sometimes a central well into an aquifer shows similar but much smaller fluctuations in water level than a peripheral well into the same aquifer and this results from the water body acting effectively as a pipeline. Where recharge exceeds discharge, storage is increasing and vice versa and the pipeline concept as applied to aquifers is just as significant as their reservoir aspects. It relates to the capacity of these bodies to transport water from one point to another. As was noted in the preceding chapter (see pp. 12–13), Darcy's law is integral to the process and applies to laminar flow (Reynolds number less than approximately 700). This is because here the velocity is proportional to the first power of the hydraulic gradient. Needless to say, almost all ground water flow is laminar, i.e. slow. However, occasional turbulent situations do arise, e.g. when water enters a heavily pumped well. Darcy's law will not apply in this case.

2.10. GROUND WATER MOVEMENT

Ground water moves in accordance with the hydraulic gradient, i.e. from high to low head. Contour lines on water table and piezometric surface maps connect points of equal head and the ground water movement is perpendicular to them. The conventional determination of ground water flow is obtainable from measurements in three wells if available, even where water table or piezometric surface maps are not. The method is illustrated in Fig. 2.1.

Another approach is the nuclear one. It gives useful information which is valid for the immediate surroundings of a borehole or well and the method may be described.

2.10.1. Tracing Ground Water Flow Direction

A suitable tracer is introduced in a segment of a borehole and is carried away in the direction of flow due to horizontal flow. With an appropriate radiotracer such as bromine-82 (as $NH_4{}^{82}Br$) or iodine-131 (as $Na^{131}I$), the activity of the cloud may be measured by an instrument such as a radial array of detectors or a directionally oriented collimated detector. The direction of maximum activity corresponds to the direction of flow. An alternative technique is to allow the tracer to become adsorbed on the wall of the borehole and this allows for a better definition of the direction. J. Mairhofer first proposed the approach.[4] Radiotracers which can be adsorbed easily include $^{199}AuCl_3$ and $^{51}CrCl_3$.

2.10.2. Ground Water Velocity

The nuclear approach is also suitable for the determination of this. One method is the borehole dilution technique from which an independent and

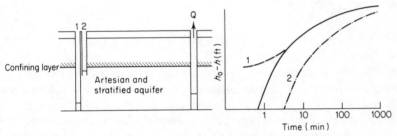

FIG. 2.1. Effects of well construction on analysis of aquifer test data. 1, 2, observation wells and data (1, --, 2, ·—·); Q, discharging well.

direct measurement of the filtration velocity in a water-bearing formation under either natural or an induced hydraulic gradient may be derived. The dilution rate of a tracer solution homogeneously distributed in a volume, V, in a borehole may be described so as to give a relationship

$$u_a = \frac{V}{Ft} \ln \frac{c}{c_0}$$

where u_a is the apparent velocity, V the measuring volume, F the cross section of the measuring volume perpendicular to the direction of the undisturbed ground water flow, and t the time interval between measurement of concentrations c and c_0. V is essentially the volume in which the actual dilution occurs.

Obviously, the horizontal flow pattern in the aquifer is distorted by the presence of a borehole and the different flows occurring in this and so a correction factor α is introduced to account for the effect, this being defined as

$$\alpha = Q_b/Q_f$$

where Q_b is the horizontal flow rate in the borehole and Q_f is the flow rate in a similar cross section of the actual formation. The filtration velocity then becomes (excluding all flows but horizontal ones)

$$u_f = -\frac{V}{\alpha Ft}\ln\frac{c}{c_0}$$

The method involves pouring tracer into the hole through a narrow pipe preferably at several depths (to facilitate mixing), thereafter inserting a probe at a chosen depth. As tracer, NaCl and tritium, ^3H, have been used.

Environmental tritium may also be utilised as may radiocarbon where the transit time of recharge is long.

2.11.   ENVIRONMENTAL TRITIUM

Artificially introduced tritium is not a very good tracer because its relatively long half-life of 12·26 years implies an environmental contamination impossible totally to eliminate before half a century or so has elapsed. Although, as will be seen below, environmental tritium contains a sizeable artificial component, the situation is different. Tritium is the radioactive isotope of hydrogen and it emits beta radiation (maximum energy 18 keV). With a half-life, $T_{\frac{1}{2}}$, of 12·26 years, it has a mean life of 18 years and, since there is a comparatively high cross section for its production in the upper atmosphere through nuclear reactions, it occurs on Earth in relatively large amounts. These atmospheric sources include:

(i) $(^{14}N,n)(^3H,^{12}C)$;
       resulting from cosmic ray-generated neutrons reacting with atmospheric nitrogen;
(ii)   solar injection;
(iii) since 1952, thermonuclear injection (irregular pulses).

Tritium in water labels precipitation, therefore, and is carried into the ground water system.

The equation of radioactive decay ought to be applicable in order to determine the time which has elapsed since a sample of water entered the ground, thus

$$C = C_0 e^{-\lambda t}$$

where C is the concentration of tritium at some observation point in an aquifer, this at a time t after recharge, C_0 is the concentration at the actual point of recharge, and λ is the decay constant for tritium ($\frac{1}{18}$).

C/C_0 should relate, in fact, to the transit time in an aquifer. However, this assumes that C_0 is constant with time and neglects dispersion effects. Also, recharge rarely occurs as a point injection.

Nevertheless, recognising these facts and knowing a particular aquifer, tritium may be utilised, but can only be applied to long distances where rapid flow occurs. Where flow takes place slowly, radiocarbon is more suitable.

2.12. RADIOCARBON IN THE ENVIRONMENT

Carbon-14 is a radioactive isotope of carbon and it emits beta radiation with a maximum energy of 156 keV. The half-life is 5730 years, but, following the decision of the Sixth Radiocarbon Dating Conference at Pullman in 1965, the figure of 5568 years is used (this facilitates comparison with earlier data).

Radiocarbon is produced in the upper atmosphere by the following reaction

$$(^{14}N, n)(^{14}C, {}^1H)$$

the carbon being thereafter oxidised to CO_2 and mixed in to the carbon reservoir. The carbon-14 content in water (carbonic acid) is constant until this enters the ground water system when the amount decreases according to the law of radioactive decay. In principle, it may be stated that the carbon-14 content of a ground water sample is a measure of the time which has elapsed since it left the zone of aeration. Theoretically, therefore, waters as old as 30 000 years or more should be datable as compared with the 50 year or so range of tritium. A disadvantage of the potential method lies in the fact that the carbon analysed is present in dissolved compounds rather than as part of the actual water molecule. Obviously, the carbonate chemistry of the water is of great significance. Practically, ^{14}C can be used to identify ancient recharge, calculate velocity of ground water movement by dating the water at different points in an aquifer, and calculate the contributions of different constituents to blends of ground water. The analytical result is expressed as the percentage of ^{14}C present relative to a modern (pre-thermonuclear) standard and the time at which the water last received atmospheric carbon in the soil zone can be calculated by the relation

$$t = 8033 \log_e \frac{A_0}{A_t}$$

where t is the time in years, 8033 is the mean life of radiocarbon, A_t is the radiocarbon activity in counts per minute per gram carbon of the sample as compared with A_0, the modern standard. The age so produced is an apparent age only, i.e. it is subject to extensive correction owing to exchange of carbon in solution with carbon in rock minerals and also to solution and precipitation of carbon compounds during the subterranean transit of water.

2.13.   TRITIUM AND RADIOCARBON SINCE THE THERMONUCLEAR ERA

Tritium is measured as tritium units (TU) where one TU is defined as one atom of tritium per 10^{18} atoms of hydrogen (7 disintegrations per minute per litre of water) or as picoCuries per litre (3·1 pC/litre = 1 TU).

First discovered in natural waters in 1951 and in the atmosphere in 1950, maximum tritium concentrations in the northern hemisphere were observed in 1963 (1964 in the southern hemisphere) to exceed normal levels by orders of magnitude as a result of thermonuclear pulse injections. Pre-bomb levels are determinable from old wine samples. Although levels have declined in subsequent years, even now they exceed normal.

As regards radiocarbon, the ^{14}C content of atmospheric CO_2 has risen, since 1954, to about 200% of modern standard. It is apposite here to mention that uranium isotopic variations in ground water can yield useful data. For example, measurements were made by J. B. Cowart and his associates on water samples from four wells from the Florida main aquifer 300 to 400 m below mean sea level in the south-east part of the state. These showed $^{234}U/^{238}U$ activity ratios significantly lower than the secular equilibrium value of 1·00. The four wells in question differ from six others all producing from the same general horizon in that they are in a highly transmissive zone. The results may indicate a relic circulation pattern whereby water from the surface aquifer was channelled to lower levels when sea level was much lower. In the deeper Boulder Zone, 800 to 1000 m below mean sea level, the uranium isotopes show progressive changes with increasing distance from the inferred flow source in the Straits of Florida. This tends to support the hypothesised landward flow (though with a more northerly component) of cold sea water in the extensively transmissive Boulder Zone. See COWART, J. B., KAUFMAN, M. I. and OSMOND, J. K., 1978. Uranium-isotope variations in groundwaters of the Floridan aquifer and Boulder Zone of south Florida. *J. Hydrol.*, **36,** 161–172.

2.14. WATER TABLE AND PIEZOMETRIC SURFACE MAPS

Where available, these provide important data. For instance, a radial dispersal of ground water from an area shows that this is probably a point of recharge. Conversely, convergence indicates a point of discharge, e.g. a lake, a spring, a well or even a river. Alternatively, where such discharges do not occur at the surface, a change in lithology or geological conditions may be the reason.

2.15. AN EXAMINATION OF DARCY'S LAW

This may be written as

$$K = \frac{Q}{A(\mathrm{d}h/\mathrm{d}L)}$$

Q being flow rate, A the cross sectional area of flow, $\mathrm{d}h/\mathrm{d}L$ the hydraulic gradient and K the coefficient of permeability.

Since water level contour maps, i.e. either water table or piezometric surface ones, graphically represent $\mathrm{d}h/\mathrm{d}L$, changes in the spacing of contours, that is to say changes in the hydraulic gradient, represent changes in Q, K or b (because $A = Wb$, where W is the width and b is the saturated thickness of an aquifer). Darcy's law may also be expressed, therefore, as

$$Q = KWb\frac{\mathrm{d}h}{\mathrm{d}L}$$

and in the USA is quantified in terms of K equal to gallons daily per square foot. W and b are given in feet and $\mathrm{d}h/\mathrm{d}L$ is given in feet per foot, so that

$$Q = (\mathrm{gpd/ft^2}) . \mathrm{ft} . \mathrm{ft} . \mathrm{ft/ft}$$

or

$$Q = \mathrm{gpd} . \mathrm{ft^3/ft^3}$$

or

$$Q = \mathrm{gpd}$$

As regards transmissibility, the coefficient of this defines the capacity of a unit cube of material to transmit water.

In dealing with aquifers, the thickness, b, is a factor of significance. In fact, transmissibility is interrelated thus:

$$T = bK$$

therefore

$$Q = TW\frac{dh}{dL}$$

The determination of transmissibility may be effected by observing declines of ground water levels near a pumping well and analysing them, using several formulae describing the hydraulic response of aquifers to water withdrawal. Another approach is to determine coefficients of permeability for the various layers in an aquifer, multiply them by the thicknesses of the layers and sum the results. Here, it must be borne in mind that permeability shows much greater variation across such layers than along them. Hence, water movement in aquifers is mainly parallel to such layers, especially if they are almost horizontal.

2.16. THE CONVENTIONAL DETERMINATION OF GROUND WATER VELOCITY

If the basic velocity equation

$$v = Q/A$$

of hydraulic studies is rewritten

$$Q = vA$$

and substituted into Darcy's law, this result is obtained:

$$vA = KA\frac{dh}{dL}$$

therefore

$$v = K\frac{dh}{dL}.$$

assuming the water moves through the entire cross sectional area.

A porosity correction is applied because ground water actually only moves through pores and the corrected equation becomes

$$v = \frac{K(\mathrm{d}h/\mathrm{d}L)}{n}$$

and the insertion of n, porosity, as the divisor gives the same units as permeability. To avoid getting a result of v in terms of gallons daily, this result is again divided by 7·48 (number of gallons per cubic foot) to give a velocity as feet per day and the final equation is

$$v = \frac{K(\mathrm{d}h/\mathrm{d}L)}{7 \cdot 48n}$$

Of course, the overall result is an approximation only because K and A are average values. It may be added that the condition of the aquifer, i.e. whether it is artesian or under water table conditions, does not affect the calculation. Using this approach, results concordant with nuclear-derived ones (cf. section 2.10.2 above) have been obtained, for instance in Florida. Actual velocities resemble permeabilities in that they vary greatly. In some cases, rates of yards or more a day are attained while in others, the movements are more like yards annually. These differences reflect environmental variability, i.e. differing stratal lithologies, rates of recharge, variations in precipitation, etc. The determination of permeability is very important.

2.17. PERMEABILITY

The coefficient of permeability, K, is always higher for a particular stratum if this constitutes part of the saturated zone than if it is in the zone of aeration. Permeability may be thought of as a governing factor in flow and its estimation is critical, but unfortunately usually rather inaccurate because of the great range of variability in the porosity of natural materials.

If the grain diameter of a bed is d, then the specific permeability is given by

$$k = Cd^2$$

where C is a dimensionless constant. This expression makes no reference to viscosity, specific weight and shear resistance of the liquid involved. It is, in point of fact, a simplification and k assumes areal dimensions referring to a pore area governing flow. The Fair/Hatch permeability formula is more apt and, where n is porosity, this may be expressed

$$k = \frac{1}{m\{(1-n)^2/n^3\}\{(\theta/100)(p/d_m)\}^2}$$

m being a packing factor, θ a grain shape factor (6 for spherical, 7·7 for angular grains), p is a percentage of the sediment which is held between adjacent sieves and d_m is the geometric mean of rated sizes of adjacent sieves.

Laboratory instruments have been devised actually to measure permeability and these comprise permeameters.

Perhaps the best known is the constant head permeameter. Basically, this permits water to enter and pass through a sample from below and be collected as overflow, the supply of water coming from a side arm tube continuously supplied and maintained at a constant level. If V is the flow volume over a time t and A is the cross sectional area of a sample, L being its thickness and h the distance between the constant water level in the side arm and the tube reservoir (above), then by Darcy's law

$$K = \frac{VL}{Ath}$$

Other approaches include a falling head permeameter in which water is added to that in the side arm tube, flows up through the medium cylinder and is collected as overflow.

Permeability may also be measured in the field. For open-end tests, a drill rig or other means of excavating a borehole and driving pipe casing are required together with a watermeter, pressure gauge, pump and the necessary water pipe and connections. For packer tests, a supply of packers, perforated water pipe and the relevant fittings are needed.

Tests involved are of the pumping-in type, i.e. they measure the quantity of water accepted by the ground through the open bottom of a pipe through an uncased section of the hole. Certain requirements are mandatory. One is that the water is clear (to avoid plugging and therefore permeability results that are too low). Another is that the temperature of the added water should be higher than that of the ground water (to preclude the formation of air bubbles in the ground which lead to reduction in the acceptability of water). In open-end tests, water is metered in order to maintain gravity flow at a constant head and the appropriate expression is

$$K = \frac{Q}{5 \cdot 5rH}$$

where K is the permeability, Q is the constant rate of flow into the hole, r is the internal radius of casing and H is the differential head of water. Any consistent set of units may be utilised. In packer tests, a part of the borehole below the casing may be used and the test may be made both above and below the water table. Common application is for testing bedrock using packers where the top packer can be placed just inside the casing. The writer has discussed packers in his book on grouting to which reference may be made.[5]

The procedure is to drill a hole, remove the core barrel, seat the packer, test, remove the packer, drill deeper, re-set the packer and repeat the test. A suitable formula is

$$K = \frac{Q}{2\pi LH} \sinh^{-1} \frac{L}{2r} \qquad 10r > L \geqq r$$

where K is permeability, Q is the constant rate of flow into the hole, L is the length of that part of the hole tested, H is the differential head of water, r is the radius of the hole tested and $\sinh^{-1}$ is the arc hyperbolic sine. Best validity is achieved where the thickness of the bed tested is at least $5L$. Optimal results are derived where the test is below the ground water table. A well permeameter method may also be employed.

Tracing methods can be useful in field determination of permeability. A suitable tracer is introduced into the ground water and monitored later. Chemical dyes, salts or radioisotopes are possible. Dispersion is a consequence of microvelocity variations occurring in laminar flow through porous media. Molecular diffusion is believed to be negligible unless the flow velocity is unusually small. Suitable tracers may be appended (see Table 2.1). Tritium is not very good because of its relatively long half-life and also because tritiated water, the compound used, is preferentially adsorbed by the montmorillonite group of clay minerals.

Much important information is derived from boreholes and wells. Some observations on these may be appropriate.

TABLE 2.1

Chemical	Colorimetric	Nuclear	Stable isotopes
B, $CuSO_4$, NaI, dextrose	Na fluorescin, methylene blue	Bromine-82, Cobalt-60, Iodine-131, Phosphorus-32, Rubidium-86, Tritium	Deuterium, Oxygen-18, Helium-4

2.18.   WATER WELLS

These are usually defined as vertical holes excavated in order to obtain
ground water or artificially to recharge an aquifer or to disperse sewage or
to dispose of industrial waste products or to effect subterranean
exploration. Shallow types, i.e. those under 50 ft deep, may be hand-dug,
bored, driven or jetted.

Deep wells are drilled by cable tool, hydraulic rotary or reversed rotary
methods. After completion, they are treated in order to afford optimal yield
and they are tested prior to pump installation. To ensure longevity, they
should be sealed to prevent the ingress of contamination and, of course,
they must be adequately maintained.

Test boreholes may be put down before any permanent well is
constructed. Normally, these are 10 in or so in diameter and they are
carefully logged.

Construction methods for *shallow* wells may involve manual labour as
recorded in the Bible and practised to this day in the Middle East and Africa
as well as elsewhere. Bored wells may be made by using either manual or
power-driven augers and function optimally in strata not subject to cave-in.
Driven wells are made by pounding connected lengths of pipe down to
below the water table and depths of as much as 100 ft have been achieved by
this impaction approach. Jetted wells are made by a downwardly directed
stream of water which cuts earth away, inserted casing removing both water
and cuttings. Diameters up to a foot may be obtained to depths exceeding
fifty feet.

Construction methods for *deep* wells, i.e. high capacity wells, include the
cable tool method, i.e. a percussion approach capable of drilling a 2 ft
diameter hole through consolidated materials. A normal well drilling rig
with percussion tools and a bailer is employed. The bailer removes drill
cuttings and comprises a section of pipe with a valve basally and a ring at the
top for attachment to the bailer line. A faster method used in
unconsolidated beds is the hydraulic rotary method which can excavate
deep wells as much as $1\frac{1}{2}$ ft in diameter. Reverse rotary drilling is a variant
capable of excavating wells up to 4 ft in diameter. It is basically a suction
method, i.e. cuttings are removed through a suction pipe by water, not
drilling mud.

Completion of wells requires various techniques. In consolidated beds,
casing is unnecessary, but it is mandatory in loose ground and it must either
be perforated or replaced by a well screen, If water quality is satisfactory,
water should enter the well along all the length penetrating a permeable

aquifer. Other sections should be sealed, sometimes by cement grout. Perforations may be effected *in situ* or pre-perforated casing may be employed. Well screens of various slot sizes are obtainable and should be made of metal which resists corrosion. Sometimes the perforated parts of a well are enclosed by a gravel packing which increases the effective diameter of the well as well as protecting the casing from cave-in. After drilling and developing, a well for water supply is subjected to a pumping test. This will not only afford information on aquifer characteristics, but also enable an assessment of the availability of ground water resources to be made. Programming is so arranged as to determine as far as possible:

(i)   yield characteristics and potential;
(ii)   hydrogeological and hydraulic properties of the aquifer;
(iii) effect of permanent abstraction of water;
(iv)   safe yield of the well and of the aquifer.

The significant hydraulic properties will be the hydraulic conductivity, i.e. the rate of flow of ground water in gallons daily through a cross sectional area of one square foot ($1 \, ft^2$) of the aquifer under a hydraulic gradient of one foot per foot ($1 \, ft/ft$) at a fixed temperature in gallons per day per square foot, and a transmissibility of T and the coefficient of storage, S, i.e. the ratio of the volume of water in cubic feet derived from storage from a vertical column on a base of one square foot ($1 \, ft^2$) extending through the entire thickness of the aquifer during a reduction in head equivalent to a fall in water level of one foot ($1 \, ft$) to one cubic foot ($1 \, ft^3$) of that aquifer expressed decimally.

The basic theory of pumping tests assumes that total penetration of the aquifer occurs because, if this is not the case, flow lines will be distorted and converge towards the bottom of an unscreened well. Analysing flow conditions will provide a solution of aquifer properties. Changes in these can lead to variations of overflow or alterations in head. In this connection, it must be pointed out that conventional analysis is often unable to give consistent results and sometimes not all data can be utilised. This is invariably so where the drawdown in the well is a significant proportion of the saturated depth. Conventionally, analytic solutions are used as the basis of curve-fitting methods, but a discrete time–discrete space numerical approach may be employed. For details of this, see RUSHTON, K. R. and BOOTH, S. J., 1975. Pumping test analysis using a discrete time–discrete space numerical method. *J. Hydrol*, **28**, 13–27. Another important paper may be mentioned and this is: TOMLINSON, L. M. and RUSHTON, K. R.,

1975. The alternating direction explicit (ADE) method for analyzing ground water flow. *J. Hydrol.*, **27**, 267–274.

Both drawdown and recovery of water levels can be analysed and these phenomena parallel hysteresis in that confined aquifers possess a state of elasticity. However, analysing them in a recharging or discharging well is not as satisfactory as effecting the exercise in observation wells some distance away. In fact, an empirical approach is just about the only way in which the problem can be tackled.

But J. Ineson has shown that computed curves can match water level data quite closely.[6]

Maximum yields for comparable depressions of water level are achieved solely when total penetration has been obtained and, as a result of exponential increase in available yield for increase in penetration, the first increase in yield exceeds that derived in the final penetration phase, i.e. the initial 50% of penetration will produce relatively *more* water than the last 50%.

A frequently used method of effecting a pumping test is by determining pumping water levels at differing abstraction rates and this is termed the step-drawdown technique. Rates of abstraction may be plotted against the corresponding drawdown of water level for individual wells and the curve so produced is called a yield–depression curve. Sometimes wells in one aquifer are characterised by a definite group of such curves while a different group may occur in another aquifer. It has been shown by multiple correlation techniques that values of transmissibility obtained from the discharging well are statistically related to the shape of the yield–depression curves. It is to be expected, therefore, that if such a curve can be obtained for a particular well, then the transmissibility of the aquifer can be defined within a set of probabilities. In practice, pumping tests are normally effected in *new* wells, although this does not mean that wells in service cannot also be analysed. There is of course a degree of wait and see involved with all pumping tests and these are economic if wells are later continuously to be operated. Where this is not the case, a simpler procedure may be adopted, namely a bailer test.

2.18.1. Parameters for Pumping Tests

These include the following:

(i)   Static water level, i.e. the water level in a well when pumping is not proceeding (distance below ground surface);

(ii)   Pumping level, i.e. the water level in a well undergoing pumping (the so-called dynamic water level);

(iii) Drawdown (extent of lowering of water level) during pumping;

(iv) Yield, i.e. volume of water per unit time discharged either by pumping or by free flow;

(iv) Specific capacity, i.e. yield per unit of drawdown (gal/min/ft of drawdown).

Depth to water is usually determined by employing the wetted tape method in which a lead weight is attached to a steel measuring tape, the lowest two or three feet of which is chalked. The tape is lowered into the well until part of the chalked section is below water and one of the foot marks is held precisely at the top of the casing. The tape is then removed and the wetted line on the tape is read to a fraction of an inch accuracy. Other methods include electric sounding and the installation of an air line. Bailer testing effects the same investigations, but a bailer is used, the average rate of bailing being the volume of the water bailed from the well during a given time interval divided by the time in minutes. The only snag is that depth to water during bailing is rather hard to estimate.

2.18.2. Specifications for Water Well Construction

It seems appropriate to summarise these at this point. This is because wells are as it were essential tools in investigating aquifer characteristics and their proper installation is therefore a critical matter indeed.

Clearly, specifications constitute a legal contract, but this is possible to conclude orally as well as in writing. However, the latter is a better idea since in this form, description of materials can be supplemented by plans. Unlike other construction work, parts of wells cannot be inspected either during drilling or subsequent to completion. Probably too there is greater variability in method because of the wide spectrum of subterranean geological conditions. The reference book for the well industry indicates that the lowest responsible bidder should be selected which appears self-evident.[7] Of course, this implies a degree of skill and ability as well as financial adequacy in the bidder. Quality as cheaply as possible is the desired result.

Where the specifications of the owner are followed, a guarantee of yield is, to say the least, very difficult to give. Nevertheless, it is often given! A contract should describe location, boundaries and protection both of site and environment and also include data on adjacent wells, availability of power and any unusual circumstances.

2.18.3. Materials

Where casing is used, this ought to be of new material supplied according to stipulated diameter, weight per foot and thickness of wall, joints being watertight. Steel pipe is optimal.

Wells deriving water from gravel or sand aquifers require screening and screens come in two series of sizes. One is telescopic in type, i.e. designed for installation by telescoping through pipe of the same size designation. The other provides pipe-sized screens having the same diameter as pipe of the corresponding designations. The diameter of the screen used depends upon the method of installation and the basic well design. After well completion, of course, the installation of pumps is necessary.

2.18.4. Pumps

Two fundamentally different types exist. One is the constant displacement type which delivers essentially the same amount of water against any head within operating capacity. The second is the variable displacement type giving water inversely with the head against which it operates.

Sometimes the terms shallow and deep well pumps are applied to pumps within these two groups. The basic difference between the two is that, in the shallow type, the pump is located *above* the well and takes water from the latter by suction lift whereas the deep type involves placement of the pumping unit *inside* the well casing with the pump inlet below the pumping level and therefore under positive pressure head.

The terms suction lift pump and positive submergence pump are occasionally employed for the two types noted above. Suction lift, of course, works through a negative pressure head at the pump intake. Water is moved by the creation of a partial vacuum which reduces pressure to below one atmosphere (1 atm); in consequence, the atmospheric pressure on a free surface of the water in a well forces water up into that part of the pump under reduced pressure. Maximum lift is limited by atmospheric and vapour pressures, frictionally induced head losses and the required inlet head of the pump itself. Atmospheric pressure is variable, but on the average it may be taken as 14·7 psi at mean sea level, i.e. equivalent to 34 ft of water head. However, a water column cannot be lifted 34 ft by a pump even if a perfect vacuum can be produced, mainly because of pipe friction.

Vapour pressure is very important in all pumps, but becomes especially so as the temperature of the water rises. The most efficient constant displacement pumps need boiling water to be delivered under positive pressure in order to be pumped. This is because vapour pressure at boiling point is equal to atmospheric pressure and therefore no suction lift is possible.

Cavitation sometimes takes place in pumping water if the pressure at any point in the suction line or in the pump is reduced to the vapour pressure of the water. Vapour bubbles form and, on moving to points of higher pressure, implode. The formation and implosion phenomena, i.e. cavitation, can interfere with pumping as well as damage parts of pumps. Cavitation occurs where the hydraulic head at the pump inlet is too low for a particular operation. The head must be sufficiently high so that, with increase in velocity and pressure decreases within the pump, pressure is unable to drop to the vapour pressure point of the water at any place in the flow path. This head, necessary at the pump inlet, is the net required inlet head. It is a function of the pump design and can be less or more than atmospheric pressure. As a characteristic of the pump, its value is independent of atmospheric pressure. The necessary inlet head is expressed as a positive value, i.e. a pressure head relative to zero, namely as the net required inlet head (absolute) or required positive suction head. The constant displacement type pumps alluded to above discharge the same quantity of water irrespective of the head against which they operate (theoretically—in practice, slippage past operating parts to some degree invalidates the statement). Positive displacement pumps include the following subtypes: piston, rotary and screw.

The variable displacement pumps mentioned earlier include the following subtypes: centrifugal, jet and air-lift.

Selection of the pumps for any installation system requires accurate information on required capacity, location and operating conditions and total head. This latter is derived from

$$h_t = h_e + h_f + h_v$$

where h_e is the total vertical lift from the level of pumping to the delivery point, h_f is the total frictional loss and h_v is velocity head, with h_t being the total head. All may be expressed in suitable units such as feet.

2.19. THE CONE OF DEPRESSION

Where a situation exists in which water is being removed from an aquifer surrounding a well by pumping, then the water table or the piezometric surface (depending upon the type of aquifer, unconfined or confined) is lowered, drawdown at any given point being the distance through which the lowering occurs (see Fig. 1.6). This latter shows, in part, a drawdown curve which indicates the variation of drawdown with distance from the well itself. In three dimensions, this describes that conic shape known as a cone of depression.

In a confined aquifer, the shape depends upon Darcy's law expressible as a system of plane polar coordinates with the discharging well at its origins. The analysis of this leads to a famous equation.

2.20. THE THIEM EQUATION

The amount of water moving towards a discharging well at a distance r is given by

$$Q = KA \frac{dh}{dL}$$

or

$$Q = 2\pi r b K \frac{dh}{dr}$$

which, rearranged to integrate, becomes

$$dh = \frac{Q}{2\pi} \frac{dr}{rbK}$$

Further integration between two points r_1 and r_2 distant from the discharging well on the cone of depression and with respective heads h_1 and h_2 gives

$$\int_{h_1}^{h_2} dh = \frac{Q}{2\pi bK} \int_{r_1}^{r_2} \frac{dr}{r}$$

and, as integral dr/r is equal to $\ln r$, therefore

$$[h]_{h_1}^{h_2} = \frac{Q}{2\pi bK} [\ln r]_{r_1}^{r_2}$$

where ln is the natural logarithm. Therefore

$$h_2 - h_1 = \frac{Q}{2\pi bK} (\ln r_2 - \ln r_1)$$

$$h_2 - h_1 = \frac{Q}{2\pi bK} \ln \frac{r_2}{r_1}$$

$$Q = 2\pi bK(h_2 - h_1)/\ln (r_2/r_1)$$

this latter constituting the equilibrium equation first developed by G. Thiem and often termed the Thiem equation.[8] It enables the aquifer permeability to be determined from a pumped well and also transmissibility after steady state conditions have been achieved. Clearly, as Q is a constant, the quantity $Q/2bK$ is also a constant and

$$h_2 - h_1 = 2 \cdot 303 \log_{10} \frac{r_2}{r_1}$$

h will indefinitely increase with increasing r and hence, theoretically, steady radial flow in a large aquifer cannot exist. In practice, however, h approaches the initial uniform head as distance from the well increases.

In fact, regardless of discharge rate, head varies linearly with the logarithm of the distance. Permeability may be determined, of course, through the rearrangement

$$K = \frac{Q}{2\pi b(h_2 - h_1)} \ln \frac{r_2}{r_1}$$

The applicability of the Thiem equation is rather restricted because it only applies to steady state conditions which, strictly speaking, can never obtain. This is a consequence of the fact that, in order to attain them, the aquifer should be of infinite extent.

2.21. DUPUIT'S ASSUMPTIONS

In a confined aquifer, it may be shown that $h = vx/K$ where h is the head above a given datum, v is the velocity of ground water flow and x is the direction of flow in a uniformly thick aquifer (K having its usual significance), i.e. head decreases linearly, flow direction being $-x$.

In an unconfined aquifer, J. Dupuit obtained a solution by assuming that the flow velocity is proportional to the tangent of the hydraulic gradient and that flow is horizontal and everywhere uniform in a vertical section.[9] However, it is somewhat unrealistic to make such assumptions because the actual water table deviates from the computational position.

2.22. THE THEIS EQUATION

In nature, non-steady states are encountered and for them, C. V. Theis in 1935, using the analogy between heat flow and ground water flow, developed an appropriate equation.[10] This was a great improvement and the relevant (non-equilibrium) equation is

$$h_0 - h = \frac{Q}{4\pi T} \int_{u_k}^{\infty} \frac{e^{-u}}{u}\,du = \frac{QW(u)}{4\pi T}$$

where $u = \dfrac{r^2 S}{4Tt}$

$h_0 - h$ = drawdown at any point in the vicinity of a well discharging at a constant rate

Q = discharge of well

T = transmissibility

$$W(u) = -0{\cdot}577216 - \log_e u + u - \frac{u^2}{2 \times 2!} + \frac{u^3}{3 \times 3!} - \frac{u^4}{4 \times 4!} \cdots$$

r = distance from the discharging well to the point where the drawdown is $h_0 - h$

S = storage coefficient, a dimensionless fraction

t = time since the commencement of pumping.

As T occurs in the argument of the function and also as a divisor of the exponential integral, it cannot be determined directly from the equation. Theis devised a graphical method for obtaining a solution, utilising a 'type curve', i.e. a plot of $W(u)$ versus u on logarithm paper. Drawdown measurements derived from pumping tests are plotted on logarithm paper too, against square of distance divided by t (i.e. r^2/t) and such drawdown plots are termed data plots. When superimposed over the type curve, values of $W(u)$, u, h_0 and h and r^2/t may be selected at any desired point and substituted in the Theis equation. Units must be consistent, naturally, and in the USA and UK, drawdown may be given in feet, discharge (Q) in gallons per minute, distance (r) in feet, time in days and transmissibility in gallons per day per foot. For uniformity, a conversion factor is introduced so that

$$h_0 - h \text{ (feet)} = \frac{Q}{4\pi T} \text{ (gal/min divided by gal/day/ft) } W(u)$$

$$= \frac{Q}{4\pi T}\left(\frac{\text{ft day}}{\text{min}} \times 1440\frac{\text{min}}{\text{day}}\right) W(u)$$

$$= \frac{114{\cdot}6Q}{T} W(u)\text{(ft)}$$

and, in US units,

$$h_0 - h = 114 \cdot 6 Q W(u)/T$$

Tables are available with values of $W(u)$ and u (see L. K. Wenzel[11]). Two other solutions are available.

2.23. JACOB METHOD

Where t is large and r small, u is also small and $h_0 - h$ (drawdown) versus the logarithm of t plots as a straight line. The simplified solutions are given by

$$T = \frac{264Q}{\Delta h}$$

and

$$S = \frac{0 \cdot 3 T t_0}{r^2}$$

where Δh is the drawdown difference (ft) per log cycle of time and t_0 the time intercept on the zero drawdown axis.

2.24. CHOW METHOD

This does not require the fitting of curves and is again based on measurements of drawdown in an observation well near a pumped well. Data are plotted on semi-logarithmic paper and on the plotted curve, an arbitrary point is selected and the coordinates t and $h_0 - h$ are noted. A tangent is then drawn to the curve at the selected point and the drawdown difference (Δh) determined (ft per log cycle of time). Thereafter

$$F(u) = \frac{h_0 - h}{\Delta h}$$

and corresponding values of $W(u)$ and u may be found.[12]

2.25. ASSUMPTIONS MADE BY THEIS

These include the following:

(a) Homogeneity (isotropism) of aquifer. Never found in nature, *but* if large enough volumes of suitable rock such as limestones are considered, appropriate characteristics may be displayed.

(b)   Infinite areal extent of the aquifer.

(c)   A coefficient of transmissibility which is everywhere and always constant.

(d)   Water taken from storage is discharged instantaneously with decline in head.

(e)   Complete penetration of the aquifer is achieved and water derived throughout its thickness. Clearly, this requirement can be fulfilled since it involves the drilling of a suitable well. However, it very often is not.

(f)   The well possesses an infinitesimal diameter. Obviously this is impossible, but as the actual diameter of any particular well is very small compared with that of the cone of depression even after only a short period of pumping, this assumption may be regarded as, in practice, justified.

In nature, stratification of sediments occurs and this may very greatly affect the response of aquifers during the course of pumping tests. Consequently, the phenomenon must be borne in mind in interpreting the latter. Probably, however, it is not very much more significant than the man-made factors involved, namely the actual features of construction of the pumping and observation wells. As these are screened usually only for a part of an aquifer, it is found that drawdowns often differ from Theis-type curves, particularly in the beginning of a pumping test, i.e. for the initial few minutes. The accompanying Fig. 2.1 illustrates the difficulties which may arise and shows two observation and one production wells, together with the theoretical and recorded curves which do not coincide.

2.25.1. Water Tables and the Theis Equation
Since some of the assumptions of the Theis equation only apply to artesian conditions, this cannot adequately describe drawdowns in unconfined aquifers. A case in point is transmissibility which ought to be constant everywhere and always. When water is withdrawn from an unconfined aquifer, transmissibility decreases with dewatering. The result is that, comparing an unconfined and a confined aquifer with equivalent initial transmissibility, a greater drawdown will take place in the former.[13]

Adjustment can be made for the effect in unconfined aquifers by using the equation of C. E. Jacob.[14] This is

$$(h_0 - h)' = (h_0 - h) - \frac{(h_0 - h)^2}{2b}$$

in which $(h_0 - h)'$ is the drawdown which would occur if the aquifer were *not* dewatered (i.e. if it were artesian), $(h_0 - h)$ is the actual drawdown and b is the thickness of the aquifer prior to pumping.

2.26. THE BOUNDARIES OF AQUIFERS

One of the assumptions of the Theis equation (see section 2.25 above) is that aquifers have an infinite areal extent and clearly it is necessary in order to solve many ground water problems. However, it is obvious that aquifers of this type cannot exist in reality, although some occur which, in human terms, approximate to it, for instance the Floridan aquifer in the USA. Nevertheless, it must be stated that all aquifers have boundaries and hydraulically these can be divided into two categories, namely recharge ones and impermeable ones. The former relate to the situation in which an aquifer contacts a water source such as a lake and the latter are those where an aquifer is bounded by impermeable material of some sort.

Only Darcy's law does not require the assumption of infinite extent in aquifers. All other equations do and therefore, where these bodies are analysed near their boundaries, this must be borne in mind. The requirement is to devise a hydraulic model which will suitably convert an aquifer of restricted extent into one of infinite extent. One approach often utilised is that of the method of images.[15]

2.27. IMAGE WELL THEORY

This is illustrated in Fig. 2.2. An image is an imaginary well or stream which is introduced in order to set up a hydraulic flow system which will be equivalent to the effects of a *known* physical boundary on the flow system. Considering initially a recharge boundary such as that illustrated, i.e. one along which there is no drawdown, such a boundary is to be found in the case where an aquifer is connected freely with a body of surface water. It can be duplicated by assuming an infinite aquifer wherein a recharging image well is located across the boundary from the real well. Water is assumed to be recharged through the image well in an equal and opposite sense from the rate of discharge from the real well and hence, in Fig. 2.2, $d_i = d_r$. Obviously, the figure is idealised because it is highly unlikely in nature that a recharge source could be found which hydraulically is completely connected with an adjacent aquifer.

As regards an impermeable boundary, this is the case in which no water at all crosses. Nevertheless, image well theory can be applied. Y. K. Chan in 1976 proposed an image well technique for aquifer analysis which he thought of as an improvement and he tested it thoroughly by considering

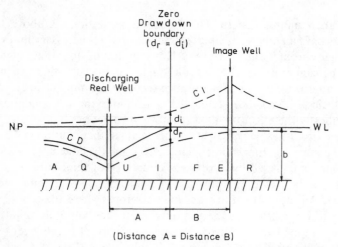

(Distance A = Distance B)

FIG. 2.2.   Image well theory. Idealised cross section of a semi-infinite aquifer bounded by a recharge boundary. CI, cone of impression; CD, resultant cone of depression; NP–WL, non-pumping water level; d_i, accumulation component of image well; d_r, drawdown component of real well; b, aquifer thickness. The shaded area represents the aquiclude and the broken line represents the cone of depression.

examples for non-leaky and leaky aquifers, indicating that, where an aquifer is enclosed by rectangular boundaries, care must be taken in order to avoid obtaining inaccurate results. Data from: CHAN, Y. K., 1976. Improved image-well technique for aquifer analysis. *J. Hydrol.*, **29**, 149–164.

2.28.   FLOW NETS

Flow nets which graphically represent flow characteristics are very useful when applied to the solution of hydrologic problems encountered in the vicinity of pumping wells adjacent to the boundaries of aquifers. Areal flow

Discharging Well

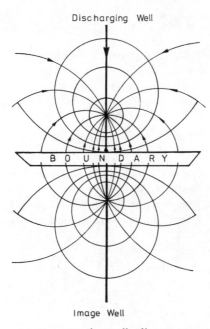

Image Well

FIG. 2.3. Flow net near a pumping well adjacent to a recharge boundary.

nets can be of course derived through empirical adjustment of ordinary
water level contour maps, and vertical ones based upon data from wells
along a line of section constitute flow nets showing the aquifer in cross
section. Another approach is to use appropriate mathematics, as C. E.
Jacob indicated.[15] This relates to a net for two adjacent wells, one
discharging and the other recharging as in Fig. 2.3 which, however, shows
equipotential lines and flow lines in the vicinity of a real well and a
recharging image well. The former comprise circles around each well and,
as the radii of these increase, the centres of the circles progressively recede
from the boundary. For any potential surface

$$\frac{(x - x_1)^2 + y^2}{(x + x_1)^2 + y^2} = C$$

where C is a constant, x_1 is the distance from the boundary either to the real
or to the image well and y is assumed to be zero (whereby, if solutions are
derived for progressively greater values of x, values for C can be obtained).
Flow lines *between* the two wells comprise circles centred on the boundary
(the y axis).

2.29.   MULTIPLE WELLS

In a well field, the drawdown anywhere in the area of influence of the wells is obtained by summing the drawdowns caused by each well itself. Where pumping is from a confined aquifer

$$h_0 - h = \sum_i^n \frac{Q_i}{2\pi Kb} \ln \frac{R_i}{r_i}$$

where $h_0 - h$ is the drawdown at any given point in the area of influence, R_i being the distance from the ith well to a point at which the drawdown becomes negligible and r_i is the distance from the ith well to the given point.[16] In an unconfined aquifer with small drawdowns, the expression becomes

$$h_0^2 - h^2 = \sum_i^n \frac{Q_i}{K} \ln \frac{R_i}{r_i}$$

2.30.   WELLS PENETRATING PARTIALLY

Here the flow patterns will differ from the radial flow which is thought to exist around wells which fully penetrate. Where penetration is achieved in an unconfined aquifer having uniform recharge W, the flow Q increases as the well is approached and the increase (dQ) through a cylinder dr thick with radius r may be expressed

$$dQ = -2\pi r \, dr \, W$$

and

$$Q = -\pi r^2 W + C$$

The modification of this for partial penetration of a confined aquifer is available.[16]

REFERENCES

1. MEINZER, O. E., 1928. Compressibility and elasticity of artesian aquifers. *Econ. Geol.*, **23**, 263–291.

2. JACOB, C. E., 1940. On the flow of water in an elastic artesian aquifer. *Trans. Am. Geophys. Union*, **21**, 574–586.
3. JACOB, C. E., 1944. Correlation of ground water levels and precipitation on Long Island, New York. *Trans. Am. Geophys. Union*, **25**, 928–939.
4. MAIRHOFER, J., 1963. Bestimmung der Strömsrichtung des Grundwassers in einem einzigen Bohrloch mit Hilfe Radioaktiven Elemente. *Atompraxis*, **9**, 2.
5. BOWEN, R., 1975. *Grouting in Engineering Practice*. Applied Science Publishers, London and The Halsted Press, New York.
6. INESON, J., 1963. *Ground Water: Geological and Engineering Aspects*. Symposium, Joint Geol. Soc. and Institution of Water Engineers Meeting, 27 February 1963, *J. Inst. Water Engrs*, **17**, 3, 283–284.
7. ANON, 1975. *Ground Water and Wells*. Johnson Division U.O.P., St Paul, Minn.
8. THIEM, G., 1906. *Hydrologische Methoden*. J. M. Gebhardt, Leipzig.
9. DUPUIT, J., 1863. *Études Théoriques et Pratiques sur la Mouvement des Eaux dans les Canaux Découverts et à travers les Terrains Perméables*. Dunod, Paris.
10. THEIS, C. V., 1935. The relation between the lowering of the piezometric surface and the rate and duration of discharge of a well using ground water storage. *Trans. Am. Geophys. Union*, **16**, 519–524.
11. WENZEL, L. K., 1942. *Methods for Determining Permeability of Water-bearing Materials with Special Reference to Discharging Well Methods*. USGS Water Supply Paper 887, Washington, D.C.
12. CHOW, V. T., 1952. On the determination of transmissibility and storage coefficient from pumping test data. *Trans. Am. Geophys. Union*, **33**, 397–404.
13. HEATH, R. C. and TRAINER, F. W., 1968. *Introduction to Ground Water Hydrology*. John Wiley, New York.
14. JACOB, C. E., 1963. *Determining the Permeability of Water Table Aquifers*. USGS Water Supply Paper 1536-I, 245–271.
15. JACOB, C. E., 1950. Flow of ground water. In *Engineering Hydraulics*, ed. H. Rouse. John Wiley, New York, pp. 321–386.
16. TODD, D. K., 1959. *Ground Water Hydrology*. John Wiley, New York.

CHAPTER 3

Nuclear Techniques and Ground Water

The application of nuclear techniques to some problems of aquifers such as permeability, transmissibility and the direction and velocity of ground water flow has already been indicated. It is important to examine how they may be utilised in regard to other properties.

3.1.   DETERMINATION OF POROSITY

The basis of the approach is the rough equality between this property, n, and partial volume of water, s, where

$$s = V_w/V_0$$

(V_w is the volume of water and V_0 the total volume). A suitable tracer is introduced at one well and pumped at another and, if the effects of dispersion are neglected, then the arrival at the second denotes that the volume of water pumped, V, may be given as

$$V = \pi r^2 b s$$

where b again refers to the thickness of the aquifer, r is the distance between the two wells in question, and s relates to *effective* porosity.

The relevant flow pattern may be considered as radial because the velocities induced by pumping greatly exceed the velocity of natural flow. For optimum results, it has been found that the thickness of the confined aquifer, or alternatively the height from base to water table in unconfined aquifers, should be much less than r, the distance between wells. Of course, the effects of exchange must be borne in mind, i.e. exchange with the bound waters. The tracer should be of such a type that exchange with the actual matrix of the aquifer does not occur. The technique has been used, for instance by E. Halevy and A. Nir on a dolomite formation in the Carmel Range in Israel.[1] In this experiment, r was 250 m and the radioactive tracer $K_3{}^{60}Co(CN)_6$ was employed. W. A. Wiebenga and his associates also utilised the technique in a sandy aquifer in the Burdekin Delta area of North Queensland, Australia, r being 18·3 m and the tracers tritiated water and iodine-131.[2]

3.2. THE STRATIFICATION OF AQUIFERS

Obviously this can be detected by drilling and the subsequent study of cores, but this is not always satisfactory because it may be difficult to obtain samples which are structurally intact where friable rocks are involved.

An alternative method is to use radiotracers and these may be injected as pulses in upper and lower zones, activity being monitored in a central well together with observation wells between the points of injection and pumping. Peaks in the pulses reveal stratification. Each layer will have different transmissivity from the others.

Perhaps a better alternative is the employment of radioactive logging methods. These include gamma logging, gamma–gamma logging, neutron–neutron logging and neutron–gamma logging.

3.2.1. Gamma Logging

This records the natural radioactivity of rocks which are penetrated by boring. The relevant radioisotopes are ^{40}K, the uranium and thorium series, etc., and the method depends upon the recognition of their decay products. Energies vary and quantitative estimates are usually related to equivalent radium (RaEq), i.e. the amount of radium which would emit a similar radiation dosage.

V. I. Feronsky[3] has given interesting data regarding the matter (see Tables 3.1 and 3.2). From these, it may be inferred that homogeneous clay-free organogenic and quartzose sediments show the lowest radioactivity and claystones and shales possess the highest. Obviously, this natural relationship between a type of rock and its radioactive content can be utilised in detection of individual zones within an aquifer.

3.2.2. Gamma–Gamma Logging

Here a sonde is employed which contains both a source (emitter) of gamma radiation and a detector, the latter measuring scattered gamma radiation as the sonde is moved along a borehole. The actual amount of gamma

TABLE 3.1

RADIOACTIVITY EMITTED FROM SELECTED SEDIMENTARY ROCKS

Type	RaEq (10^{-12} g/g of rock)
Anhydrite	0·5
Brown coal	1·0
Rock salt	2·0
Dolomite	0·5–10
Limestone	0·5–12
Sandstone	1·0–15
Clayey sandstone	2–20
Clayey limestone	2–20
Carbonaceous claystone and shale	3–25
Claystone and shale	4–30
Potassium salt	10–45
Deep sea clay	10–60

radiation received is a function of the density of the surrounding rocks and fluids and this permits a distinction to be made between saturated and unsaturated materials. Of course, other factors may interfere with the results, notably drilling mud, and, bearing in mind that the extent of lateral investigation permissible is a mere 10 to 15 cm, they constitute an obstacle to accurate density measurement.

3.2.3. Neutron–Neutron Logging

Here a sonde is utilised which records through a suitable detector the scattered neutron radiation which is emitted by a fast neutron source. Hydrogen atoms have a large cross section for moderating these to epithermal energy levels around 1 eV and the approach therefore indicates,

TABLE 3.2

RADIOELEMENTAL CONTENT OF SELECTED SEDIMENTARY ROCKS

Type	Ra (10^{-12} g/g of rock)	U (10^{-6} g/g of rock)	Th (10^{-6} g/g of rock)
Sandstone	up to 1·5	up to 4·0	—
Quartzite	0·54	1·6	—
Clay	1·3	4·3	13·0
Claystone and shale	1·09	3·0	—
Limestone	0·5	1·5	0·5
Dolomite	0·11	0·3	—

along the profile of a borehole, moisture content. Among other ways, neutrons may be produced according to the nuclear reaction $(^9Be,^4He)(^1n,^{12}C + 5\cdot74\,MeV)$, ^4He being alpha particles. Suitable alpha emitters include ^{226}Ra (half-life 1620 years), ^{227}Ac (half-life 22 years), ^{210}Po (half-life 138 days), ^{239}Pu (half-life $2\cdot4 \times 10^4$ years) and ^{241}Am (half-life 458 years). The yield of appropriate neutron sources may vary from 2×10^6 to $2 \times 10^7\,n/sec/Ci$. As detectors, scintillation and gas proportional counters may be used. In this technique also, extraneous factors may interfere with results and these are connected with drilling and well design.

3.2.4. Neutron–Gamma Logging

This records the gamma radiation emitted by nuclei in the formation when they capture thermal neutrons emitted by a fast neutron source in the sonde. Rough calculations demonstrate that neutron-capture gamma yield in a homogeneous medium depends upon the moderating properties of that medium. The technique is particularly suitable for detecting the boundaries between fresh and saline waters as a result of the fact that, if chlorine occurs, high neutron-capture gamma yield is noted.

A point against is that elements such as boron, cadmium, iron and potassium, if present, decrease the apparent moisture content due to neutron-capture effects. The 'sphere of importance' of a neutron probe is usually 70 cm (nil moisture) to 20 cm (moisture content 35 %).

Ground water occurs in the zone of saturation, but reaches this through the overlying zone of aeration (see Fig. 1.2). These shallow occurrences of subterranean water may also be investigated using the same methods. Soil density is determined by a transmission type density gauge based upon the principle of attenuation of gamma radiation by matter, thus

$$I = I_0\,e^{-\mu\rho z}$$

where I is the transmitted intensity of gamma rays, I_0 the primary intensity, μ is the mass adsorption coefficient of soil, ρ is the density of the soil and z is the distance between the detector and source of radiation. A soil moisture gauge is based upon the thermalisation of fast neutrons by hydrogen ions.

Radiologging is important in stratification determination when used in deep wells. Normally, there are three components, namely logging sondes, a surface unit for controlling these and recording data from them and a cable on a winch which transmits data to the surface and also powers the sondes and sources. Properly effected operations will give information regarding the profile of formations which are penetrated by a borehole or well. They can be carried out almost to any depth and give high accuracy.

3.2.5. Summary
It may be stated that stratification of aquifers is due to one or more of the
following phenomena:

(a) permeability barriers such as clays;
(b) normally higher horizontal permeability as compared with vertical
     permeability found in sediments;
(c) causes unconnected with permeability *per se*, such as variations in
     density and vertical differences of age of water due to inadequate
     mixing.

As well as the detection techniques alluded to above, i.e. radiologging ones
involving the introduction of instruments and monitoring of their emitted
radioactivity, environmental isotope analysis may be utilised in identification of discrete water bodies.

Obviously, the most important property here is radioactive decay and
both tritium and radiocarbon are relevant.

In phreatic aquifers, i.e. those in which recharge is directly from the
surface, a tritium gradient is usually observed which reflects the high input
of this radioisotope in recent years, higher concentrations being found in
the shallower waters with a decrease being demonstrated with depth. On a
wider chronological scale, the same effect may sometimes be noted with
carbon-14. Occasionally, where this wider time span is present, *long-term*
climatic changes can be recognised and identified even from the stable
isotope content.

Stratification of ground water indicated by isotopic differences is very
well shown by results obtained from the Vienna Basin.

3.2.5.1. *The Vienna Basin*
This is a flat valley which, in its southern part, encompasses about 1600 km^2
and includes the capital city itself as well as over 30 % of the population of
Austria. Geologically, it comprises a graben, i.e. a downfaulted block which
is bounded to the west by the limestones of the eastern Alps, to the east by
crystalline rock of the Alpine central zone and to the north by a structural
ridge bringing impermeable Tertiary sediments to the surface, these
constituting a barrier to ground water flow. The bordering faults do not
permit subterranean flow. Consequently, all inflow and outflow from the
basin is believed to be through surficial streams. The main aquifer is a 35 km
long by 4 km wide Pleistocene body filled with gravel to a depth of 100 to
150 m, this acting essentially as a pipe receiving recharge from an alluvial

fan at the upper end and discharging to streams in the lower portion. General isotopic results from the region reveal that:

(a) all ground water is from a common source, probably snowmelt in the Alps (oxygen analyses);

(b) those large and non-thermal springs of the eastern Alps emit waters comprising a mixture of current year recharge with an older base flow component (tritium);

(c) those thermal springs which emerge along bordering faults represent a triple blend of current year recharge, recharge from the post-1965 period and antique water with a radiocarbon content of 30% of modern (tritium and radiocarbon);

(d) the main aquifer has an upper unconfined zone (about 20 m deep) and a lower zone with uniform tritium indicative of good mixing;

(e) estimated transit time is approximately 4 m per day (this agrees well with the figure derived from conventional methods).[4]

Test wells in the Vienna Basin show marked tritium stratification. Those in question are at Mitterndorf and Haschendorf. Both of these were drilled by the percussion method and samples were obtained from the open-bottomed and cased well as the drilling went on. Naturally, it is very important to avoid any possibility of contamination from superficial waters which contain relatively high tritium contents and so enough water was pumped from each well in order to account for the volume of water in the casing prior to the commencement of sampling. Records from the two boreholes concerned indicated a rapid decrease in tritium content down to a certain depth and thereafter rather uniform *low* values. Interestingly, this phenomenon corresponded with a lithological boundary. The interpretation of the results was that there exists a sharp separation between an upper zone with incomplete mixing and a lower well-mixed zone. Active lateral flow is believed to take place between the two wells.[4]

3.3. HYDROGEN, CARBON AND OXYGEN ISOTOPES

The potential of these is well indicated by a selected case history, that of the Kalahari ground waters and this was discussed by E. Mazor and his associates.[5] The Kalahari is a particularly suitable region of southern Africa which is within the limits 19°S–28°S latitudes and 18°E–27°E longitudes and characterised by a flat sandy topography with grassland, scrubland and occasional trees covering about 600 000 km^2 with a very variable rainfall (average annual value 600 mm in the north and 400 mm in the centre; 250 mm to the south-west). There is only one area of *sustained* surface water and this is the famous Okavango delta in the north which is supplied by rains originating in Angola. Both this feature and the Makgadigadi pans act as an internal drainage basin. Because of this situation, the Kalahari has aptly been described as a desert. Mostly, it is

FIG. 3.1.   Kalahari desert.

within the country Botswana and what water exploitation takes place is by means of hand-excavated and drilled wells but these are few and have a low yield (2–10 m^3/h), so that they are far from adequate. Additionally, the ground water is sometimes saline in quality.

Figure 3.1 illustrates the region in general. It was long thought that there is negligible recharge by rain because it was believed that a sand cover more than 6 m deep absorbs annual precipitation which is subsequently lost through evapotranspiration, mostly during the dry season. Tritium and radiocarbon data indicate clearly, however, that this is not the case, providing unequivocal evidence of *recent* rain recharge within the last two decades or so within the northern and occasionally in the southern Kalahari.

As well as hydrogen, carbon and oxygen, but more rarely, nitrogen isotopes may also be employed as they were, for instance, in a study of the Melarchez Basin, Seine-et-Marne, France. Here, the $^{15}N/^{14}N$ ratio of nitrates in an intensively cultivated area was utilised in order to distinguish between three potential inputs, namely:

(a)   nitrates from the local nitrogen cycle;
(b)   nitrates from the nitrification of animal wastes;
(c)   nitrates from artificial fertilisers.

The isotope balance obtained indicated that the last source (c) was preponderant. Details may be obtained from the following publication: MARIOTTI, A. and LETOLLE, R., 1977. Application de l'étude isotopique de l'azote en hydrologie et en hydrogéologie. Analyse des résultats obtenus sur un exemple précis: le Bassin de Melarchez (Seine-et-Marne, France). *J. Hydrol.*, **33**, 157–172.

3.3.1. Tritium Results in the Kalahari

The average pre-bomb tritium content of southern hemisphere rains is estimated at about 5 or 6 TU; this rose to approximately 30 TU after 1952. In three rivers and a dam in Botswana, waters gave a content of 24 to 32 TU, representative of 1971–72 rains. The ground waters studied in various areas of the country gave data divisible into three categories which are: contents exceeding 2 TU (indicating active rain recharge through the preceding 20 years), contents not in excess of 1·5 TU (indicating *either* 20 to 30 year old waters *or* mixtures of older waters with small quantities of post-bomb rains) and contents which are not measurable (indicating ages greater than 20 years and no active rain recharge). The rain recharge pattern as shown by this tritium work can be correlated with (a) the rain distribution, and (b) the increasing thickness of the Kalahari beds from north to south.

3.3.2. Carbon Isotopic Results in the Kalahari

3.3.2.1. *Carbon*-13

The $\delta^{13}C$ values of the dissolved species of carbon in the waters studied showed a range of from $-13·7\permil$ to $-5·3\permil$. There appears to be a chemical correlation between these and the chemical composition of the waters. As regards the latter, bicarbonate is the dominant anion and sodium is the common cation. The $\delta^{13}C$ values positively correlate with the HCO_3 concentration which reflects a higher portion of fossil carbon in the higher bicarbonate waters.

There is also a positive correlation between the $\delta^{13}C$ values and pH values. It is believed that the wide range of $\delta^{13}C$ values noted in the ground waters of the Kalahari were probably the result of fast reactions under varying environmental conditions of infiltration and these latter are retained more or less unaltered in the aquifers.

3.3.2.2. *Carbon*-14

These range from 120 to 1 pmc (percentage modern carbon). The former values, i.e. the high ones, are very interesting. The bomb era has caused an increase in the atmospheric ^{14}C content in the southern hemisphere from 100 pmc in 1955 to 165 pmc in 1963, this value declining to 145 pmc in 1972.[6,7]

The average radiocarbon content in the atmosphere over the period 1964 to 1974 is thought to be about 155 pmc. At one well, Makgaba, a figure of 120 pmc was obtained and this is therefore considered to represent a *dilution* by fossil carbon to some 85 % of the initial atmospheric value. The accompanying $\delta^{13}C$ value here is $-11\cdot7\%_0$, typical of many Kalahari waters and probably indicating typical ^{14}C dilution to 85 %.

General results show that recent rain recharge definitely occurs in the Kalahari and the data indicate young ages in the phreatic ground waters in the northern part, greater ages occurring to the south (in agreement with the respective annual rainfalls). The semi-artesian Cave sandstone aquifer gave evidence of a complex situation because water obtained therefrom contained 9–20 pmc associated with 0·4–1·8 TU, this being interpreted as an admixture of shallow water containing tritium to water pumped at depth. Mazor *et al.* argued that, to assess the *real* ^{14}C of the confined water, the quantity of radiocarbon which was brought in along with the tritium of the *recent* water component has to be taken away from the measured ^{14}C value.[5] Thus, were the 0·4–1·8 TU to enter with post-bomb rain water, the accompanying radiocarbon would be 2–10 pmc. However, if the recent water component was stored in the ground for, say, two decades, then the *original* tritium value would have been greater by a factor of at least two with a corresponding value of approximately twice the radiocarbon, covering completely the actually measured concentrations. Cave sandstone water hence appears to be devoid of tritium and either lacking or poor in radiocarbon so that the inference may be drawn that it is probably over 15 000 years old (indicating *trapped* water).

Of course, it has to be pointed out that there is much debate about how ground water ages are correctly to be calculated, some workers suggesting that dilution by fossil carbon may be corrected by reference to the accompanying $\delta^{13}C$ value. This is based on an assumption, namely that infiltrating water becomes charged in the soil by biogenic carbon dioxide with $\delta^{13}C$ values around $-25\permil$ and a radiocarbon value of 100 pmc. This is neutralised by fossil rock carbonate with $\delta^{13}C$ values of $0\permil$ and of course a nil radiocarbon content. Consequently, the measured radiocarbon value is divided by $\delta^{13}C/-25$ and this value is then utilised in the age equation.

Other workers have proposed a value of $-18\permil$ for the $\delta^{13}C$ of the organic carbon. The present writer has accepted the earlier value of $-25\permil$. Then the delta value of any sample will fall between zero and $-25\permil$ depending upon the relative contribution of carbon from limestone and from organic sources. If pl and ls are used to denote plant matter and limestone, then the correction factor can be expressed as $P = pl/(pl + ls)$. Thereafter, the delta value of the sample as regards carbon-13 will be the weighted average of the two components:

$$\delta^{13}C_{sample} = {}^{13}C_{pl}[pl/(pl - ls)] - {}^{13}C_{ls}[ls/(pl - ls)]$$

Since the general definition of delta is

$$\delta = \frac{R_{sample} - R_{standard}}{R_{standard}} \times 10^3$$

then combination gives

$$P = \frac{\delta^{13}C_{sample} - \delta^{13}C_{ls}}{\delta^{13}C_{pl} - \delta^{13}C_{ls}}$$

and, inserting previously noted values

$$P = \delta^{13}C_{sample}/-25$$

as noted above. An extended discussion can be found in a paper by the writer on progress in isotopic hydrology.[8]

Reflecting on their results, Mazor and his associates asked whether their 'ages' are realistic and, regarding the fact that phreatic ground waters in the northern Kalahari are younger than those in the south and that this is explicable in terms of decrease in rainfall, ascribe this phenomenon to less turnover. This can be the cause of the higher ages to the south. Some young ground waters may be accounted for by flood recharge. This argument seems persuasive.[5]

3.3.3. Stable Isotopes

Waters sampled from appropriate locales such as the Mopipi Dam region and the closed reservoir of the Rakops Hospital appear to be well evaporated as might be expected. Both in phreatic and confined water samples, a range of, for deuterium

$$\delta D - 55\%_0 \text{ to } -25\%_0$$

and, for oxygen-18

$$\delta^{18}O - 8.5\%_0 \text{ to } -3.5\%_0$$

is observed. There seems to be no correlation between this and the type of aquifer and also there is no apparent correlation with ^{14}C content or age.

The ground waters have an isotopic composition falling into the range of individual rains, but they are *lighter* than the annual average. Direct infiltration is probably the mechanism of percolation and it is believed that this is rapid so that minimal evaporative losses occur.

The preferential lightness alluded to above may well result from origination of the precipitation in a previous climatic regimen although it must be allowed that the non-correlation of ^{14}C ages with the deuterium and oxygen-18 values militates against this. Perhaps there is a selective intake of individual rains with light isotopic composition, but why this takes place is not immediately clear.

3.4. SILICON-32

A word on this radioisotope may be useful here as it is one which can be important in age assessment of ground water. It has a half-life of about 600 years and thus, as it occupies a chronological slot between tritium and radiocarbon, could be employed, theoretically, to date ground waters around 2500 to 3000 years in age. Actually, the level of cosmic ray-produced ^{32}Si activity in precipitation is quite low—0.5 dpm/t on average —and this probably exists in solution as monomeric silicic acid. The low activity means that this radioisotope is practically unobservable. Fortunately, however, it decays to phosphorus-32 (half-life 14 days) which can be extracted from large quantities of silica in essentially carrier-free form and thereafter measured by techniques of low level counting. This nuclear tool has not found wide application. The reason for this is that large volumes of water are required in the field sampling associated with the technique, approximately 5 tons being necessary for extraction of silica and a very long counting time later being involved. By comparison, radiocarbon sampling can be done with only 200 litres of water.

Some other aspects of nuclear techniques in ground water studies may now be considered and these may be categorised as below.

3.5. INFILTRATION AND PERCOLATION

These are essential parts of the process of ground water recharge, a matter investigated conventionally by measuring the level of the water table in observation wells (cf. sections 2.2 and 2.18.1 in the preceding chapter, for instance). Lysimeter measurements may also be made.

3.5.1. Lysimeters

These are devices which collect downwardly moving soil moisture and are usually funnel-shaped. Unfortunately, they are quite expensive and, of course, only give results for a rather localised spot. Additionally, they can locally alter the naturally occurring conditions. Ocasionally, they are filled with artificially introduced material which is non-representative of the actual soil itself. A funnel device again is not particularly useful because it can seriously change the hydraulic gradient in the reference plane (horizontal) and thus the moisture flux. This is especially the case where the soil under examination is fine-grained.

3.5.2. Nuclear Methods in Determining Recharge Rates to Ground Water

One approach is to isotopically tag or label soil moisture with tritium or some other suitable isotope and K. O. Münnich's work in this field has already been referred to in Chapter 1, section 1.12.[9]

Another approach is to deduce the average ground water recharge since 1962 on the basis of the bomb tritium found in a soil moisture profile. In this case, the radioisotopic tracer results from the increased atmospheric contribution due to thermonuclear testing (cf. section 2.11, environmental tritium, above in Chapter 2). In point of fact, this was at its maximum during the years 1963 and 1964 because this was immediately after the nuclear moratorium and soil profiles taken in those years manifested such a marked leading edge of the bomb peak that this could be utilised in evaluating ground water recharge. Consequently, the approach is no longer so useful (although atmospheric tritium levels remain above normal, they are much lower than they were at the time in question).

Stable isotopes are very important because they show variation in soil moisture with depth and hence provide natural tracer marks. If these relate to seasonal variations in stable isotope contents in rains, they can be employed in calculating recharge rates but only if all associated factors are properly understood. Thus, for instance, diffusion occurs and so does a kind of seasonal weighting, this latter because rains are often commoner in winter and those falling in summer are mostly lost to the ground water system as a result of evapotranspirative processes. It may be more practical to analyse deuterium in some cases and this is because the isotope is easier analysed in small amounts of water than is oxygen-18, thus less water needs to be collected. Often, deuterium profiles in soils exhibit errors, however, as a result of fractionation effects.

3.6.　FLOW THROUGH FRACTURES

Water often occurs in fractured rocks such as karst, i.e. in materials with a very high capacity for infiltration and few surficial streams. Infiltration may occur in concentrated points, sink holes for example, or more generally. The tracing of connections between such points and emergent springs is difficult in most cases and radioisotopes are applicable to the problem.

David J. Burdon and his associates utilised the method in order to study the possible interconnections between two sinkholes on the high plateau of Tripolis and a number of springs situated near the coast of the Peloponnese.[10] Activation analysis has also been applied, a non-radioactive material being made radioactive in order to detect it, measurement of the induced radioactivity being a measure of the concentration of the tracer.[11]

Environmental isotopes may also be employed. For instance, Bryan R. Payne determined that Lake Chala, Kenya, a volcanic crater lake without surface inflow or outflow, did *not* supply springs in the area. This was

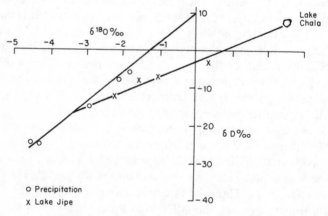

Fig. 3.2.　D and ^{18}O composition of Lake Chala and other lakes in the area.

inferred from deuterium and oxygen-18 measurements.[12] The isotopic composition of the lake is, in fact, completely different from that of the springs and while the waters of the former show all the characteristics associated with high evaporation rates, those of the latter, of course, do not. Figure 3.2 illustrates the matter (see also Chapter 13). Environmental isotope analysis has also been used in the case of a volcanic island, Cheju, off the coast of South Korea, the data indicating that there is rapid infiltration and sub-surface flow.

3.7.   NUCLEAR METHODS IN FRACTURED ROCKS

There can be little doubt that the optimal manner in which to tackle the problem is firstly to effect a reconnaissance survey of the environmental isotope content of the relevant waters, therefore elucidating the situation. Later, if required, a further stage would comprise the employment of artificial tracers (and this might also include chemical dyes as well as radioisotopes) which can deal with specific investigations such as those outlined, i.e. interconnections between water bodies. Care is necessary because of dispersal of the tracer and possible subsequent contamination. It is interesting to consider what are the respective advantages of radiotracers and inactive ones followed by activation analysis. Of course, a nuclear reactor is necessary for the latter and a merely nominal irradiation charge may be used. Both methods must conform to considerations of health and safety.

REFERENCES

1. HALEVY, E. and NIR, A., 1962. The determination of aquifer parameters with the aid of radioactive tracers. *J. Geophys. Res.*, **61**, 2403.
2. WIEBENGA, W. A., 1967. Radioisotopes as ground water tracers. *J. Geophys. Res.*, **72**, 4081.
3. FERONSKY, V. I., 1968. Stratification of aquifers. In *Guidebook on Nuclear Techniques in Hydrology*, Tech. Rep. Ser. No. 91, International Atomic Energy Agency, Vienna, 156–164.
4. DAVIS, G. H., 1968. Saturated zone. In *Guidebook on Nuclear Techniques in Hydrology*, Tech. Rep. Ser. No. 91, International Atomic Energy Agency, Vienna, 125–126.
5. MAZOR, E., VERHAGEN, B. T., SELLSCHOP, J. P. F., ROBBINS, N. S. and HUTTON, L. G., 1974. Kalahari groundwaters: their hydrogen, carbon and oxygen

isotopes. In *Isotope Techniques in Groundwater Hydrology*, International Atomic Energy Agency, Vienna, 203–225.

6. RAFTER, T. A. and O'BRIEN, B. J., 1972. ^{14}C measurements in the atmosphere and in the south Pacific Ocean. *Eighth International Conference on Radiocarbon Dating, Proc. Conf. N.Z.*, 1972. Roy. Soc. New Zealand.

7. VOGEL, J. C., 1972. Radiocarbon in the surface waters of the Atlantic Ocean. *Eighth International Conference on Radiocarbon Dating, Proc. Conf. N.Z.*, 1972. Roy. Soc. New Zealand.

8. BOWEN, R., 1969. Progress in isotopic hydrology: the combined environmental isotope approach. *Science Progress*, **57**, 559–575.

9. MÜNNICH, K. O., 1968. Moisture movement. Sect. IV A 3. In *Guidebook on Nuclear Techniques in Hydrology*, Tech. Rep. Ser. No. 91, International Atomic Energy Agency, Vienna, 109–118.

10. BURDON, D. J., ERICSSON, E., PAYNE, B. R. and PAPADIMITROPOULOS, T., 1963. The use of tritium in tracing karst groundwater in Greece. *Radioisotopes in Hydrology, Proc. Symp. Tokyo*, 1963. International Atomic Energy Agency, Vienna, 309–320.

11. DIMITROPOULOS, C., PAPADIMITROPOULOS, T. and PAPAKIS, N., 1962. Groundwater investigation by the use of neutron activation analysis. *Mémoires de l'Association Internationale des Hydrogéologues*, V, Athens, 83.

12. PAYNE, B. R., 1970. Water balance of Lake Chala and its relation to groundwater from tritium and stable isotope data. *J. Hydrol.*, **11**, 47–58.

CHAPTER 4

The Chemical Quality of Ground Water

4.1. INTRODUCTION

The water molecule comprises two atoms of hydrogen and an atom of oxygen and both of these elements exist in nature in the form of several isotopes. Hydrogen occurs as ^1H, ^2H (deuterium, D) and ^3H (tritium, T), the latter being a radioactive isotope as previously described. Oxygen possesses three significant and non-radioactive isotopes, namely ^{16}O, ^{17}O and ^{18}O. Average abundances of ^{17}O and tritium are extremely small and therefore the water molecule may appear as $H_2^{16}O$, the usual variety, HDO and $H_2^{18}O$. The relative quantities are, in ppm

$$
\begin{array}{ll}
H_2^{16}O & 997\,680 \\
HDO & 320 \\
H_2^{18}O & 2\,000
\end{array}
$$

Actual concentrations of these stable isotopic species in terrestrial water samples undergo small variations of up to 30% for HDO and 5% for $H_2^{18}O$. As was noted earlier, relative concentration values for these are usually given rather than absolute amounts. They are related to the isotopic composition of a standard mean ocean water called SMOW and expressed in delta units, i.e. as per mil deviations from the standard, the expression being, as stated on p. 73,

$$
\delta = \frac{R_{sample} - R_{standard}}{R_{standard}} \times 10^3 \ (\text{‰})
$$

The normal range for terrestrial waters is then approximately

$$-50 \text{ to } -300\text{‰} \qquad \text{for deuterium,}$$

and

$$-5 \text{ to } -50\text{‰} \qquad \text{for oxygen-18}$$

As regards surface waters, differences in isotopic composition reflect isotope fractionation processes occurring in the hydrological cycle. Hydrometeorological phenomena result in identifiable differences in the isotopic composition, for instance, of precipitation as a function of latitude, topography, climate and season. Increasing latitude and altitude, as well as increase in distance from the source of water vapour, all result in increasing depletion of the heavy isotopic content of the precipitation while maintaining a linear correlation of

$$\delta D = 8\,\delta^{18}O - 10\,(\permil)$$

in the major continental areas of Europe and North America.

Where local moisture sources exist where evaporation occurs under more extreme conditions such as around the Mediterranean Sea, the relation becomes

$$\delta D = 8\,\delta^{18}O - 22\,(\permil)$$

The precipitation at any specific locale therefore is characterised by its relative position on a $\delta D/\delta^{18}O$ graph and its intercept on the positive side of the deuterium axis (i.e. the so-called d-parameter). Normally, there will be a slope of 8, but surface evaporation reduces this to a slope of 4 to 6 as a result of increase in the heavy isotopes content (cf. Fig. 3.2).

All this is highly relevant to ground water undergoing active recharge. Apart entirely from isotopic considerations, the ground water encountered in a particular aquifer will contain many substances in solution, these sometimes militating against its use for one purpose or another. Clearly, it is necessary to know the quality of water in any region and also the quality requirements for the various aspects of water usage there found. The steps involved are to collect samples from the ground water system and thereafter analyse them in a suitable laboratory. Usually half gallon samples are optimal. Much smaller ones are satisfactory for stable isotope analysis in a mass spectrometer, naturally. One of the deleterious materials often carried is salt and various sources of salinity are met with in nature. For instance, excess irrigation water may add it as also may fertilisers. Other salts may be present. Ground water which passes through igneous rocks may dissolve mineral matter, especially if the CO_2 content (derived from the atmosphere) is high. Some sedimentary rocks contribute mineral matter, for example limestone which yields calcium and carbonates. Concentrations of all such inorganic constituents may be determined from appropriate samples and where these are obtained from wells, they should be pumped for some time beforehand (this is also necessary where the samples are to be used for stable isotope analysis in order to prevent exchange taking place). This way, stagnant and hence non-representative waters are avoided.

The actual concentrations of chemical substances which are dissolved in water may be reported in several ways.

4.2. PRINCIPAL METHODS OF EXPRESSING RESULTS OF CHEMICAL ANALYSES

There are at least three and these are discussed below.

4.2.1. Parts Per Million (ppm)

Concentration in terms of weight per weight, i.e. weight of solute compared with weight of solution, is expressed as parts per million; 1 ppm is equivalent to 1 mg of solute in 1 kg of solution, i.e. ppm equals mg/litre.

In irrigation, unit tons of dissolved solids per acre-foot of water (taf) are utilised and 1 taf equals 735 ppm.

4.2.2. Milligrams Per Litre (mg/litre)

Concentration in terms of weight of solute per volume of solution is expressed as milligrams per litre. It is essentially metric and hence used in countries employing this system. The equivalent unit in English measure is grains per gallon, 1 grain per US gallon being equal to 17·1 mg/litre.

4.2.3. Equivalents Per Million (epm)

Concentration of substances in solution in terms of their chemical equivalence is expressed as equivalents per million. The equivalent weight of an ion is, of course, the ratio of its atomic weight to its valency. Some relevant data are appended in Table 4.1.

One equivalent weight of any cation will combine with one equivalent weight of an anion *exactly*. Hydrogen has an equivalent weight of unity and therefore the equivalent weights of other elements refer to it and are, in fact, equivalent weights of hydrogen. It may be stated that the equivalent weight in grams of an ion or a compound (i.e. the gram equivalent weight) is that weight in grams combining with or replacing one gram of hydrogen.

If a water sample contains a known concentration of say calcium, then the amount is expressible in several ways. For instance, where 30·6 ppm of this element are present, the epm may be calculated thus:

$$\text{atomic weight of calcium} = 40 \cdot 08$$
$$\text{valency (ionic charge)} = 2$$
$$\text{equivalent weight} = 40 \cdot 08/2 = 20 \cdot 04$$

TABLE 4.1

SOME CHEMICAL CONSTITUENTS OF GROUND WATER

Commonly occurring cations	Equivalent weight	Commonly occurring anions	Equivalent weight
Calcium, Ca	20·04	Carbonate, CO_3	30·00
(at. wt. 40·08, valency 2)		Bicarbonate, HCO_3	61·01
Magnesium, Mg	12·16	Sulphate, SO_4	48·03
(at. wt. 24·32, valency 2)		Chloride, Cl	35·46
Sodium, Na	23·00	Nitrate, NO_3	62·01
(at. wt. 23·00, valency 1)			
Potassium, K	39·10		
(at. wt. 39·10, valency 1)			

Other common elements dissolved in water

Carbon, C	atomic weight 12·00	valency 2, 4	
Nitrogen, N	atomic weight 14·01	valency 3, 5	
Oxygen, O	atomic weight 16·00	valency 2	
Sulphur, S	atomic weight 32·06	valency 2, 4, 6	
Hydrogen, H	atomic weight 1·01	valency 1	

Minor constituents

Iron, Fe	Aluminium, Al	Selenium, Se
Silica, SiO_2	Boron, B	Fluoride, F

therefore

$$epm\ Ca = 30·6/20·04$$
$$= 1·52$$

It must be added that epm are usually employed for reporting substances in solution in the ionic form and hence substances such as silica and iron which occur in solution in *non*-ionic form are *not* reported in epm.

4.3.   ELECTRIC CONDUCTIVITY

Total dissolved solids in ground water may be determined rapidly using appropriate instruments to measure the electrical conductance of a sample. This is done in preference to making measurements of resistance, the reciprocal of conductance, because this latter increases with salt content. Conductance is expressed in mhos (i.e. reciprocal ohms), usually as specific electrical conductance, mhos/cm.

Since conductance is a function of temperature, it is necessary that measurements of it be related to a standard temperature normally taken as 25 °C.

4.4. WATER HARDNESS

The total hardness of a water sample is a measure of the content of magnesium and calcium, usually expressed as the equivalent of calcium carbonate; thus

$$\text{Total hardness} = Ca \times \frac{CaCO_3}{Ca} + Mg \times \frac{CaCO_3}{Mg}$$

Total hardness is measured in ppm as are Ca and Mg and the ratios in equivalent weights, so that the equation may be given as

$$\text{Total hardness} = 2 \cdot 497\,Ca + 4 \cdot 115\,Mg$$

4.5. THE PHYSICAL ANALYSIS OF GROUND WATER

Temperature in °C is taken immediately subsequent to sampling and colour may also be noted and reported in ppm by comparison with appropriate standards. Colour is due to mineral or organic material in solution and turbidity results from suspended and colloidal matter such as silt or clay in water. Turbidity is often reduced or eliminated by natural filtration processes in unconfined aquifers, but where present, it may be measured by a technique depending upon the length of a path of light through the water. Taste and aroma may arise from bacteria, dissolved gases or mineral matter.

4.6. BACTERIA

These are contaminants and their occurrence must be monitored if water quality is to be ensured. The isolation of pathogenic bacteria is a difficult job, but those of the coliform group can be both identified and separated and may therefore serve as an indication of the safety or otherwise of drinking water. Results of tests on them are reported as most probable numbers in a given volume of water (MPN).

4.7. ION EXCHANGE

A great number of naturally occurring minerals possess the ability of exchanging one ion for another, such processes usually involving cations. The cations which figure most often in them are calcium, magnesium and sodium and the exchange actually takes place when ions adsorbed on mineral grain surfaces are not the same as those in the ground water. The process of exchange terminates when equilibrium is established between the cations of the matrix and the cations in the ground water. Obviously, such a phenomenon has a great bearing upon the chemical composition of ground water, cf. for instance, the zeolites. These constitute a group of hydrous, aluminium silicates possessing calcium and sodium as important components. They also have potassium and aluminium and in many ways, their composition is analogous with that of the feldspars. In fact, they result from alteration of feldspars and aluminous minerals of igneous rocks and occur almost exclusively as secondary minerals filling cavities, joints, fissures, etc., in rocks such as basalts and scoriaceous lavas. They are soft minerals and their hardness varies from 3·5 to 5·5. Their specific gravities range from 2 to 2·4. The fibrous varieties have framework structures of linked silica tetrahedra arranged in groups of five and some of the best known of these are natrolite, $Na_2(Al_2Si_3O_{10}) \cdot 2H_2O$, scolecite, $Ca(Al_2Si_3O_{10}) \cdot 3H_2O$ and mesolite, midway between these in composition. When ground water traverses such minerals, sodium ions exchange with calcium and magnesium ions in the water and thus reduce its hardness. Eventually, equilibrium is established and therefore no further ion exchange occurs unless a new factor is introduced. Such a new factor is the possibility of sea water intrusion into an aquifer whereby the sodium in the sea water is exchanged for the calcium and magnesium ions.

4.8. CRITERIA FOR THE QUALITY OF WATER

Since ground water may be utilised for drinking, irrigation and industry, it must conform to certain standards.

4.8.1. For Drinking
Most countries have standards set up for evaluation of drinking water and these will include unobjectionable colour and taste with unnoticeable aroma and low turbidity as well as low bacterial content (MPN about 1 per 100 ml) with the chemical characteristics listed in Table 4.2.

TABLE 4.2

DESIRABLE CHEMICAL CHARACTERISTICS OF DRINKING WATER

Constituent	Maximum permissible level (ppm)
Lead, Pb	0·1
Fluoride, F	1·5
Arsenic, As	0·05
Selenium, Se	0·05
Hexavalent chromium, Cr	0·05
Copper, Cu	3·0
Iron, Fe—Manganese, Mn	0·3
Magnesium, Mg	125
Zinc, Zn	15
Chloride, Cl	250
Sulphate, SO_4	250
Phenol	0·001
Total permitted solids	1 000

Limits for the first five constituents are mandatory.[1]

4.8.2. For Industry

As well as suitable quality, the criteria here include consistency as regards the various components. Fluctuations in ground water temperature may also be of importance although it must be mentioned that this property is one of the most conservative since the insulating effect of the planetary crust reduces extremes. Generally speaking, the temperature of ground water at a depth of 50 or 60 ft has been found to exceed air temperatures by a couple of degrees Celsius and thereafter, temperatures rise about 1 °C per 100 ft of depth following the geothermal gradient. This latter and associated phenomena have been discussed by the writer in *Geothermal Resources*.[2]

4.9. ADULTERATION OF GROUND WATER

This can occur as a result of a number of factors such as the introduction of sewage and industrial wastes. If such pollutants constitute a threat to public health, they comprise contaminants. Clearly, attention must be given to the matter in order to safeguard a supply of ground water.

Organic pollution is not as important as that due to inorganic solutions because the latter penetrate more easily down to an aquifer and are much

TABLE 4.3
CAUSES OF DEGRADATION OF GROUND WATER

(a) *Natural*
  Inflow of juvenile water
(b) *Associated with development programmes*
  Return water from irrigation
  Interchange between aquifers due to factors such as improperly constructed wells
  Overdraft conditions: these result from taking more than the safe yield from an aquifer (safe yield = the quantity of water which can be withdrawn annually *without* producing any unwanted result of a deleterious nature)
  Sea water intrusion
  Diffusion, either upwards or laterally, of connate brines due to over-pumping
(c) *Mineralisation caused by plant transpiration and/or evaporation*

more difficult to remove. This is because natural dilution is very slow and artificial flushing is expensive.

4.10. THE GRAPHICAL REPRESENTATION OF CHEMICAL ANALYTICAL DATA

John D. Hem has referred to numerous graphical methods for facilitating both the presentation and also the interpretation of chemical analyses.[3] These include scatter diagrams, ionic-concentration diagrams, percentage-composition diagrams, frequency diagrams, quality of water maps, etc. Data may be plotted on nomograms, i.e. alignment charts so arranged that the value of one variable can be determined without calculation from values of one or two other variables which are known. In this manner, chemical

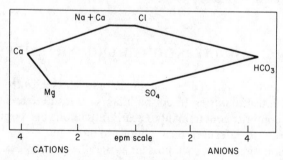

FIG. 4.1. 'Shape' diagram.

analyses can be compared. For instance, bar graphs may be drawn showing epm of analyses and, for example, the left half of such a bar might show cations Ca, Mg and Na; the right half will consist, in the same order, of anions HCO_3, SO_4 and Cl.

The chemical composition of a ground water sample may also be shown by means of a shape diagram (see Fig. 4.1). Here, cations and anions are plotted on the epm scale and a characteristic 'shape' produced.

REFERENCES

1. TODD, D. K., 1959. *Ground Water Hydrology.* John Wiley, New York and London, p. 185.
2. BOWEN, R., 1979. *Geothermal Resources.* Applied Science Publishers, London.
3. HEM, J. D., 1959. *Study and Interpretation of the Chemical Characteristics of Natural Waters.* USGS Water Supply Paper 1473.

CHAPTER 5

Ground Water Basins

Ground water may be considered as one of Man's major resources and it is, to a degree, renewable both through natural and artificial recharge. Of course, its uses are extremely diverse and, to consider a single country, the USA, water usage in general may be surveyed. Total use is approximately 9860 million m³ daily, mostly for the generation of electricity. Industry occupies second place with agriculture third and it may be stated that water is primarily utilised for purposes which do not consume it. It is interesting that a regional variation exists, so that in the east the uses are mainly not consumptive while in the west they are. Although ground water is important, by far the bulk of the annual supply is composed of precipitation. Per capita use is continually increasing and industrial use, for instance, doubled from 1950 to 1965. This is also true for ground water which therefore assumes an ever-increasing significance. The existing supply of water is considered quite adequate and there appears to be no danger of a shortfall. Of course, problems exist, but are technically and financially soluble.

To develop ground water resources efficiently, it is thought best to consider it in terms of entire basins. Obviously, a hydrologic equilibrium ought to exist between input and output of water from such a basin. Safe yield in aquifers has been referred to previously and exactly the same concept may be applied to basins, i.e. the optimal draft of water from one is that which can be continued indefinitely without adverse effects. Excess pumpage is again referred to as overdraft. If ground water is to be safeguarded, then only a certain amount of water can be taken annually from a basin and the difficulty of assessing this accurately is demonstrated by the fact that the biggest single ground water problem in the USA arises from the withdrawal of too much, i.e. overdrafting. At the least, this promotes temporary depletion and at worst, it can cause permanent damage. In the first place, of course, safe yield must on no account be greater than the long-term average annual supply to the basin because withdrawals exceeding this must perforce come from storage. If storage is being tapped, permanent depletion or *mining* results. To some extent, this can be overcome by artificial recharge and this is being done, for instance, north of Miami where enormous water-conservation districts exist in which water of the Everglades is ponded and permitted to soak into the ground, i.e. to percolate into the ground water system. Water supply to a basin may be restricted as a result of several factors. For example, the actual physical size of the basin may limit it. Also, the velocity with which recharge water transits the basin to the point of withdrawal may be unfavourable. It is possible, therefore, to distinguish between quantity and rate in determination of safe yield. H. E. Thomas, in fact, considered the matter under the designations reservoir and pipeline problems.[1]

Another phenomenon may be significant in assessing safe yield within a basin and this is pollution. Sometimes, pumping may be continued long enough to produce saline waters resulting from induced sea water intrusion. Again, lowered water levels may promote the inflow of deeper lying connate brines. The equation of hydrologic equilibrium has already been stated, for instance in Chapter 1, section 1.9, as

$$I = O - \Delta S$$

where I is the input, O the output and ΔS the change in storage. An expanded expression of this might be:

(Surface inflow + subsurface inflow + precipitation + imported water + decrease in surface storage + decrease in ground water storage) = (Surface outflow + subsurface outflow + consumptive use + exported water + increase in surface storage + increase in ground water storage)

This includes all waters entering and leaving a basin. Naturally, some items may be omitted in particular situations. One of the pertinent ones is that of a confined aquifer to which there is no contribution of overlying surface waters. Obviously, every item represents a discharge (volume of water during a unit time) and appropriate consistent units must be employed (for instance, acre-feet per year). Obviously, too, both sides of the equation must balance.

Another expression of the fundamental balance equation for *any* hydrologic system is given by

$$\Sigma \Delta V_i = \Sigma I \Delta t - \Sigma O \Delta t$$

where ΔV_i are changes of storage in the surface and subsurface reservoirs during Δt, Is represent inputs to the system such as precipitation or inflow and Os are the outputs, for example runoff at an outlet and evapotranspiration. Essentially, the concept relates to water budget studies and these may also be approached using environmental isotopes so that

$$\Sigma C_i \Delta V_i + \Sigma V_i \Delta C_i = \Sigma C_i I \Delta t - \Sigma C_o O \Delta t$$

where ΔV_i is the change of storage, C_i the mean isotope concentration in the storage, ΔC_i the change of concentration during the period, V the mean storage and C_i and C_o the isotope concentrations in the inflow and outflow components. The relevant isotopic species of water here are HTO, HDO and H_2O.[2]

5.1. DETERMINATION OF SAFE YIELD IN A BASIN

A quantity of data is requisite, particularly surface inflow and outflow, imported and exported water (measurable by conventional hydrographic and hydraulic methods), precipitation (available from meteorological services such as the Weather Bureau), consumptive use (including *all* water released into the atmosphere by evapotranspirative processes), changes in surface storage (computable from alterations in water levels of surface reservoirs), changes in ground water storage (obtainable from detailed studies on an appropriate grid of measuring wells) and subsurface inflow and outflow. These latter items are perhaps the most difficult accurately to determine because it is impossible to measure them directly. However, it is possible to estimate them because often one of them is the only unknown in the equation.

5.1.1. Hill Method
This is based upon the work of R. A. Hill in Arizona and Southern California.[3] Yearly alterations in the elevation of ground water levels, either water table or piezometric, in a particular basin are plotted against annual drafts. The points usually fall on a straight line if the water supply to the basin in question is nearly constant. The draft which corresponds to a zero change in elevation will be the safe yield.

5.1.2. Harding Method
This was developed by S. T. Harding and is based upon an annual retained inflow and alteration in water table elevation.[4] Yearly values for the former

are plotted against yearly alterations in the elevation of water table. Points are again best fitted by a straight line and the retained inflow which corresponds to zero change in water table elevation is the safe yield.

5.1.3. Simpson Method

T. R. Simpson originated this and it is based upon a pumping trough in a coastal aquifer.[5] Obviously, where overdrafts occur in coastal aquifers, sea

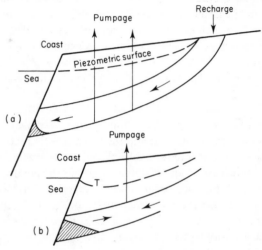

FIG. 5.1. Confined aquifer intersecting a coastline. (a) Safe yield; (b) overdraft. Note intrusion of wedge of sea water in (b) cf. its stationary position in (a). Aquifer water flow direction near the coastline is reversed in (b), i.e. is directed inland, as compared with (a). T, Trough in piezometric surface.

water intrusion results if water table or piezometric levels decrease below mean sea level. Figure 5.1 shows a confined aquifer intersecting a coastline and in case (a) the piezometric surface slopes *towards* the ocean; here, the basin draft is equal to safe yield. When overdraft arises, however, the piezometric surface falls as a result of the fact that down-valley flow is less than the draft. A pumping trough in the piezometric surface forms. Consequently, from hydraulic gradient considerations, it may be seen that draft on the inland side of the trough is supplied by down-valley flow from the area of recharge; on the other hand, draft on the seaward side of the trough derives from ground water moving inland from the sea. This latter phenomenon extends the sea wedge further into the body of the aquifer and wells near the coastline begin pumping highly saline water from the aquifer.

This renders them useless. Obviously, the basin draft immediately before the appearance of the trough or immediately subsequent to its disappearance is the safe yield.

5.1.4. Darcy's Law Method
If lateral inflow occurs into a basin from a known direction, the safe yield is obtainable from the long-term inflow by application of this law where average hydraulic gradient, permeability of the aquifer and the cross-sectional area of the latter in a direction perpendicular to flow are known. Of course, these parameters are determinable from ground water levels, the results of pumping tests and the geological information. The method has been used by the US Geological Survey in respect of confined aquifers possessing unidirectional flow. O. E. Meinzer has outlined the technique in greater detail.[6]

5.1.5. Zero Net Ground Water Level Fluctuation Method
Where the elevation of ground water at the beginning and the end of a time interval is the same, the average annual net draft on the basin is a measure of the safe yield. In the case of an unconfined aquifer, the net draft will be the consumptive use of pumped ground water together with any exported ground water. In the case of a confined aquifer, the net draft will be the gross pumpage. The average yearly supply ought to approximate the long-term mean and the draft prior to and subsequent to the period ought to approach overdraft conditions.

5.1.6. Specific Yield/Average Yearly Rise in Water Table Method
In an unconfined aquifer, yearly recharge may be expressed as the product of the specific yield, yearly rise in the water table and the area of the particular aquifer. All these parameters are determinable. The average yearly rise should approximate the long-term mean.

5.2. CHRONOLOGICAL ASPECTS OF SAFE YIELD

It appears that safe yield will show variation with time in almost all natural situations. In fact, the concept has been critically evaluated, for instance by R. G. Kazmann.[7] This is because it is possible to interpret it incorrectly. Also, it is rarely ascertained prior to the arising of overdrafts in a ground water basin. Changes in it can be caused by a number of factors. For instance, in an unconfined aquifer, adequate recharge occurring, increasing pumpage or rearrangement of pumping patterns may increase the safe yield.

Modifications of one sort or another can also change the safe yield of a basin. These can be in crops or vegetation which may affect infiltration processes. Urbanisation can reduce recharge as a result of the fact that pavements and streets in place of fields can increase runoff.

Some change in utilisation may alter safe yield as well. For example, if the pumped ground water was used for irrigation and is now used in industry, the effective safe yield will perhaps *increase*.

Some of the effects alluded to can have long-term deleterious consequences. A case in point is the High Plains of eastern New Mexico and western Texas where rainfall is very low and evaporation high. Here, the aquifers have been isolated from an abundant water supply by the downcutting of river valleys. Of course, this did not matter until the present century, at the turn of which it was realised that water could be obtained from them to utilise an ideal farming climatic regimen. Almost total lack of planning has resulted in creation of a rich farming community on a perched water supply which, after over half a century, decreased in places by over 40%.[8] The actual water table declined almost 100 ft, so that the cost of the pumping activities has increased greatly. It has been estimated that the situation will not return to normal for 4000 years! Obviously, artificial recharge could be tried, but this might well be too expensive a procedure to justify in terms of the yields from farming. Consequently, the farmers would seem to have a rather bleak and limited future in the region.

5.3. THE DIVISION OF BASIN WATER

Effecting this is difficult because of social problems. A classic instance is the Colorado River Basin which carries a fluctuating volume of water arising from the Rockies in Wyoming and Colorado. The river flows through Utah and Arizona and along the California/Nevada border and supplied Mexico also. Actually seven US states are concerned and in 1922, the Colorado River Compact split the river into an Upper Basin and a Lower Basin with the junction at Lees Ferry in northern Arizona. *In perpetuum*, the latter was allotted 9·250 billion m³ annually together with 1·232 billion m³ extra when available. Mexico was to receive 1·850 billion m³. On the other hand, the Upper Basin received 9·250 billion m³ less whatever would prove necessary to supply the Lower Basin *and* Mexico in a dry year. It would also receive any wet year surplus. Of course, all this presupposed an *average* flow at Lees

Ferry of 22·800 billion m^3 annually (based upon previous records). Most unfortunately, however, the climate entered a dry phase, hence the average flow reduced to a mere 16·0 billion m^3/year between 1930 and 1964. At the same time, of course, Los Angeles expanded enormously and agriculture was booming throughout the entire basin. The Upper Basin states then reduced the allocation to each from the diminished quantity available, but legal disputes grew in the Lower Basin. Also, Mexico complained because, by 1972, its allotment became too saline to employ. This was afterwards rectified and from it, authorities learned that, in the future, water quality as well as water quantity had to be taken into account.

5.4.   INTER-BASIN TRANSFERS

These have gone on for many years, so that, for instance by 1968, 20 % of the population of the western US (i.e. in the seventeen western states) received water which was imported from more than 100 miles away. Usually, in the west, water is normally transferred from one drainage basin to another, but not across state boundaries. Hence, Los Angeles for instance draws water from the Colorado River Basin, but only from that part of it which lies in California.

Inter-transfer between basins in the year 1969 amounted to over 22·2 billion m^3 annually, i.e. 13 % of *all* withdrawals from streamflow in the west. Subsequently, the California State Water Project commenced draining vast quantities of water from northern to southern California.

Future developments include possible transport of water from the Columbia River or the Mackenzie River in the Arctic Basin down to the dry southwestern states of the USA. It has also been suggested that Long Island Sound might be converted into a *fresh* water reservoir for New York and especially Long Island.

Obviously, such plans are expensive, but they are also technically feasible. Of course, natural hazards will increase with their grandiosity. Earthquakes and volcanism might interfere with their functioning and these phenomena are particularly likely in precisely those regions which stand most to benefit such as Southern California. Canals there, for instance, cross a plate boundary and are therefore peculiarly vulnerable. It seems likely, therefore, that periodic damage to water systems will arise.

Some of the developments which may lie in store have been suggested by the North American Water and Power Alliance (see for instance Simons[9]).

5.5. CONJUNCTIVE UTILISATION OF SURFICIAL AND GROUND WATER RESERVOIRS

This is the optimal method of obtaining the maximum possible water development in a region. It requires that surface reservoirs impound streamflow which is afterwards transferred at an optimum rate to ground water storage.

Surface storage provides most of the annual water requirements in many areas, but ground water reserves are usually much larger and can be considered as invaluable backup resources in the event of drought conditions arising. Technically, the transference of water from above ground to aquifers must be so arranged that the lowering in level of the surface reservoirs is adequate for the retention of the next input of runoff. The mechanism of transfer is artificial recharge, but quite ordinary seepage processes, for instance from canals, contribute also. It may be stated that artificial recharge is the basic essential of the conjunctive utilisation approach and this subject will be discussed in the next chapter.

David K. Todd has listed positive and negative economic factors in respect of conjunctive use and these may be appended.[10]

5.5.1. Positive Factors

(a) Better conservation of water through the provision of larger storage facilities.

(b) Smaller surface storage. Subterranean storage available for dry years.

(c) Smaller distribution system above ground. More ground water used from wells.

(d) Smaller drainage system.

(e) Less canal lining necessary because seepage contributes to ground water system.

(f) Better flood control. Stored surface water used for artificial recharge.

(g) Easy integration with existing development.

(h) Stage development facilitated.

(i) Lower losses through evapotranspiration.

(j) Greater control of outflow.

(k) Improving of power load and pumping plant use factors.

(l) Lesser danger from dam collapse—smaller dams and hence lesser impounded water are feasible.

(m) Reduced weed seed distribution. The smaller the surface area, the less noxious weed can grow.
(n) Better timing for water distribution.

5.5.2. Negative Factors

(a) Less possibility to develop hydroelectric power.
(b) Greater consumption of power because of more pumping from greater depths.
(c) Decrease in pumping efficiency because increased fluctuations in ground water levels lower pumping efficiency.
(d) Greater mineralisation of water.
(e) More supervision of project operation is necessary.
(f) Cost allocation assessment is more difficult.
(g) Requisite artificial recharge is expensive and sometimes hard to effect.
(h) There may arise dangers of possible land subsidence.

REFERENCES

1. THOMAS, H. E., 1951. *The Conservation of Ground Water*. McGraw Hill, New York.
2. DINCER, T., 1968. Water balance. In *Guidebook on Nuclear Techniques in Hydrology*. Tech. Rep. Ser. No. 91, International Atomic Energy Agency, Vienna. 206–212.
3. CONKLING, H., 1946. Utilization of ground water storage in stream-systems development. *Trans. Am. Soc. Civ. Engrs*, III, 275–354.
4. HARDING, S. T., 1927. *Ground Water Resources of Southern San Joaquin Valley, California*. Bull. 11, Calif. Div. Eng. and Irrig., Sacramento, 146 pp.
5. SIMPSON, T. R., 1946. *Salinas Basin Investigation*. Bull. 52, Calif. Div. Water Resources, Sacramento, 230 pp.
6. MEINZER, O. E., 1932. *Outline of Methods for Estimating Ground Water Supplies*. USGS Water Supply Paper 638-C, Washington, D.C., 99–144.
7. KAZMANN, R. G., 1956. 'Safe yield' in ground water development, reality or illusion? *Proc. Am. Soc. Civ. Engrs*. **82**, IR3, 12 pp.
8. MENARD, H. W., 1974. *Geology, Resources and Society*. W. H. Freeman, San Francisco.
9. SIMONS, M., 1969. Long term trends in water use. In *Water, Earth and Man*, ed. Richard Chorley. Methuen and Co, London, pp. 535–544.
10. TODD, D. K., 1959. *Ground Water Hydrology*. John Wiley, New York and London, pp. 215–216.

CHAPTER 6

Artificial Recharge

Artificial recharge of ground water basins may be defined as the augmentation of the natural infiltration of precipitation or surface water into subterranean formations by appropriate methods. These may include spreading of water on the ground, pumping to induce recharge from surface water bodies and recharge through boreholes, wells, mineshafts or other suitable access features. The approach actually selected for a particular location will depend upon a variety of factors such as topography, geology and soil state, the amount of water to be recharged and the end use of the water. Artificial recharge is a process which has been employed for many years, in fact from the end of the last century in the USA. A quarter of a century ago, California recharged as much as 375 million gallons daily of surface water, at that time over half of all the water artificially recharged in the United States when the national total amounted to 1·5% of the total ground water use in that country. As noted above, the activity is sometimes accomplished by water spreading or ponding on the surface whereby up to several feet of water depth daily may be infiltrated into pervious ground. In the case of shallow beds where ponding is impracticable or with confined aquifers, recharging is effected by pumping water down wells at rates somewhat less than the corresponding withdrawal rates. This method has been applied in the Netherlands where fine sand beds are recharged with treated water from the Rhine river both to provide water storage for supply and also to act as a barrier against the inward seepage of sea water from the North Sea.

6.1. WATER SPREADING

Water is released over the surface of the ground so as to increase infiltration and thus increase the quantity which percolates down to the water table.

The efficiency of the process is measured by the recharge rate which is expressed as the velocity of downward movement of water over the relevant wetted area. Feet per day may be employed as a unit, alternatively given as acre-feet per acre daily. Various means may be utilised in order to accomplish the water spreading activity and these include the following:

6.1.1. Flooding
Where flat land is involved, water may be diverted so as evenly to spread over quite a large area and thus constitute a thin sheet moving downwards slowly and hence not disturbing the soil overmuch. Levees may be erected in order to control the whole operation and the approach is the cheapest way of water spreading.

6.1.2. Basin Injection
Water is recharged by release into specially made basins defined by dikes or dug. These may be anything from several to hundreds of feet across. Series of such features have been constructed in California and operated also in abandoned stream channels. As an initial basin is filled, it flows into a second and so on. At the lowest point, water is available and its excess recycled to the main channel.

6.1.3. Ditches
Water may be distributed through a series of these which are proximate in order to derive the maximum water contact area possible.

6.1.4. Natural Channels
These are particularly suitable for water spreading activities and in use may be combined with any of the above-described techniques.

6.1.5. Irrigation
During non-irrigating parts of the year such as winter, water in excess may be employed in spreading and the approach is especially attractive economically because there is no cost for land preparation, the distribution system already existing.

6.2. RECHARGE THROUGH SEWAGE

This is practised in many parts of the world because sewage is an important water source. However, the unaesthetic aspects of this matter sometimes

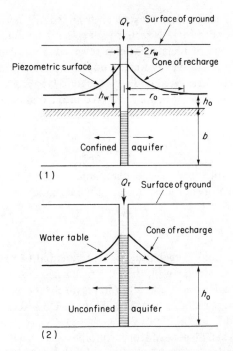

FIG. 6.1.   Radial flow from recharge wells penetrating (1) confined, (2) unconfined aquifers. After D. K. Todd.[1]

arouse public resentment and opposition. Suitable units for small scale recharge include septic tanks and sewage farms are common in Europe and the USA. Average rates for these latter vary, but 0·5 to 1 ft daily and even more are found. Attempts to utilise sewage recharge through well injection have often failed because of clogging effects and obviously the rate of blockage will depend upon the suspended solids content.

6.3.   IMPERVIOUS REGIONS

Here it is not possible to spread water with any degree of efficiency and so alternative means must be sought in order to effect the downward movement of water. Pits and shafts may be excavated and, should they reach permeable beds, these may convey water into an aquifer. Another approach is to utilise wells. Recharge wells of this type operate in a manner directly opposite to that of normal pumping wells because they transmit water *to* subterranean levels, not extract it *from* them. They are particularly useful where it is necessary to recharge deep-lying confined aquifers and they develop a cone of recharge, i.e. a reversed cone of depression (see Fig. 6.1). With the aid of the Dupuit assumptions, an equation for the curve may be derived and David K. Todd gave the following expressions: (1) for a confined aquifer with water being recharged into a completely penetrating well at a rate Q_r

$$Q_r = \frac{2\pi K b (h_w - h_o)}{\ln (r_o/r_w)}$$

(symbols identifiable from the accompanying Fig. 6.1), and (2) for a recharge well which penetrates an unconfined aquifer

$$Q_r = \frac{\pi K (h_w^2 - h_o^2)}{\ln (r_o/r_w)}$$

Obviously, if the cone of recharge is of a size equal to that of a cone of depression for a particular well, then the recharge capacity will equal the pumping capacity. However, this situation is rarely, if ever, encountered in nature. The recharge rates for various wells in the USA were summarised by Todd and ranged from 0·1 cfs to 2·2 cfs.[1]

Recharge wells can dispose of storm runoff as has been done in Orlando, Florida, for instance, where some attain depths of 1000 ft in limestone. Because of the type of country rock, clogging seldom takes place.

6.4.   RECHARGE INDUCTION

The technique differs from the above approach in that ground water is withdrawn adjacent to a river or lake with the result that its level is lowered and therefore water from these surface sources is induced to enter the subterranean system. Of course, ground water must be extracted in order to initiate the process and the actual quantity of recharge is hard to determine. Nevertheless, such induced infiltration where it is supplied by a perennial river can assure a continuing supply of water and, in fact, has proved remarkably useful in unconsolidated formations of permeable sands and gravel hydraulically connected between a river and an aquifer, cf. for example F. H. Klaer, Jr.[2]

It is interesting to note that induced infiltration appears to provide water which is practically free of organic material and pathogenic bacteria. Certainly, the water, which is a mixture of surface and ground water, has better quality than ground water alone because surface water is less mineralised. Consequently, collector well installation often results in improvement in regard to such factors as hardness, iron content and chloride content in the obtained water.

6.5. THE EUROPEAN EXPERIENCE

This is long, having begun early in the last century, and the first infiltration basin for recharging was constructed at Göteborg in Sweden in 1897. Actually, in that country, such basins are components of a great number of municipal water supplies and they are located mostly on glacial eskers which, of course, function very efficiently as conduits conveying recharged water to pumping installations. Adjacent river or lake waters are transmitted through mechanical and rapid sand filters prior to recharging and most of the plants utilise rectangular basins with unprotected side slopes of 1:2 with a layer of uniform sand up to a metre thick on their bottoms. V. Jansa has given some interesting data on a number of these Swedish infiltration basins and a selection from these is given in Table 6.1. Of course, these are unusually high infiltration rates which is explained by the high degree of permeability available. Additionally, the distances between the basins and the actual pumping wells which collect the recharged water are sufficient to ensure that the latter is of a high quality, i.e. bacteriologically pure. In the Federal Republic of Germany, artificial recharge activities are effected in several locations, notably on the Ruhr,

TABLE 6.1
JANSA DATA[3]

	Capacity (cfs)	Height of basin above water table (ft)	Infiltration rate per day (ft)	Distance from basins to the pumping wells (ft)
Västerås	16·3	50	13	700–1 600
Hälsingborg	6·5	9	13	over 1 000
Eskilstuna	5·3	72–82	13	1 600
Södertälje	4·1	30–56	16	1 300–5 600
Luleå	3·7	43	8	700
Landskrona	2·0	0–6	16	300–1 600
Malmö	2·0	16–33	7–10	1 600–3 300
Katrineholm	1·6	23	52	1 500
Kristinehamn	1·2	9	33	750
Eksjö	0·4	0–6	10–16	1 000

Rhine and Main rivers which are polluted. The Netherlands have been mentioned already and it is only necessary to add that artificial recharge waters are utilised there in municipalities such as Amsterdam, Leiden and The Hague. Coastal sand dunes retain fresh water from rainfall, but overdraft induces penetration of underlying saline waters, unfortunately, hence the introduction of recharge water into them stabilises the salt water, increasing the volume of ground water storage and providing natural filtration of polluted surface water. As regards the UK, artificial recharge was attempted first in the Lea River Valley near London where, before 1965, a scheme started and became operational later. In 1970–71, a recharge borehole and eleven observation boreholes were made in the Bunter sandstone (Triassic) near Clipstone, Nottinghamshire, and experiments were made in them during the period June 1971 to March 1974. In describing these and other works, K. J. Edworthy and R. A. Downing concluded that:

(i)   the technique is applicable to main aquifers in the UK;
(ii)   an average recharge rate of 0·3–0·5 m per day can be expected where lagoons are used to recharge aquifers, for instance the Permo–Triassic sandstones;
(iii) the quality of a water is improved by recharge through an *unfissured* aquifer.

See: EDWORTHY, K. J. and DOWNING, R. A., 1979. Artificial groundwater recharge and its relevance in Britain. *J. Inst. Water Engrs. and Scientists*, **33,** 2, 151–172.

6.6.   PROBLEMS ENCOUNTERED IN ARTIFICIAL RECHARGE PROJECTS

A number of these may arise and have been discussed by various authorities.[4] In discussing them it must be borne in mind that some are associated with aspects of clogging and hence result in alteration in infiltration rates which may be deleterious. Silting is a case in point. Particles of this grain size may well block the interstices of the soil at a quite superficial level and *lower* the infiltration rate. De-silting must then be undertaken and fortunately, there are several useful approaches to this. Suitable flocculating agents may be employed; one is 'Separan'. Water may be bypassed until the concentration of silt attains a non-detrimental amount; the increase in velocity of water introduced through ditches ensures its infiltration even where higher concentrations of silt exist. Also, silt may be sluiced out of such ditches. Additionally, injection wells may be pumped so as to loosen silt from the interstices and remove it altogether from the wells.

The growth of weeds may *raise* the rate of percolation which can be, in itself, good. However, a fire hazard may then develop. Control using appropriate chemicals is possible or manual removal methods may be utilised. Weeds are not considered very significant as negative factors in operating pits or injection wells.

Another organic danger lies in the activities of animals, particularly rodents, which may cause leakage in and often failure of levees and dikes. Clearly, the remedy is the use of traps and poisons. Rodents and mosquitoes can also constitute a menace to public health and may require fencing of areas, patrolling and the use of chemicals as well as the erecting of warning signs.

The maintenance of correct rates of percolation may be achieved by properly treating the water, not only by desilting, but also by chemicals such as chlorine or copper sulphate to control bacteria and algae. Chemicals may also be used to prevent the possibility of chemical encrustation, especially through the deposition of calcium carbonate. Aeration of the water must also be prevented. Intermittent drying periods should also be scheduled in order to obviate problems which could arise because of the swelling of soil particles, especially those of the clay grade. The head of water ought to be increased as far as possible by increasing the depth of water. Injection wells may be reconditioned by employment of dry ice, hydrochloric acid and/or sulphuric acid. Continuous spreading should be used in winter to prevent water from freezing. The possibility of base exchange reactions must also be explored. Soil also may be reconditioned by utilising organic material such as cotton gin trash or appropriate chemical agents such as krillium.

The problem of maintenance to diversion structures which manifests itself in the breakdown of spreading operations may be solved in several ways. One is preventive, namely the carrying out of systematic and routine checks coupled with patrolling during operation. Deterioration of wooden structures and settlement (which may change flow conditions) must be monitored. Another is to examine the undercutting of structures especially on the downstream end of operation, a process which may be arrested by application of riprap. Additionally, the sluicing of channel may be carried out in order to de-silt and remove other debris which may have accumulated near or at the diversion structure.

6.7. ARTIFICIAL RECHARGE OF GROUND WATER IN THE USA

Table 6.2 summarises data as of 1955 derived from the US Geological Survey.[4]

TABLE 6.2

Water source	Quantity (million gpd)
Air-conditioning return	41
Industrial wastes	49
Surface water	540
Public water supplies	71
Total	701

TABLE 6.3

1. Spreading basins Location	Rate (ft/day)	2. Recharge wells Location	Rate (cfs)
California		California	
Los Angeles Cty	2·2–6·2	Fresno	0·2–0·9
Madera	1·0–4·1	Los Angeles	1·2
San Gabriel River	1·9–5·4	Manhattan Beach	0·4–1·0
Santa Ana River	1·8–9·6	Orange Grove	0·7–0·9
Santa Clara Valley	1·4–7·3	San Fernando Valley	0·3
Tulare Cty	0·4	Tulare Cty	0·12
Ventura Cty	1·2–1·8		
New Jersey		New Jersey	
East Orange	0·4	Newark	0·6
Princeton	0·1		
New York		New York	
Long Island	3·1	Long Island	0·2–2·2
Iowa		Florida	
Des Moines	1·5	Orlando	0·2–2·1
Massachusetts		Idaho	
Newton	4·3	Mud Lake	0·2–1·0
Washington		Michigan	
Richland	7·7	Jackson Cty	0·1
Arizona		Texas	
Santa Cruz River	1·1–3·8	El Paso	2·3
		Virginia	
		Williamsburg	0·3

6.8. RATES OF RECHARGE OF GROUND WATER BY ARTIFICIAL MEANS IN THE USA

Table 6.3 summarises data as of 1959 derived from the US Geological Survey.[4]

REFERENCES

1. TODD, D. K., 1959. *Ground Water Hydrology*. John Wiley, New York and London.
2. KLAER, F. H. JR., 1953. Providing large industrial water supplies by induced infiltration. *Min. Eng.*, **5**, 620–624.
3. JANSA, V., 1952. *Artificial Replenishment of Underground Water*. International Water Supply Assn., 2nd Cong., Paris.
4. TODD, D. K., 1970. (Ed.) *The Water Encyclopedia*. Water Information Center, Water Research Building, Manhasset Isle, Port Washington, N.Y.

CHAPTER 7

Problems of Sea Water Intrusion

Salinity is a factor which renders water unfit for usage as water supply and occurs in nature in a number of forms such as oceans and seas, waters in interior closed drainage basins, connate marine waters and in easily dissolved saline deposits. In Table 7.1, the classification of water based upon the total dissolved solids concentrations is that of the US Geological Survey.

Clearly, so long as salinity is as it were immobile, it does not constitute a problem, but difficulties arise where saline waters encroach upon or mix with fresh waters. They may arise in situations where coastal aquifers contact the ocean and increasing demands for ground water reverse its normal seawardly directed flow thereby causing sea water to penetrate inland. This phenomenon is termed sea water intrusion. When it takes place, subterranean water supplies become contaminated with salt and this may take many years to remove. As a result, measures exist which should be applied to prevent or at least control sea water intrusion in cases where this is likely to happen. In certain situations, filtered salt water may be useful, for instance in the fish-processing industry. Under such circumstances, a

TABLE 7.1
CLASSIFICATION OF WATER

Type	Concentration of dissolved solids (total) ppm
Fresh	0–1 000
Brackish	1 000–10 000
Salty	10 000–100 000
Brine	More than 100 000

saline well which has become contaminated by salt water encroachment may be utilised *between* a fresh water well zone and the coast. See VANDERBERG, A., 1975. Simultaneous pumping of fresh and salt water from a coastal aquifer. *J. Hydrol.*, **24**, 37–43.

7.1. SEA WATER INTRUSION

Obviously, this phenomenon is associated with overdraft conditions in a coastal aquifer as a consequence of which the water table in unconfined aquifers or the piezometric surface in confined ones may be substantially lowered. This causes the natural gradient sloping towards the ocean to be reduced, or in extreme cases to be reversed. Two fluids having different densities are in contact and so a boundary (interface) forms here and study of the shape and movement of this is essential. Sea water intrusion has been recognised for a long time and was described by F. Braithwaite as early as 1855.[1] As populations have increased and associated water demands have risen, it has become ever more common, for instance in the Netherlands, Germany and Japan as well as along the coasts of the USA. In Israel, an interesting case of faults probably acting as conduits for the active contamination of an aquifer by sea water has been described from the Na'aman catchment area where the water in the Judea Group aquifer varies from fresh to saline. An irregular distribution of high salinities along the major east–west trending faults indicates this. The relevant report is to be found in: ARAD, A., KAFRI, U. and FLEISHER, E., 1975. The Na'aman springs, northern Israel: salination mechanism of an irregular fresh water–sea water interface. *J. Hydrol.*, **25**, 259–274.

7.1.1. Ghyben–Herzberg Relation
This exists between fresh and saline waters and was indicated independently by W. Baydon Ghyben in 1888–89 and B. Herzberg in 1901.[2,3] They found that salt water occurred underground at a depth below sea level of approximately forty times the height of fresh water above sea level. This results from a hydrostatic equilibrium existing between the two fluids of different densities. Figure 7.1 illustrates the relationship which may be expressed

$$h_s = \frac{\rho_f}{\rho_s - \rho_f} h_f$$

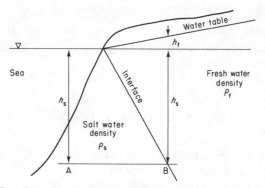

FIG. 7.1.   Illustrating the Ghyben–Herzberg relation.

symbols having the meanings apparent from the figure. ρ_s normally is taken as $1\cdot025\,\text{g/cm}^3$ and ρ_f as unity, hence

$$h_s = 40h_f$$

and this result has been substantiated by actual field measurements in a number of coastal areas. Certain limitations exist. One is that proximate to the shoreline there must be a seepage face for fresh water outflow and here the relationship cannot hold. If hydrostatic equilibrium fully existed, no flowage is implied, but ground water is observed to flow near coastlines. Nevertheless, under special conditions, the relation is quite accurate, for instance in the cases where flattish gradients are found. From it may be derived the idea that a saline wedge should be present at the intersection of an aquifer with the ocean and this is probably the usual state of affairs.

Examination in the field of interfaces has shown that these are actually narrow zones of mixing which may be several feet in width and they result from dispersion effects, from fluctuations produced by tides, from molecular diffusion and from seasonal water table variations. When steady, the sea water–fresh water interface in a coastal area is parabolic, but in nature it is rarely stationary, see VAPPICHA, V. N. and NAGARAJA, S. H., 1976. An approximate solution for the transient interface in a coastal aquifer. *J. Hydrol.*, **31**, 161–173.

To maintain good water quality, see NUTBROWN, D. A., 1976. Optimal pumping regimes in an unconfined coastal aquifer. *J. Hydrol.*, **31**, 271–280. See also KISHI, Y. and FUKUO, Y., 1977. Studies on salination of ground water. 1: Theoretical consideration of the three dimensional movement of the salt water interface caused by the pumpage of confined ground water in fan-shaped alluvium. *J. Hydrol.*, **35**, 1–30.

7.2. PREVENTION AND CONTROL MEASURES

H. O. Banks and R. C. Richter have proposed several approaches.[4]

7.2.1. Pumping Modifications

Obviously, this would be a simple solution, i.e. reducing demand and thereby eliminating overdraft. However, the cooperation of water users is necessary and this is not at all easy to get.

Alternatively, therefore, a *rearrangement* of the pumping patterns of a basin may be undertaken. Pumping may be concentrated near the inflow region, inflow may then increase and this, together with reduced pumping near the coast, may raise water levels and help to resist the penetration of sea water.

7.2.2. Artificial Recharge

This is an obvious method of control (see Chapter 6).

7.2.3. Ground Water Trough

This involves constructing a line of wells both near and along a coastline which, when pumping, will cause a depression (trough) in the level of ground water in the aquifer. Clearly, the resultant gradient will limit the intrusion of sea water.

7.2.4. Pressure Ridge

This may be regarded as the reverse of the trough situation. Where unconfined aquifers are concerned, surface water spreading may be utilised in order to create a fresh water pressure ridge. In confined aquifers, a line of recharge wells can produce a similar effect in the piezometric surface. In both cases, the ridge must be high enough above mean sea level to repel sea water. Some of the introduced fresh water will constitute waste to the sea, but most of it will pass landward and supply a portion of the pumped supply inland. The exact location of the ridge is very important. If it is not sufficiently inland away from the sea water front, then sea water lying inland from it will actually be driven more and more inland.

7.2.5. Grout Curtaining

This approach, admittedly an expensive one, might well be optimal. It involves forming a subterranean impermeable part of the aquifer to prevent the inflow of water and this can be done in shallow situations by introduction of asphalt, concrete or puddled clay. A line of holes may be used for injecting grouts such as bentonite slurry or silica gel and optimally, the barrier so created ought to be permanent in nature. For further discussion of appropriate grout materials, see the present writer's book on grouting.[5]

7.3.   IDENTIFICATION OF SALINE WATERS

Naturally, this is not a problem, but in many cases it is important to find out the source of the salinity itself. Additionally, it is often important to know, the actual path of movement in order that saline contamination may be either prevented or at least ameliorated.

Perhaps the most difficult matter in this connection is to distinguish between sea water intrusion on the one hand and other sources of salinity in coastal regions on the other. For instance, at Long Beach, California, there existed no less than *four* local possible saline sources, namely: (a) the sea itself, (b) oil field brine wastes, (c) irrigation wastes, and (d) shallow connate waters.

It is hard to utilise conventional chemical analysis in resolving such questions because almost all of the common ions found in natural waters are liable to change while in ground water transit—cations by base exchange with mineral matter, sulphate by bacterial reduction and bicarbonate by precipitation and solution. Chloride ions are not affected to any large extent, but they are far too common in nature to be employed as tracers.

Consideration may be given to isotopic analyses because isotopic contrasts may be anticipated among the various possible sources of salinity. Those isotopes of the water molecule not usually subject to what may be termed transit changes include deuterium, tritium and oxygen-18, although the last one may exchange with oxygen-16 in rock material under certain circumstances. Stable isotope analysis is very useful as a result of the fact that marine waters are almost always distinguishable from meteoric waters. Saline waters which originate from evaporative concentration in lake environments are much enriched relative to precipitation and marine waters. Oil field brines and deep fossil waters usually show oxygen-18 exchange when compared with sea water and precipitation. Isotope analyses for tritium and carbon-14 are significant because modern precipitation is labelled with these isotopes and, of course many tritium-dead fossil saline waters may be 'dated' by their radiocarbon content. Near surface sea waters possess a low, but consistent, tritium content and a rather high, but also consistent, radiocarbon content.

It appears, therefore, that a distinction may be made between the various possible sources of saline contamination on the basis of the isotopic contents of the waters. Reconnaissance sampling is normally effected and is often sufficient to arrive at a result. If stable isotope contents do not show appreciable contrasts, then tritium and radiocarbon may be employed.

Some examples may be cited:

(a)   terrestrial waters concentrated by evaporation may be easily distinguished from waters of marine origin. This is because the former, affected by evaporation, will be relatively enriched in deuterium and oxygen-18.

(b)   modern sea water may be distinguished from connate waters occasionally, although often there is little stable isotope contrast.

(c)   sea water can be distinguished from deep brines because these latter are relatively enriched in oxygen-18 with respect to deuterium due to the exchange of oxygen with rock minerals.

One interesting phenomenon should be mentioned and this is that, if connate water entered an aquifer while the planetary-wide cooler conditions of any of the Pleistocene glacial periods prevailed, analyses of deuterium and oxygen-18 can show great depletion relative to modern sea water. Here, the radioisotopes are also valuable because modern sea water is labelled by thermonuclear-injected tritium and radiocarbon.

In principle, $^{13}C/^{12}C$ and $^{34}S/^{32}S$ ratios might also be utilised in the problem of distinguishing sea water from meteoric waters.

Robert N. Clayton and his associates have used deuterium and oxygen-18 ratios in studying ninety-six brines from oil fields in the Illinois and Michigan basins as well as the Gulf Coast and in the Alberta Basin (USA, Canada).[6] The major findings were as follows:

(a)   variation in deuterium content among basins was much larger than that noted in individual basins and showed a relationship to geographic location;

(b)   the oxygen-18 contents showed a wide range in each basin and this correlated with salinity and formation temperatures.

The conclusions reached were that:

(a)   the water is not of marine but mainly of local meteoric origin,

(b)   the deuterium contents had not suffered much exchange or fractionation,

(c)   there had been quite extensive exchange between the water and the
      rocks of the reservoir,
(d)   some samples may well have originated as Pleistocene glacial
      precipitation.

Marked depletion effects at higher latitudes are noticeable despite those of
oxygen-18 exchange.

REFERENCES

1. BRAITHWAITE, F., 1855. On the infiltration of salt water into the springs of wells under London and Liverpool. *Proc. Inst. Civ. Engrs.* **14**, 507–523.
2. GHYBEN, W., 1888–89. *Nota in Verband met de Voorgenomen Putboring nabij Amsterdam.* Tijdschrift van het Koninklijk Instituut van Ingenieurs. The Hague, 21.
3. HERZBERG, B., 1901. Die Wasserversorgung einiges Nordseebäder. *J. Gasbeleuchtung und Wasserversorgung*, **44**, 815–819, 842–844 (München).
4. BANKS, H. O. and RICHTER, R. C., 1953. Sea water intrusion into ground water basins bordering the California coast and inland bays. *Trans. Am. Geophys. Un.*, **34**, 575–582.
5. BOWEN, R., 1975. *Grouting in Engineering Practice.* Applied Science Publishers, London and The Halsted Press, New York. 187 pp.
6. CLAYTON, R. N., FRIEDMAN, I., GRAF, D. L., MAYEDA, T. K., MEENTS, W. F. and SHIMP, N. F., 1966. The origin of saline formation waters. I: Isotopic composition. *J. Geophys. Res.*, **71**, 16, 3869–3882.

CHAPTER 8

Ground Water in Construction

Ground water may constitute a considerable hazard in construction work. For instance, in tunnelling activities, its presence may require expensive corrective labour and, with soft rock tunnels with relatively low tensile and shear strengths, the water table can be an important factor. This is because combating water influx may come to be an almost continuous activity and necessitate sinking well points in order to lower the water table to acceptable levels. Basically, such well points are perforated and screened pipes usually about $1\frac{1}{2}$ in. in diameter and several feet in length. Such a well point is fixed to a riser pipe of the same diameter and the entire unit is driven into the ground with or without jetting. Individual riser pipes are attached to a header pipe or manifold which leads to a pump. Lines of well points are arranged in conformity with the physical characteristics of the unconfined aquifer's water table surface. Here, they operate in a sense as a piece of dewatering equipment. In normal building construction work, well points may be placed from 3 to 6 ft centre to centre and the suction lifts which may be attained range from 15 to 25 or more feet. Obviously, a lot depends upon the efficiency of the system utilised and the altitude at which the operation is carried out is an important factor also. If very deep excavation work is being done, well points are usually arranged on a series of descending steps from 15 to 20 ft high; this is termed a multiple stage set up. An example may be cited of the effects of ground water influx on a soft rock tunnel. This is the well known Box Tunnel excavated under the direction of Isambard Kingdom Brunel on the main line of the Great Western Railway between London and Bristol and commenced in 1836. It was planned to be 3·2 km long, a daring concept in its day, and its completion was delayed until June of 1841, partly by ground water problems. The various beds encountered included clay, blue marl and the inferior oolite (for about three-quarters of the length) and great oolite (for the remaining quarter). Lining was effected, specially made bricks being utilised to the number of about 30 million. It is interesting to record that the sole illumination then possible for the carrying out of this work was candles! Actually, one tonne of candles was used every single week. Another famous tunnel which had water problems was the Kilsby Tunnel (UK) which Robert Stephenson had temporarily to drain. This too will lower the water table. Although well points and other methods can effect this, it may not always be feasible to use them. This is because damage in urban areas may easily arise through such lowering. Hence, freezing is sometimes resorted to as an alternative. In hard rock tunnels also, water may inflow and tends to do so in a sudden, sporadic and violent manner. For instance, in the case of the Simplon Tunnel, this was begun in 1898 and completed in 1906 to create what is still the longest continuous *railway* tunnel in the world (over 19 km). The work involved extraordinary difficulties including, at one point, a water influx of no less than just under 40 m³/min.

8.1. DELETERIOUS EFFECTS OF LOWERING GROUND WATER TABLES

A number of instances may be cited. In the Brooklyn area, where there is a very great consumption, sewer construction and street paving work combined to drop the water table to as much as 10·7 m below sea level. Of course, this caused sea water intrusion to occur and serious contaminational problems to arise at some wells. Continuous monitoring of this situation from its inception in the 1930s produced cessation of almost all ground water pumping for public supply by 1947. Thereafter, Brooklyn and its environs were supplied from surface water sources available through the New York Board of Water Supply. Ground water was still pumped, but only for the purpose of air-conditioning and it had to be returned underground. As a consequence of all this, the water table rose once more. Due to inadequate foresight, subways, etc., had been constructed below ground without any problems, but now that the ground water reverted practically to its original level, flooding of basements, etc., occurred. Thus, remedial action had to be taken and at considerable cost.

8.2. BUILDING FOUNDATIONS

Ground water can be very significant and the case of Winchester Cathedral in England may be instanced. Some of the very old piles made of timber under the building show decay as a result of variations in ground water levels through history. The influence on construction of better methods of pumping ground water and the utilisation of well points for drying wet excavations are demonstrated here. Various grout approaches may be employed. For example, the lignochrome grout TDM was utilised in underpinning work necessary because of the reconstruction work at Great Cumberland Place (Bilton Towers) in London. Here, underground garages were planned as a feature of a new fourteen storey block and deep excavations for foundations had to be carried out. Some of the nearby buildings were over 200 years old and had to be protected. Strata involved included the Taplow Terraces of the River Thames, sands of various types associated with saturated gravels, these being underlain by the London Clay. Injection of the grout was specified and after treatment, practically uniform results were attained in sandy gravels while adequate results of lower consistency were obtained in laminated sands.

If pile rotting cannot be prevented in time, expensive remedial work may have to be carried out. This happened, for instance, with the famous Strasbourg Cathedral. This was commenced in 1439 with stone footings supported on timber piles. A new drainage system was installed in the eighteenth century and this interfered with the local ground water conditions, subsequently causing damage to the piles. In consequence, a large scale underpinning operation for the foundation had to be effected during the early part of this century.[1]

A similar problem arose around 1929 with the Boston Public Library, Mass., under which almost half of the piles were found to have rotted. As a result, these had to be attended to and almost 40% of the building underpinned.[2]

At Milwaukee, Wisconsin, an interesting set of factors is involved. There is a normally rather high local water table and the central portion of the city is underlain by variable soils. Close to the waterfront is the head office building of the Northwestern Mutual Life Insurance Company erected in 1912, and in 1930 it was proposed to add to this an extension which would complete a city block belonging to the company. The latter was founded on timber piles grouped under mass concrete footings. To make certain of a completely satisfactory result, the architectural design provided every concrete footing with a 10 cm pipe capped at the level of the sub-basement floor. Ground water levels have been recorded in these in every subsequent month. Where a drop in level occurs, water is introduced until the restoration of the usual level. The foundations have given every satisfaction. Obviously, careful forethought pays off.[2]

8.3. SULPHATES IN GROUND WATER

These can be highly deleterious if present in unacceptably high quantities. Such contaminants occur in many parts of the world, for instance in the United Kingdom and western Canada, and an instance of their bad effects may be cited.[3] In 1938, the St Helier Hospital at Carshalton in Surrey, England, was constructed with a capacity of 750 beds and comprising four multi-storey ward blocks with the central services in one main block; subways connect the various parts. Concrete foundations were placed on brown clay overlying the famous London Clay. In the spring of 1959, some foundation concrete was exposed during maintenance work and it was noted that this had deteriorated badly. A general study then divulged that most of the foundation was deteriorating progressively. A high sulphate content was also found in the substrata, although the latter possess quite adequate load-bearing capacity. Clearly, the concrete had been subjected to a chemical attack and this had weakened the highly aluminous cement which had also been adversely affected by a warm and damp atmosphere. A major underpinning operation had to be undertaken and this necessitated the provision of new foundations for the entire building complex.

8.4. GROUND WATER AND OPEN EXCAVATIONS

In building, the subsurface conditions are determined and thereafter the design of a particular foundation is made and a contractor realises it. Nearly all such activities require excavation, often in confined areas. An interesting and relevant case history is that of the New York World Trade Center located near to the lower part of Manhattan and costing US$600 m. The two buildings concerned, the tallest in the world when completed, are supported by concrete piers lying directly on the Manhattan schist, a rock with a high bearing capacity but steeply dipping and often showing slippage along joint planes. The actual rock level was just over 21 m below the level of the street and a six-storey basement had to attain this depth also. It was discovered by means of a survey of maps dating back to 1783 that then the Hudson River shoreline ran two blocks inland from the currently existing shoreline. Many wharves and other structures had been built on it and these have been later covered up by miscellaneous fill and lay upon mixed beds of organic silt, overlying inorganic silt and sand. All of these beds are water-bearing, naturally. Clearly, therefore, ground water lies quite near to the existing ground surface. Now in the prevailing circumstances of streets and buildings, not to mention subterranean services, it is impossible to lower the water table around the selected site. It was decided, therefore, to enclose this by means of a wall of concrete placed using a slurry trench. Of course the latter had to be very carefully excavated and was thereafter infilled with bentonite and water. Concrete was then placed in the trench, commencing at the bottom, by using a tremie (submerged) pipe. Steel grills were also placed in the trench so that they would become encased in the concrete and reinforce the structure. As the concrete ascended, it displaced bentonite and reinforced the sides of the trench thus making it safer. After excavation was effected to total depth, the walls were anchored by inclined steel tiebacks drilled into and grouted into the underlying schist. All excavation material was trucked to a nearby site in the Hudson River which was enclosed by a sheet pile retaining structure and, after dumping, the fill has created a new land region said to be worth US$90 million to New York City.

8.5. ROTTERDAM: EXCAVATION *BENEATH* A CITY

Robert F. Legget has referred to the subway system of this beautiful city of The Netherlands, a tasteful blend of antiquity in its older streets and modernity in its elegant centre which was rebuilt after World War II when it was subjected to devastation by low flying German bombers.[2] Ground water is involved in this and some discussion on it is therefore relevant. There is a river associated with the city, namely the Nieuwe Maas, actually an extremely busy waterway and also a port, in fact the largest one in the world which handles not only ocean ships, but also Rhine traffic. Although there are bridges over the river, its presence constituted a hindrance to passengers travelling to central Rotterdam and so, between 1938 and 1942, a vehicular tunnel was constructed under it. Subsequently, another was driven and comprises part of a rapid transit urban subway system.

The geology involved is interesting, consisting of a Pleistocene sand and gravel deposit 16 to 18 m below local datum (i.e. mean sea level) transported by two rivers, namely the Rhine and Meuse. It is water-bearing and sometimes extends to a depth exceeding 40 m in the east of the city. It has been proved useful as a foundation bed, many city structures lying on it and imposing their loads through piles. Above it is a bed of alluvial clay of approximately 1 m thickness and above that is a peat layer and finally a bed of marine clay about 2 m thick. Man-made fill, peaty layers and shallow clays infill to the surface. Obviously, roads, etc., have to be founded on these. Settlement is a constant problem and has to be compensated for by infilling and rebuilding. The general level of the city is below sea level and hence it is not surprising that the ground water lies everywhere quite near the surface, in fact never more than 2 m below it. However, it is quite constant in elevation and as a result, there is practically no deterioration in the numerous timber piles widely utilised in Rotterdam. *Deep* excavations, on the other hand, seriously interfere with the water table and therein lies the problem encountered in construction of the subway system. All rapid transit lines on the north side of the Nieuwe Maas in the city centre had to be constructed in a tunnel which emerges into an elevated line south of the river. The initial 7·6 km of tunnel had 3·1 km in it and 4·5 km on a prestressed reinforced concrete superstructure. The bottom part of the tunnel actually lay 11 m below ground and construction, very near many pilings, was hazardous due to these, also because of the high water table. It was reckoned that the excavation of open trenches by normal cut and cover methods would have necessitated a large scale pumping operation for every section of trench over a quinquennial period even with controlled pumping and efficient well points. Hence, in order to avoid pumping, it was decided to build inner sections of the subway tunnel as precast concrete tubes and *float* them into position in the city centre. This was done and the work completed by 1967, the first section of the subway actually opening on 9 February 1968.

8.6. GROUND WATER AND SETTLEMENT

An excellent example of this is afforded by the case of Long Island, this being approximately 192 km long and having a maximum width of 35 km. The feature constitutes a coastal plain bordering New York State and Connecticut and is politically divided into four counties, two of which, the smallest (at the western end), also constituting boroughs of New York. The geology of the island is interesting, comprising bedrock which approaches the surface on the northern side, but lies about 600 m below the surface on the southern side. Overlying this is a set of beds which are mostly water-bearing, althouth there are two, the Raritan and Gardiner clays, which are not. Surficial glacial deposits were laid down during Pleistocene times and they are quite pervious, quite sufficiently so for water to seep down through them to sands and gravels below. Originally, when settlement began, ground water conditions were in equilibrium. The infiltration of precipitation maintained the water table at a high level and the balance was preserved as a result of the movement of water through springs and also in small water courses on the island. There was most likely a seepage effect into the sea as well. Under the sea, of course, the ground water is sea water and hence there must be an interface under the island separating overlying fresh water from underlying sea water. The depth of this may well be 300 m or so. Initially, the inhabitants obtained an excellent water supply from springs and rather shallow wells and used cesspools for waste disposal, these draining back into water-bearing beds. Naturally, contamination problems arose and so deeper wells had to be drilled. Water was drawn from the Jameco gravel (Pleistocene) and the Magothy formation (Cretaceous) and, although pumping increased, the equilibrium was not seriously disturbed because most of the water returned into the water-bearing beds after it had been utilised. As Brooklyn developed, servicing there meant that much waste water was no longer recycled, but was returned directly to the sea or to Long Island Sound. Of course, this resulted in a decline in the level of the water table which was corrected by restriction of the usage of ground water, but resulted in flooding. Correction of this was expensive as indicated above, section 8.1.

As Legget indicated, the ground water situation under Long Island shows all phases of the development at the western end referred to above, but, at the eastern end, the natural conditions are still in existence.[2] Nowadays, the western end is much more developed and culminates in Brooklyn which obtains all of its water supply from the New York system. Sea water contamination of the ground water occurs to an unknown extent. Long Island is a very interesting area for ground water study and is thought to represent one of the largest usage regions for any single well-defined subterranean reservoir anywhere in the world. It is not surprising, therefore, that plans have been drawn up for future conservation measures including employment of recharge wells, water reclamation from sewage and desalination of sea water. In fact, an atlas of Long Island's water resources has been compiled by the US Geological Survey and the NY State Water Resources Commission.[4] Current consumption is not known, but, in 1963, it amounted to 1438 million lpd from Long Island wells.

Obviously, construction activities throughout the island have had a close relation with ground water supplies and may be categorised as, from the east westwards, few (hence retention of natural conditions), settlement of individual dwellings and usage of public wells, urban zones with sewerage, but deriving water by pumping (accompanied by depression of the water table) and a well-developed region ending in Brooklyn (this latter deriving water from the New York system, water table slowly regaining its natural level, sea water contamination occurring to an uncertain extent).

8.7. DAMS

These constitute the dearest and potentially most dangerous of all engineering structures, their construction involving the accumulation of huge masses of building material and water on limited regions of the surface of the Earth, these exerting tremendous compressive stresses on foundations. Their associated reservoirs impound large volumes of water which have a destructive effect both on them and their dams with consequent leakage, erosion and possibly structural failure which may have catastrophic results. Hence the observation of E. Grunner that *every* impounding dam is potentially dangerous.[5]

Foundation studies are essential in dam construction and ground water conditions must be carefully studied prior to constructional work beginning. A single case of great interest may be cited and that is a tailings dam constructed on a very loose and saturated sandy silt foundation soil.[6] The location was Kimberley, British Columbia, and the investigation and design were completed in 1974. The dam was needed in order to replace an existing embankment of marginal stability and allow for the extension of a waste pond to a total height of 30 m or so. The dam was so designed as to be capable of retaining iron tailings to the north in a first phase and gypsum tailings to the south later, after recovery of the iron tailings in the future. Especially important was the presence of a very loose saturated layer of iron tailings which, in the design stage, was envisaged as forming the foundation for some 240 m length of the dam. Actually, iron and silica tailings waste have been stored in an area to the north of the dam site for more than half a century and south of the site, recent gypsum pond construction is expected to result in gypsum tailings contacting the southern edge of the dam. Over most of the length, gravel or glacial till comprises the foundation soils, according to K. E. Robinson who concerned himself specifically with design considerations for the dam where it rests on iron tailings.[6] Several embankment failures have occurred in the old iron tailings disposal area and they took place when the embankments were situated some 0·8 km north of the new dam. The worst was in 1948 when a shear failure in the retention dyke caused liquefaction of the contained tailings. Approximately a million tons of tailings flowed down valley where the new dam is located and a part of this is situated on up to 6 m of loose saturated tailings. It was found that gypsum tailings were accumulating to the south much faster than the iron ones. The planned embankment had to satisfy several requirements. These included adequate storage for iron tailings, containment of gypsum tailings and allowance for future removal of the former. Stability under static and dynamic loading conditions had to be achieved also.

8.7.1. Kimberley Site Conditions

The area is rather flat and grassy with occasional boggy or peaty ground and two ground water zones in the foundation materials. Immediately above or at the surface of bedrock, there is an artesian aquifer with a piezometric level exceeding 3 m above the surface of the ground. Ground water within the iron tailings is within 0·3 to 0·6 m of the surface. Glacial till provides a rather impervious barrier between these two zones. There exists, therefore, a high water table and very loose tailings from which a quick condition can easily develop if, for instance, someone so much as walked over the tailings. Actually, during probe tests, the tailings liquefied underfoot where a person stood too long in one place.

8.7.2. Liquefaction Failures

These occurred previously as a consequence of dyke displacements when the phreatic level rose to critical height in late winter and the safety factor fell below unity. Resultant high pore pressures induced overstressing of tailings and the resultant displacements were sufficient to liquefy saturated sandy silt. Vibration-induced liquefaction of impounded tailings was considered and various concentrations of saturated materials at low relative density modelled in different positions relative to the dam face. Various positions of the phreatic surface within the tailings with regard to toe drains and the embankment were simulated in a wedge analysis. Foundation liquefaction was also considered. The dam design had to be such that long-term stability conditions could be satisfied. Stability also had obtained during construction and, as a result of pore pressure build up during initial filling over the tailings foundations, it was thought advisable to monitor activities using piezometers and settlement plates. Normally, the former were installed to depths equal to 75 % of the thickness of tailings. Daily measurements were made.

8.7.3. Construction

As quick response was anticipated from the tailings, simple standpipe piezometers were utilised and comprised 1·3 cm PVC coated conduits with slots cut in the lower 0·3 m, the slotted part being protected by a 200-mesh brass screen surrounding the pipe. Additionally, the interior was sand-filled to a depth of almost half a metre. Settlement plates were located over the piezometer pipes.

There occurred a response in the piezometers as the initial lift of fill neared a few metres of each piezometer location and pore pressure build up sufficed to cause overflow of the PVC tubes. Initial settlements were rather high.

8.8.   GENERAL CONSIDERATIONS

In the case of masonry dams, ground water observation wells or holes must be established during the exploration phase and maintained in order when the actual construction commences. The water levels in such holes must be read periodically, for instance monthly, for a minimum of 1 year after filling of the reservoir or until the post-constructional ground water regimen is established. Urban areas near the reservoir which depend upon ground water for water supplies may find that their wells are running dry, particularly downstream from the dam. Ground water observations can be very useful in assessing whether such a situation may develop and, if so, what remedial or preventive measures may be undertaken.

REFERENCES

1. ANON., 1923. Modern engineering to save medieval tower. *Eng. New Record*, **91**, 505.
2. LEGGET, R. F., 1973. *Cities and Geology*. McGraw Hill, New York, p. 233.
3. ANON., 1965. Foundation reinstatement without interference to services. *The Engineer, London*, **220**, 791.
4. COHEN, P., FRANKE, O. L. and FOXWORTHY, B. L., 1968. *An Atlas of Long Island's Water Resources*. NY Water Resources Commission Bull. 62.
5. GRUNNER, E., 1963. *Dam Disasters*. Inst. Civ. Engrs., London.
6. ROBINSON, K. E., 1977. Tailings dam constructed on very loose, saturated sandy silt. *Can. Geotech. J.*, **14**, 3, 399–407.

CHAPTER 9

At and Below the Surface Investigations of Ground Water

Obviously, subsurface investigations will give more information regarding ground water, but work on the surface of the Earth is sometimes useful also, although this is not always easy or indeed successful. Some well-tried geophysical methods may be mentioned.

9.1. ELECTRICAL RESISTIVITY

This property of a rock determines the quantity of current actually transmitted when an electrical potential is applied and it may be defined as the resistance in ohms between the opposing faces of a unit cube of a material. Resistivity may be expressed thus:

$$\rho = \frac{RA}{L}$$

where ρ is the resistivity, R the resistance, A the cross sectional area, and L the length. In the CGS system, the units of resistivity are ohm-m^2/m.

Not surprisingly, the resistivities of the many types of rock found in nature show a very wide range of values which depends upon factors such as density, porosity, pore dimensions, temperature and especially water content. In fact, the resistivity in porous formations is much more controlled by water than by the rock itself so that in aquifers comprising unconsolidated materials, the resistivity of the ground water predominates.

The resistivity of an aquifer is expressible in terms of that of the ground water, therefore, and also relates to porosity for uniform packing together of spherical mineral grains. Consequently, where ρ is once again the resistivity (of the aquifer) and ρ_w is that of the ground water, n being porosity, then

$$\frac{\rho}{\rho_w} = \frac{3 - n}{2n}$$

a relationship which clearly does not obtain in nature because it requires isotropic conditions.

Resistivities are determined from an apparent resistivity obtained from measurements of current and potential differences between pairs of electrodes inserted into the surface of the ground. The actual process is to measure a potential difference between two electrodes which results from the application of a current through two *other* electrodes outside of, but in line with, the potential electrodes. An orthogonal network of circular arcs will be created by the current and equipotential lines if the resistivity is uniform in the subsurface region below the electrodes and the measured potential difference is a weighted value over a particular subsurface region controlled by the shape of this network. Hence, the measured current and potential differences give an apparent resistivity over a depth which is not specified, an increase in this latter occurring if the space between the electrodes is increased (a different apparent resistivity is also thereby obtained). Since it is usually the case that the actual subsurface resistivities vary with depth, the apparent resistivities also change as the electrode spacings increase, although not in a similar manner. Since resistivity changes at great depth affect apparent resistivity compared with that at shallow depth to a very small degree, the method is not really effective for the assessment of actual resistivities at depths exceeding a few hundred feet or so.

Of course, the electrodes consist of metal rods impaled into the earth and they handle the actual current, the potential electrodes comprising porous cups with saturated solutions of copper sulphate which inhibit electrical fields from arising around them. Either an a.c. low frequency current or a reversible d.c. current may be employed so as to minimise polarisation effects.

Standard electrode spacing arrangements exist and include the Wenner and the Schlumberger ones.

9.1.1. The Schlumberger Array

Here, the potential electrodes are close together and the apparent resistivity is given by

$$\rho_\alpha = \pi \frac{(L/2)^2 - (b/2)^2}{b} \frac{V}{I}$$

where L and b are the current and potential electrode spacings respectively, α is the distance between adjacent electrodes, V is the voltage difference between the potential electrodes and I is the applied current. Theoretically $L \gg b$, but in practice it is possible to obtain satisfactory results where $L \gg 5b$.

This array was utilised in the investigation of ground water aquifers in the area around Lusaka, Zambia, by K. D. Töpfer who measured apparent specific resistivity as a function of half the current electrode separation and the resultant 'sounding curve' obtained was interpreted by matching with 'master curves'.[1]

This work was in the nature of a rather small scale survey and therefore it was not considered practicable to directly interpret the field curves using a large computer as proposed by G. Kunetz and J. P. Rocroi.[2] Instead, a Compucorp desk computer was utilised in order to study the 'principle of equivalence' (see G. Kunetz[3]) and the interpretation of field curves was accomplished by application of Hummel's method discussed by A. Ebert.[4] This was considered as satisfactory and errors as to depth determination were within 15%, thought to be tolerable. In certain areas, distortion of sounding curves occurred due to lateral effects such as might be expected from limestone under a shallow soil covering. Here, it was clear that an interpretation using master curves calculated for near horizontal layer problems becomes meaningless; consequently, isoresistivity maps were made for several current electrode separations. Therefrom resistivity lows and highs showed up readily for the various depths of investigation. Qualitative interpretation is possible and larger areas of low apparent specific resistivity were considered most promising for good borehole sites.[1]

When apparent resistivity is plotted against various electrode spacings $(L/2)$ for various spacings at any one locality, then a smooth curve may be drawn through the points and this produces a resistivity-spacing curve, the interpretation of which is complex. It may be effected in terms of various layers of actual resistivities and their appropriate depths. It may also be effected by interpreting the actual resistivities in terms of subsurface geological and ground water conditions. The first alternative can be done using theoretically computed resistivity-spacing curves of 2-, 3- and 4-layer instances for various ratios of resistivities. In fact, the Compagnie Générale de Géophysique has published curves and explanations of curve-matching techniques for the Schlumberger array and these may also be derived from tables of potentials about a point electrode.[5]

The second alternative may be derived from actual data. The comparison of actual resistivity variations with depth to information from an adjacent logged test borehole facilitates establishment of a correlation with

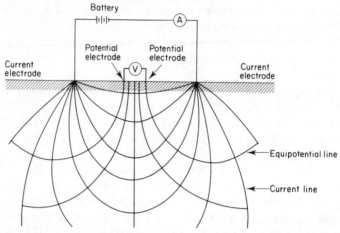

FIG. 9.1. Electrical circuit for determination of resistivity and the electrical field for an isotropic subsurface situation. A, ammeter; V, voltmeter.

subsurface ground water conditions and this may be applied in the interpretation of resistivity measurements in the environment.

As noted above, isoresistivity maps of a region can be produced by resistivity surveys. In regional studies involving an aquifer, a constant spacing may be adopted in order to measure resistivities only at its depth.

9.1.2. The Wenner Array

Here, the potential electrodes are located at the third points between the current electrodes, and the apparent resistivity is given by the ratio (voltage:current) times a spacing factor. The apparent resistivity is expressible

$$\rho_\alpha = 2\pi\alpha \frac{V}{I}$$

where symbols have the meanings already noted above.

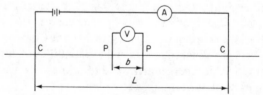

FIG. 9.2(a). Schlumberger array. V, voltmeter; A, ammeter; C, current electrode; P, potential electrode.

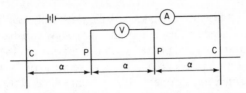

FIG. 9.2(b).   Wenner array. Symbols as Fig. 9.2(a).

Figures 9.1 and 9.2 show the general principles of the electrical resistivity method and the two arrays mentioned above in sections 9.1.1 and 9.1.2.

9.2.   SEISMIC REFRACTION

This method depends upon the initiation of a shock at the surface of the Earth. Such a shock may be produced by impact or by explosion and thereafter the velocity of the resultant wave is measured. As well as undergoing refraction, seismic waves may be reflected, i.e. they partake of the same propagation laws as light. Refraction and reflection can occur at any interface below ground at which a change in velocity takes place. The major difference between the two phenomena is that the reflection technique yields data on the geological structure at great depths (thousands of feet), but the refraction approach which is used in ground water study gives information from shallower depths only (hundreds of feet). The actual transit times for seismic waves obviously relate to the materials through which they pass. Wave velocities have been found to be anywhere between 1500 and 3000 ft/s in unconsolidated and non-saturated beds. By comparison, they increase to between 3000 and 6000 ft/s in unconsolidated aquifers and reach anything from 6000 to 10 000 ft/s in low quality aquifers, i.e. those possessing sizeable amounts of clay or silt. Alterations in velocities are related to changes in the elastic properties of the strata. Clearly, the greater the differences involved, the easier it becomes to distinguish between various formations and also to define their boundaries. Interestingly, as regards sediments texture has been found to be more significant than mineralogy. While water content increases wave velocity, porosity decreases it.

9.2.1. Theory
Considering a point at which a shock occurs, a spherical wave front will expand outwards from it and the velocity of its motion will depend upon the medium through which it passes. If an unconsolidated but isotropic aquifer

having a water table is involved, the seismic wave will actually travel along the interface produced by this. Simultaneously, waves are back-propagated into the unsaturated layer, i.e. refraction occurs. If another point at the surface of the Earth is considered, a shock wave will arrive at it and this may be either a refracted one or one which has come directly from the point at which the shock was originated. Measurement of time intervals of the arrivals at various distances from the point of shock enables a time–distance graph plot to be constructed, and reciprocals of the slopes in this give velocities of interest and, in the hypothetical case of an unconfined aquifer, facilitate distinction of a velocity *above* from one *below* the water table and, incidentally, the depth to this latter. The relevant expression may be given as

$$H = \frac{s}{2} \sqrt{\left(\frac{v_2 - v_1}{v_2 + v_1} \right)}$$

where H is the depth to the water table, s is the distance from zero to the point of alteration from velocity v_1 to velocity v_2 on a time–distance graph, this referring to a case where a horizontal two-layered situation exists, i.e. the unconfined aquifer mentioned above with a water table surface (separating the overlying zone of aeration from the underlying zone of saturation). Multiple layers may also be analysed in an analogous fashion.

In the simplest case, a shock wave may be propagated by employing a sledge hammer to strike a plate on the ground surface, but for adequate measurements to be made, a charge of dynamite is more appropriate. In this event, a very small amount may be perfectly adequate and this can be inserted into an augered hole up to 5 ft deep, this being afterwards backfilled. Geophones can be utilised in order to pick up the shock wave which is thereafter converted into electrical impulse form and, after amplification, recorded on an oscillograph or other suitable instrument. One of the assumptions of the method is that interfacial planes are bounding homogeneous (isotropic) layers and this is hardly in accordance with nature. As may be anticipated, the usual situation is that separation of layers actually comprises transitional zones. Consequently, the sharp alteration from one slope or velocity to another on the time–distance graphs which ought to occur theoretically is normally replaced by a *curve*. However, water tables may be taken as often approximating to planar surfaces and this helps in obviating difficulties arising from the actual field situations. Of course, interpretation of data does require a considerable knowledge of the geology of the particular area, especially with reference to the rock strata concerned. It is necessary for seismic wave velocities to increase with depth if acceptable results are to be obtained. If a reversal situation exists, for instance where a more consolidated layer overlies a loosely consolidated aquifer, the existence of the latter will not be apparent from seismic measurements. These are also not particularly valuable in areas of restricted size. This is because of the necessity of having a minimal distance in order to derive seismic profiles in different directions. However, where this is available, the seismic refraction method is very useful as it enables those areas unsuitable for test drilling to be identified and avoided.

Certain factors such as noise from roads or airports, etc., and vibrations from basements containing heavy machinery militate against obtaining valid seismic data and they have to be borne in mind when assessing the potential of the method for application in any particular area.

Nevertheless, seismic investigations have been used very successfully, for instance as long ago as 1949 by D. Linehan and S. Keith in reconnoitring for ground water development.[6] This was in Massachusetts and Connecticut, USA.

More recently, K. D. Töpfer and C. A. Legg utilised the method in exploring for ground water in the region of Lusaka, Zambia.[1] Here, they utilised seismic refraction as supplementary to geoelectric resistivity measurements in order to obtain some additional information in a region of limestone, quartzite and sediments of Karroo age near Kafue, south-west of Lusaka. It is pertinent to point out that the Karroo derives its name from a Hottentot word which means dry and this system occupies a unique position in the geology of southern Africa. Correlation through glaciation effects enables the system to be demonstrated as correspondent with parts of four European systems, namely the Carboniferous, the Permian, the Triassic and the Jurassic. In fact, it is believed that a widely distributed and thick outpouring of basalt which caps the Karroo is of Rhaeto-Liassic, i.e. lowermost Jurassic, in age. The total thickness of the Karroo is no less than 25 000 ft in some places. The best known member of it is the famous Dwyka tillite series.

Töpfer and his associate employed a continuous profiling technique, that of A. J. Barthelmes, because this permitted a detailed investigation of bedrock velocities and bedrock irregularities, e.g. solution hollows and fracture zones in the limestone.[7] Their interpretation was based upon the 'plus–minus method' of J. G. Hagedoorn and was done using a desk computer.[8] A 'Huntec FS 3' seismic equipment was utilised and used a 5 kg hammer as a source of energy, cf. N. R. Paterson's work on the portable facsimile seismograph.[9] This proved to be very suitable for geophone lines of up to 120 m. The geophone array was fixed and the hammer source was moved in 2 m intervals for the initial 20 m and thereafter in 5 m intervals. Each shock stroke was repeated thrice so that signals could be distinguished from noise. This is of course an application of the 'sledge hammer' and 'plate' technique alluded to above and here, it proved to be quite successful as a technique, although unfortunately contributing little of value in addition to data already available from electrical resistivity measurements.

9.3.   GRAVITY AND MAGNETIC METHODS

The gravity approach is based upon the measurement of differences in density on the planetary surface which may perhaps indicate geological structure. The method is not especially useful in ground water prospecting because the differences in water content in subsurface beds usually do not involve measurable differences in specific gravity at the surface.

Magnetic methods enable the mapping of the magnetic fields of the Earth to be undertaken. Again, there is little relevance to ground water studies because magnetic contrasts are not normally associated with the occurrence of ground water. However, they can be employed in oil and mineral exploration. Using an accuracy of ± 1 gamma, fluxgate and proton magnetometers are often utilised on surveys where magnetic anomalies of between 5 and 1000 gammas are interesting. The fluxgate magnetometer is very useful in regions of very high magnetic gradients and when used with digital sampling at 8 times per second has an advantage over proton magnetometers. These latter are used widely, however, and in the best installations can provide a noise envelope of ± 0.5 gamma.

In certain kinds of exploration work, a higher sensitivity optical pumping magnetometer can be utilised. In flat magnetic areas with very good control of all survey variables, it is possible to produce magnetic contour maps with a contour interval of 0.25 gamma, although this is a more costly approach.

Every type of magnetometer can be combined with both analogue and digital recording. The latter, where applicable, can be said to possess many advantages such as the filtering of high frequency noises, removal of regional gradient, non-linear filtering to separate shallow magnetic effects from deeper components and, when appropriate, automatic contouring.

9.4.   RADIOMETRICS

While these surveys are useful in locating uranium mineralisation, they are not usable in ground water work.

9.5. AERIAL PHOTOGRAPHY

This is useful in ground water work because terrain characteristics are to some degree determinative of ground water occurrence. Features which are relevant include vegetation, drainage, erosion, colour and physiographic phenomena such as eskers, kames, river terraces, flood plains and gravel pits. The technique is to take a large number of individual aerial photographs and later assemble them into a map covering the area, i.e. a mosaic map. Studying this and also the stereoscopic study of individual photographic pairs facilitates the construction of drainage and soil maps. These can be utilised to prepare a ground water prediction map.

9.6. SIDE LOOKING AIRBORNE RADAR

This technique is now a well-established regional mapping tool utilisable in bad weather conditions or regions in which persistent cloud renders normal aerial photography both difficult and slow, hence expensive. Unaffected by haze and nearly all cloud conditions and equally effective whether flown by day or night, SLAR can survey without problems areas which have frustrated photographic aircraft using visible or infrared methods. Unfortunately, however, it must be pointed out that it does not give such detailed interpretations as ordinary aerial photographs. Of course, where SLAR is applicable, aerial photography is not, so it is a case of employing it as a necessity if planimetric, geomorphic, geologic or other maps are required in regions obscured in one way or another.

High resolution radar mapping is based on pulsed microwave energy beamed obliquely towards the ground to one side of the survey aircraft. The returned pulses are confined to a vertical plane and cover an angle between $20°$ and $70°$. These are converted to a modulated light signal which is exposed on film to give a photograph-like image. This can then be interpreted in a manner similar to that used in aerial photography. Although the system has the oblique approach mentioned above, it is electronically adjusted to simulate a correct scale vertical view and typically the aeroplane operational altitude is at 20 000 ft or more, the imagery strip obtained covering a belt of country 12 miles in width. One of the disadvantages of the method at present is that the US Department of Defense limits the employment of radar systems with resolution better than 10 m, but this does not have an adverse effect on regional geological and ground water studies. Obviously, because the radar illumination of the ground is from the side, shadow effects are produced similar to those of low sun angle photography and this enhances the impression of morphological relief in the imagery, thus assisting interpretation. Shadows should be placed so as to lie towards the observer (to avoid giving an effect of inverted relief). For the same reason, surveys are flown using the same looking direction throughout.

SLAR surveys can be carried out fairly quickly, for instance a 100 000 km² area could be covered in a couple of weeks. Such surveys can identify faults and other linear structures as well as salt domes and additional features which may be relevant to the presence of ground water. A variety of wavelengths is available to operators and it must be remembered that the one actually selected is significant as a consequence of the fact that the reflectance of a particular surface varies with that utilised. Additionally, the penetration of the surface increases with wavelengths.

9.7.   INFRARED LINE SCAN

This technique was first used commercially (by Huntings) in 1968 in Africa. It is capable of mapping by day or by night temperature contrasts at the surface of the Earth as small as 0·5 °C and is applicable to hydrology in detection of spring lines and water seepage along faults.

9.8.   SATELLITES

Some relate to hydrology and among these is the METEOR system of the USSR which is equipped with instrumentation for the sensing of basic meteorological and hydrological parameters on both an operational and an experimental basis. These satellites are launched in a polar orbit at a height of about 900 km and the inclination of the plane of the orbit to the equator is 81 °. The system comprises two or three such satellites which survey almost four-fifths of the planetary surface twice during a period of 24 hours. METEOR satellites are equipped with the following sensors:

(a)   TV cameras which are sensitive to radiation in the visible spectral band for obtaining information on clouds, ice and snow;

(b)   infrared TV-type instrumentation for deriving data relating to quantity of cloud and ice cover;

(c)   scanning radiometer for measuring intensity of reflected radiation and outgoing radiation, temperature of the underlying surface and of cloud tops.

Additionally, experimental METEOR satellites are equipped with:

(d)   scanning telephotometer for automatic direct transmission of pictures in the visible spectral band;
(e)   eight-channel scanning radiometer for measuring vertical temperature profiles;
(f)   passive microwave instrumentation for detection of areas of precipitation and ice cover;
(g)   four-channel TV-type scanning instrumentation for deriving multispectral images of cloud and underlying surface.

There is also the European Meteorological Satellite Programme (METEOSAT) executed by the European Space Agency (ESA) and the Meteorological Satellite Programme of Japan. Naturally, NASA/NOAA have an extensive US programme.

There is also a global observing system (GOS) which comprises the coordinated system of methods, techniques and facilities for making observations on a planetary scale within the framework of the World Weather Watch. GOS consists of two sub-systems, namely a surface-based one and a speca-based one. The WWW plan envisages near-polar orbiting and geostationary satellites to form part of the integrated GOS.

9.8.1. Requirements in Soil and Ground Water Studies

Exploration for ground water and the development of aquifers would be aided by the detection of ground water discharge or leakage to rivers and lakes or in the form of springs. As is well known, changes in the ground water storage component of the balance equation are determinable by observation of alterations in the ground water levels. Above these lies the zone of aeration, i.e. unsaturation, and it is important to measure conditions in this for the purposes of water balance assessment, study of vegetation and prediction of runoff. Obviously, ground water flow is complex and detailed investigation requires data such as subsurface geological structure and the hydraulic conductivity of the aquifer. It is probable that satellites will be able ultimately to provide information on these matters, but unlikely that they can do so in the immediate future.[10]

TABLE 9.1

SPECIFIC NEEDS AS REGARDS SOIL AND GROUND WATER[10]

Hydrologic element	Resolution[a] A	B	C	Accuracy[b]	Frequency[c]
Ground water detection					
Aquifer mapping	100	100	100	—	(5 years)
Location of discharge to rivers	30	30	30	—	(weekly)
Location of discharge to lakes	100	100	100	—	(weekly)
Location of springs	30	30	30	—	(5 years)
Ground water level	300	1 000	1 000	(1 cm)	(daily)
Soil type	100	1 000	1 000	—	(5 years)
Unsaturated zone					
Moisture content profile[d]	100	300	1 000	10 % of field capacity	(daily)
Temperature profile[d]	100	300	1 000	(0·5 °C)	(daily)
Infiltration/percolation	100	300	1 000	(10 %)	(daily)
Depth of seasonal frost	100	300	1 000	(10 %)	(weekly)
Detection of permafrost	100	300	1 000	—	(5 years)

[a] Expressed in metres, for drainage basins of the hydrologic elements of the following sizes: A, less than 100 km², B, between 100 and 1 000 km² and C, more than 1 000 km².
[b] Not in brackets, as given in relevant WMO guides or technical regulations; in brackets, as recommended by the Informal Planning Meeting for review and possible revision by appropriate WMO bodies.[10]
[c] Reference may be made to WMO publication number 168 of 1974, paragraph 2.11.2.1.
[d] In depths of 5, 10, 20, 50 and 100 cm.

Explanation of the hydrologic elements mentioned in Table 9.1:

(a) aquifer mapping: this will indicate the region in which ground water is found;
(b) location of discharge to rivers and lakes and of springs: these indicate the existence of ground water;
(c) ground water level: this refers to the level of the water table in an unconfined aquifer and of the piezometric surface of a confined aquifer at specific times and locations;
(d) soil type: relates to the composition and classification of the loose materials occurring on the surface of the Earth (Regolith);
(e) unsaturated zone (zone of aeration): that zone lying between the surface of the ground and the water table;
(f) soil moisture: the amount of water stored in the unsaturated zone;

(g)   infiltration: flow of water from the surface of the soil into the soil itself;

(h)   percolation: flow of water through a porous medium, principally downwardly directed gravitational flow;

(i)   depth of seasonal frost: this is the distance from the surface of the ground to the level of freezing (0 °C);

(j)   detection of permafrost: indication of regions where the ground is permanently frozen.

Of course, areal assessments as a result of satellite imagery can contribute some very valuable data on hydrologic catchment areas relating to supply to ground water reservoirs and these include extent of open water, saturated soil regions, flood extent and flood plain boundaries.

All these techniques fall under the general heading of remote sensing.

9.8.2. Remarks about Remote Sensing

This may be defined as the detection at distance of variations in the planetary surface and its chemical and physical properties. It includes not only satellites and aircraft, but also rockets and balloons.

Detectors are operated in the electromagnetic spectrum from the UV end through the visible to the thermal IR end and then out to microwave and radar wavelengths (1–3 cm). Within the EM spectrum, there is a number of 'windows' permitting detectors to be operated in aeroplanes and satellites with minimal distortion of measurements by the atmosphere.

Since depth penetration is restricted to at most a few centimetres, remote sensing techniques mainly provide data on the surface characteristics of the planet, any deeper information being inferred by downwardly directed extrapolation or derived by geophysical techniques such as aeromagnetics and seismic already described and applicable solely to land areas. It may be stated, therefore, that aircraft, rockets and satellites may be regarded as complementary sensory platforms. A particularly useful (earth resources technology) satellite, ERTS-1, was launched by NASA in July 1972 and this is now orbiting the Earth at an altitude of 496 nautical miles and a period of 103 min. ERTS-1 can give global coverage every 18 days, crossing a particular point at the same local time (although the angle of the sun alters with time). Information is collected from strips of width 100 nautical miles and overlapping by 14 % at the equator, increasing to 70 % at 70 °N. On the equator, the distance between successive tracks is 86 nautical miles. The satellite carries two imaging systems. The return beam (RVB) system has not functioned since early in the mission and geologists are now working with the multi-spectral scanner system (MSS). This is a line scanning device using an oscillating mirror to scan continuously at right angles to the path of the satellite. It operates in four bands, two in the visible wavelengths and two in the near IR. Detector outputs are sampled and periodically transmitted to ground stations located in North America. Of course, the great advantages of this ERTS satellite's imagery include global synoptic coverage irrespective of military and political factors (i.e. human stupidity, as might well be said), repetition of imagery every 18 days with constant sun angle and shadow effects, provision of accurate and uniform exposure over enormous areas (hence the mosaic assembling of aerial photographs is avoided), giving a regional picture, and cheapness (NASA supplies ERTS satellite imagery below its real cost).

The major disadvantage of the satellite is that the present scale of imagery leaves quite a lot to be desired since it is one to one million. Consequently, only features possessing excellent spectral contrast and a diameter exceeding 100 m can be resolved. In this connection, it might be indicated that the so-called Big Bird spy satellite can do much better, resolving to less than 2 m. Then too, there is lack of stereoscopic vision with ERTS and no cloud penetration capacity.

Nevertheless, it has become clear that the advantages of ERTS-1 far outweigh its disadvantages. However, it is a pity that the ERTS tape recorders have failed and the coverage is now obtainable over North America alone. Receivers should be installed elsewhere in order to obtain coverage there, for instance in Europe. Additional satellites of this type will be launched and provide more evidence useful to geologists, particularly as regards long linear features which are occasionally traceable for hundreds of miles. Interestingly, some of these cannot be seen fully on aerial photographs, but why this is so remains rather obscure. Such linears probably correspond with faults and afford vital clues to regional geology and structure. ERTS imagery is particularly useful in quick regional geological mapping, but field checking is still necessary for validation. Also, it seems likely that ERTS-1 does not give detail sufficient for up-to-date sedimentological studies.

9.9.   GEOLOGICAL METHODS

These comprise the utilisation of existent published and unpublished geological information supplemented by field work. Both approaches can give a useful initial appraisal of ground water potential in a region and have the advantage of being non-instrumental and therefore inexpensive. The geological history and especially the accumulatory and erosional happenings in a region are invaluable in determining ground water bearing formations and the actual type of rock found may well give a clue to the amount of water which is to be expected. This is very important because that suitable for domestic purposes may well be totally inadequate for application to industrial requirements. In a classic study, O. E. Meinzer long ago indicated the influence of rock structure and type on ground water.[11]

9.10.   DOWSING (WATER WITCHING)

This is mentioned because of its psychological interest. However, there is absolutely no scientific evidence whatsoever that it has the slightest value in the search for ground water. It is not surprising that the US Geological Survey advises against employing the 'technique'.

Having dealt with investigations of ground water *at* the surface of the Earth, it is now time to direct attention to *below* surface investigations.

9.11.   BOREHOLE INVESTIGATIONS

Obviously, test drilling activities will provide maximal information on subsurface conditions and a bore so constructed may well be converted into a pumping well or used as an observation well either for pumping tests or measuring water levels. Practically any method may be employed for test drilling, although in loose materials the optimal ones are cable tool and hydraulic rotary. These have been mentioned briefly in Chapter 2 above, but some amplification may be useful.

9.11.1. Cable Tool Technique
Holes up to 2 ft or more in diameter may be so constructed and the actual excavation work is accomplished by regularly raising and dropping a string of appropriate tools. This comprises a rope socket, a set of jars, a drill stem and a drill bit having a total weight of as much as several tons. The components are made of steel and joined with tapered box-and-pin screw joints; on the whole, it may be said that the bit is the most important part of

the assembly because this is the part which actually effects the drilling. Bits can reach lengths of 10 ft and weigh well over a ton and they may be of various shapes according to the nature of the particular job in hand. The drill stem is a long steel bar adding to the drill in order to improve its cutting and penetrating ability and it may well be over 30 ft long and 6 in. in diameter. The set of jars constitutes a pair of narrow connecting links. They loosen the tools if sticking occurs.

Drill cuttings are removed by a bailer, essentially a pipe with a basal valve and a summit ring attached to a bailer line. When it is admitted to the well, the former allows cuttings to enter and prevents their escape. After it is full, the bailer is hauled up to the surface and emptied.

A drilling rig is associated with the above assembly. In loose formations, casing may have to be inserted and this is usually made of corrosion-resistant steel. In a deep drilling, alignment must be properly maintained, i.e. deviations from the vertical should not exceed 0·5 % or less. This is more difficult to achieve in solid rock than in unconsolidated materials.

9.11.2. Hydraulic Rotary Technique

This is a more rapid method and operates continuously with a hollow, rotating bit of various designs through which lubricant is forced, material loosened by it being transported to the surface by the ascending lubricant. Normally, casing is not necessary. The bit is attached to a drill rod of heavy pipe screwed to the end of a square section of drill rod; the drill is rotated by a rotating table fitting closely around this square section and permitting the drill rod to slide down as the hole deepens. A drilling rig is associated with the above assembly. A variation on this technique is the reverse rotary method which involves a suction dredging approach by means of which cuttings are removed using a suction device.

Although quicker, this approach does not give such accurate sampling as the cable tool technique, especially in the case where very fine grained material is being collected—this tends to mix with the lubricant. At greater depth, the hydraulic rotary technique is cheaper to use and accurate samples may be obtained by pulling the drill stem and using a sampler at the base of the hole.

9.11.3. Augering

This can be done in soft ground and at shallow depth. Auger borings may be utilised for any purpose where disturbed samples are satisfactory and they are valuable in advancing holes to depths where *undisturbed* sampling is necessary. Depths are limited by the ground water table and also by the quantity and maximal size of gravel, cobbles and boulders as these relate to the size of the equipment actually in use. Hand-operated post hole augers from 4 to 12 in. in diameter can be used for exploration up to about 20 ft deep, but, employing a tripod, holes as deep as 80 ft have been drilled successfully. Machine-driven augers may also be used. These are of three

TABLE 9.2

ROTARY DRILL CORE SIZES

Designations	Diameters (in.)
NX	$2\frac{1}{8}$
BX	$1\frac{5}{8}$
AX	$1\frac{1}{8}$
EX	$\frac{7}{8}$

Range of rotation speeds:
In medium-hard rock from 300 to 1 500 rev/min for diamond bits and from 100 to 500 rev/min for metal bits

types, namely helical augers from 3 to 16 in. in diameter, disc augers up to 42 in. in diameter and bucket augers up to 4 ft in diameter.

An auger boring is made by turning the auger as far into the soil as is desired, withdrawing it and removing the soil specimen for examination.

9.11.4. Jetting
This is a cheap method of drilling shallow small-diameter holes and it is a rapid method also. Unfortunately, it does not always yield good samples.

9.11.5. The Log
This is a vital concomitant of the drilling and comprises an accurate record of the time (minutes, seconds) to drill each foot of hole. It is most practical with hydraulic rotary drilling and should also contain details of the various materials and conditions encountered during the work. It lists all those fundamental facts upon which all the later conclusions should be based and these latter will include need for additional testing, site feasibility, etc. In fact, the log may be used again and again and can later delineate changes in conditions with time. The *Earth Manual* gives excellent examples of the various types of drilling log.[12]

9.12. RESISTIVITY LOGGING

In a well which is not cased, it is possible to measure the electrical resistivities of the surrounding media by simply lowering current and potential electrodes into it and observing variations of these with depth. Obviously, the presence of a fluid (such as water), the diameter of the well in question, the occurrence of ground water and the nature of the rock strata encountered will all have a bearing on the log obtained.

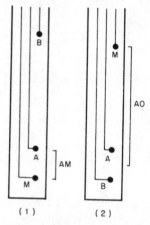

FIG. 9.3.   Arrangements of electrodes for (1) normal, (2) lateral resistivity well logs. AB, current electrode; MN, potential electrode.

There are various methods of effecting the actual measuring and perhaps the commonest is the multielectrode one. This lessens the influence of the well dimensions and the drilling fluid while facilitating a direct comparison of a number of recorded resistivity curves. The technique requires the utilisation of four electrodes, two for the emission of current and two for potential measurements. Normal and lateral recorded curves may be produced according to the arrangement of electrodes used. The alternatives are shown in the accompanying Fig. 9.3. In the normal arrangement, the effective space is AM and the recorded curve is termed AM also whereas in the lateral arrangement, the effective space is AO which is measured between M and a point halfway between the electrodes A and B. An additional possibility is to increase the effective spaces AM and AO. Short spaces are useful in determining the boundaries of formations possessing different resistivities whereas long ones are optimal in deriving data on the fluid contents of permeable formations. Resistivity curves can provide information regarding the lithology of various beds of rock and also facilitate the distinction between fresh and saline water sometimes required in particular jobs. The actual resistivity of ground water will depend upon both the ionic concentration and mobility of contained salts, the latter relating to molecular weight and electric charge. It is not surprising that there are large differences between various chemical compounds—for instance a solution of $NaCl$ is much more mobile than one of $Ca(HCO_3)_2$.

Temperature is an important factor in that, as it increases, so does the ionic mobility of ground water; consequently, there exists an inverse relationship between resistivity and temperature. This may be expressed as a correction factor in order to multiply resistivities at measured temperatures and produce resistivities at a standard temperature taken as $25\,^\circ C$.

Resistivity measurements are useful also in determination of porosity by means of the following relationship:

$$n^m = \frac{\rho_w}{\rho}$$

where ρ is the formation resistivity *in situ*, ρ_w is the water resistivity and m is a void-distribution coefficient (cementation factor).[13]

Electrical resistivity logs are very useful. For instance, they are employed to find out the optimum placing of well screens. Also, they can be utilised in the estimation of concentrations of salts in waters derived from wells, these possibly deriving from sea water intrusion or connate origins. Additionally, such logs can facilitate the location of aquifers, the delineation of sequences of beds, the monitoring of alterations in the quality of ground water and the correlation of different aquifers.

9.13. POTENTIAL LOGGING

This method measures natural electrical potentials occurring within the Earth and these may be termed self-potentials or spontaneous potentials (SP). Appropriate measurements may be derived using a recording potentiometer connected to two like electrodes, one usually being lowered into the well and the second one connected to the surface of the ground. Interpretation of the resultant logs is a complex matter and it reflects uncertainty regarding the actual cause(s?) of the phenomenon. Actual recorded values can range up to hundreds of millivolts and positive values occur when flow from a formation into a well is examined, negative ones occurring for the reverse flow. The logs themselves are read in terms of positive and negative deviations from a quite arbitrary base (perhaps a thick, impermeable formation), hence they indicate permeable zones and, if the differences between these are not very marked, deviations will also not be very marked and results rather vague. Care must be exercised also near urbanised areas where such factors as electrical instrumentation may induce artificial earth currents to arise.

Spontaneous potentials which derive from electrochemical potentials (arising from fluid concentration differences) are expressible as

$$SP = M \frac{\rho_f}{\rho_w}$$

in which ρ_f is the drilling fluid resistivity in ohm-m, ρ_w is the ground water resistivity (also in ohm-m), and M is a factor which depends upon the chemical composition of the two fluids and additionally upon the nature of the formations which adjoin any particular aquifer. A value of $M = 70$ has sometimes been found to be satisfactory. Using such a value and measuring SP and ρ_f is a means of estimating the ground water resistivity.

In normal work, both potential and resistivity logs are recorded together and they frequently indicate the same subsurface conditions, thereby supplementing each other.

9.14.　CALIPER LOGGING

This involves using a hole caliper in order to measure well diameters down a well. A suitable instrument has four extensible arms with an electrical resistor which is motivated by these. The technique is to insert the device with the arms folded into a well until the bottom is attained. Then the arms are released by detonation of a small charge and the average hole diameter logged as a continuous graph by the recording of resistance changes while the caliper is being raised.

9.15.　RADIOACTIVE LOGGING

Gamma, gamma–gamma, neutron–neutron and neutron–gamma logging have been discussed already in Chapter 3 and can be used, for instance, in determination of stratification of aquifers.

Radioactive logging (RL) applications may also be made to logging of deep exploratory wells and also, in conjunction with well-boring techniques, in the study of the structure of friable deposit profiles in the use of shallow occurrences of ground water.

RL equipment comprises three components, namely a surface unit and a set of logging sondes controlled by it together with a cable on a winch for transmitting data to the surface and for powering the sonde and sources.

RL of hydrogeological boreholes is similar to that effected for petroleum, gas or coal, but, as water wells are usually shallower, less cumbersome equipment can be employed. The sonde ought to fit against the side of the well bore as closely as is feasible. Sometimes this is not so easy, for instance where a large diameter hole is involved. Here, the sonde may be *pressed* against the side by means of a mechanical device such as a bow spring. To compensate for separation of the sonde from the well bore, it is advisable that caliper logging should be utilised in conjunction with RL. In actuality, it is advisable to use electrical resistivity and conductivity logs as well as sonic ones plus standard hydraulic tests also in utilisation of RL in the assessment of the hydrogeological parameters of a bore hole. RL can give good accuracy. Individual strata only 20 cm thick have been distinguished. It is certainly clear that the approach is sometimes the sole means of obtaining certain lithological and hydrological parameters. Optimally, RL can give invaluable information on porosity, formation bulk density and the chemical and mineral composition of a formation.

9.16. TEMPERATURE LOGGING

A recording resistance thermometer may be used in order to obtain a vertical traverse measurement of the ground water temperature. Ordinary temperatures will increase with depth in accordance with the usual geothermal gradient of approximately 1 °C per 100 ft depth. Departures from this may give information about unusual conditions, for instance abnormally low temperatures may demonstrate the presence of gas, while high temperatures indicate perhaps local heat sources. This whole matter will be discussed below in Chapter 10.

9.17. VERTICAL FLOW DETERMINATION

Measurement of vertical flow in wells can give important data regarding such matters as water production, waste disposal, artificial recharge, etc., and mechanical current meters are efficient in effecting it. For low velocities, i.e. those of less than 2 cm/s, however, the precision of these deteriorates because of friction and radiotracing may be preferable.

9.17.1. Principle of Tracing

Peak to peak velocity can be measured and the discharge Q is given by

$$Q = u_v F_v = \frac{x}{t} F_v$$

where u_v is the vertical velocity, F_v the horizontal cross section of the filter tube, t the peak to peak time between two measuring points at a distance x apart. An alternative is the total count technique where the concentration time integral is measured at each measuring point and the total count N is related to the concentration c by

$$N = E_H \int_0^\alpha c \, dt$$

where E_H is the detector sensitivity. Then if A is the activity of the added tracer

$$Q = \frac{A E_H}{N}$$

This latter technique is sensitive to added inflows but insensitive to outflow. Consequently, if between two points of measurement there is interchange of flows, the inflow can be detected by the *decrease* in total count even where the total discharge shows no alteration owing to equal in- and out-flows. This means that for all practical purposes, *both* methods should be utilised because one measures the velocity while the other one is proportional to the discharge and does not necessitate a knowledge of the cross section.

Obviously, measurement of the vertical flow in a bore hole is not as straightforward as it initially appears; thermal effects, etc., may set up density currents (the tracer itself contributes to these, at least potentially) and must therefore be considered. The approach normally is carried out by injecting an appropriate tracer and measuring its motion in the direction of flow by using a series of suitable detectors arranged along the bore or by using one detector and moving it along the bore. The commonest tracers for the purpose are iodine-131 and bromine-82 which are short-lived. A lot of information has been derived by use of the method in determining vertical flows in dam sites and building foundations and in turbulent flow conditions, accuracies better than 10 % may be achieved. The accuracies in laminar flow are not so well known.

9.18. INTERNAL INSPECTION METHODS

One method is to use fluid samplers which can collect water samples at specified depths and thus enable water quality to be measured and also to check on electrical log results. Another is to employ photography, i.e. to photograph interior well surfaces in order to inspect variations in lithology and also casings and their condition.

REFERENCES

1. TÖPFER, K. D. and LEGG, C. A., 1974. Geophysical exploration for ground water in the Lusaka district, Republic of Zambia. *J. Geophys.*, **40**, 97–112.
2. KUNETZ, G. and ROCROI, J. P., 1970. Traitement automatique des sondages électriques. *Geophys. Prospecting*, **18**, 2, 157.
3. KUNETZ, G., 1966. *Geoexploration Monographs*, Ser. 1, No. 1. Gebrüder Bornträger, Berlin.
4. EBERT, A., 1943. Grundlagen zur Auswertung geoelektrischer Tiefenmessungen. *Z. Angew. Geophys.*, **10**, 1.
5. MOONEY, H. M. and WETZEL, W. W., 1956. *The Potentials about a Point Electrode and Apparent Resistivity Curves for a Two-, Three- and Four-layered Earth.* Univ. of Minnesota Press, Minneapolis.
6. LINEHAN, D. and KEITH, S., 1949. Seismic reconnaissance for ground water development. *J. New Eng. Water Works Assn.*, **63**, 76–95.
7. BARTHELMES, A. J., 1946. Application of continuous profiling to refraction shooting. *Geophysics*, **11**, 1, 24.
8. HAGEDOORN, J. G., 1959. The plus–minus method of interpreting seismic refraction sections. *Geophys. Prospecting*, **7**, 158.
9. PATERSON, N. R., 1968. Portable facsimile seismograph; the equipment and its application. *Mining in Canada*.
10. WORLD METEOROLOGICAL ORGANISATION, 1976. Informal planning meeting on the satellite applications in hydrology. Final Report (25–27 October 1976), Geneva, 35 pp. plus annexes.
11. MEINZER, O. E., 1937. *The Occurrence of Ground Water in the United States.* USGS Water Supply Paper 489, 321 pp.
12. US Department of the Interior, 1968. *Earth Manual.* Bureau of Reclamation, US Govt. Printing Office, Washington, D.C., 783 pp.
13. JONES, P. H. and BURFORD, T. B., 1951. Electric logging applied to ground water exploration. *Geophysics*, **16**, 115–139.

CHAPTER 10

Ground Water and Geothermal Energy

In the previous chapter, section 9.16, allusion was made to the fact that ordinary temperatures increase with depth into the crust in accordance with the normal geothermal gradient which is about 1 °C per 100 ft.

Visually, natural phenomena such as volcanoes, geysers, fumaroles, hot springs and boiling mud pools confirm the presence of terrestrial heat inside the Earth and often relate to the occurrence of earthquakes.

In a book on geothermal resources, the author has discussed the reason for this and also the probable source of this internal heat, complex subjects into which it is not possible to enter in any great detail here.[1] A summary of some important facts and hypotheses may be given, however.

10.1. PLANETARY STRUCTURE

Figure 10.1 illustrates the concentric layered structure of the Earth and Fig. 10.2 shows the crust in section. That part of the crust underlying the oceans is about seven times thinner than that part underlying continents which are themselves fringed by a sediment zone, the shelf, of varying width. The crust is separated from a deeper mantle by the famous Mohorovičić discontinuity, the so-called Moho, lying about 10 km below the ocean base and about 35 km below continents.

High stresses can accumulate in the upper mantle and in the crust and when relieved by material movements, earthquakes result. Mostly, these take place along ribbon-like regions, principally the well-known 'Pacific Girdle of Fire' bordering that ocean and along the Mediterranean–Himalayas zone and East Africa (the Rift Valley). Why this is so is explicable on the basis of a hypothesis called plate tectonics. This postulates that the crust comprises several discrete 'plates' continuously in

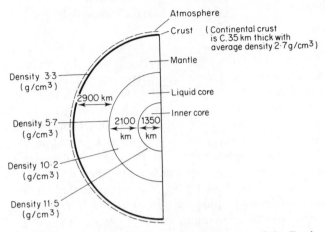

FIG. 10.1.   Concentric layered internal structure of the Earth.

motion relative to each other at a rate of several centimetres annually, also continually being formed and destroyed in certain regions. The seismic regions follow lines along which plates are either separating or colliding. Volcanoes and similar manifestations of internal heat energy also lie along these lines. A development of this is that the planetary surface can be regarded as divisible into non-thermal and thermal areas. The former are those showing the normal geothermal gradient mentioned above. The latter are those possessing temperature gradients far in excess of that; they have been termed 'hyperthermal' by H. Christopher H. Armstead.[2] Pragmatically, they can be divided into vapour-dominated and water-dominated systems, the former constituted of steam which may be superheated with temperatures around 250 °C, the latter being subdivisible into (a) high enthalpy fluids with temperatures up to 388 °C, (b) low enthalpy fluids with temperatures up to 200 °C.

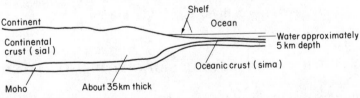

FIG. 10.2.   Sections of Earth's crust. Sial, chemical composition of continental rock (silicon, aluminium predominant). Sima, chemical composition of oceanic crust (silicon, magnesium predominant).

10.2. PLANETARY HEAT RESOURCES

These are obviously of great importance because it is they which heat up ground water and produce high enthalpy fluids and/or steam, sometimes superheated, in thermal areas of the Earth. In point of fact, the total heat potential of the planet is very hard indeed to assess. This is because it is not known how much of the internal heat could be released safely, how much radioactivity exists in crustal rocks or what are the physicochemical properties of mantle and core material. It is known, however, that the continuous natural outflow of heat from the Earth is approximately 30 000 m kW (thermal), a tiny amount compared with the heat energy received from the sun (about 0·025 %). None the less, the heat reserves of the Earth must be enormous and from this, it might be inferred that geothermal energy may constitute an almost infinitely renewable resource. However, there is no doubt that particular fields can become exhausted. For instance, the famous Italian one in Tuscany maintains its capacity of 400 MW only by continual expansion by drilling more and more wells over an ever-increasing area. Clearly, one day the field's boundary will be reached and the stored heat will begin to run down.

10.3. GEOTHERMAL AREAS

These may be contrasted with non-thermal areas, i.e. those with the normal geothermal gradient noted at the beginning of this chapter (variable, of course, and perhaps ranging from 0·3 °C/100 ft to just over 1 °C/100 ft).

H. Christopher H. Armstead has proposed subdividing geothermal areas into:

(a) semi-thermal areas, i.e. those with geothermal gradients up to around 70 °C/km depth;
(b) hyperthermal areas, i.e. those with geothermal gradients many times greater than those found in non-thermal areas.

10.4. THE CHARACTERISTICS OF GEOTHERMAL FIELDS

Geothermal fields may be distinguished from geothermal areas because the latter constitute high enthalpy regions not necessarily associated with suitable strata (permeable) and not necessarily exploitable as a geothermal

TABLE 10.1
THE DISTRIBUTION AND POTENTIAL IMPORTANCE OF THERMAL REGIONS

Frequency of occurrence	Type	Economic significance	Future value
Rare	Vapour-dominated hyperthermal	Great	As now, great
	Water-dominated hyperthermal	Great	As now, great
	Semi-thermal	Valuable	As now, valuable
Common	Hyperthermal/semi-thermal without associated permeable strata	None	Possible

resource, whereas the fields are exploitable precisely because they *are* associated with suitable (permeable) strata.

Theoretically, the interesting question is exactly how deep-seated heat is transferred upwards to shallow levels in the crust. While models may be constructed for this, knowledge is limited because with existing technology, it is simply not feasible to 'reach' subterranean fields. However, such models must be made, since it is by means of them that predictions may be made regarding the siting of boreholes designed to provide access to hot, exploitable geothermal fluids. Indeed, the accuracy of the model utilised can be gauged later by its success in predicting such sites.

A model either of a vapour-dominated or of a liquid-dominated hyperthermal field must incorporate the following information. Such fields require a heat source; strata, of permeability such as to constitute an aquifer containing steam and/or water; a source of water replenishment to replace losses of fluids entailed by natural or artificial processes; bedrock underlying the aquifer; and a cap rock overlying it (and preventing loss of heat and vapour from the field into the atmosphere).

The reason for the rarity of such hyperthermal fields is now apparent. In nature, a combination of such factors is unusual. Some observations on each may be pertinent.

(a) The heat source: from section 10.1 above, it can be seen that seismic belts are the places wherein hyperthermal fields occur, i.e. they occur at places of crustal weakness where adjacent plates are in relative motion— here the intrusion of magma into the crust is most likely to take place.

(b) The high outwardly-directed heat flow in hyperthermal fields may be due to:

(i)   local hot spots in the mantle;
(ii)   localised thinning of the crust;

(iii)   local high concentrations of radioactive minerals in the crust;
(iv)   exothermic chemical reactions;
(v)   frictional heat occasioned by the differential motion of rock masses sliding over each other at geological faults;
(vi)   latent heat which is released on crystallisation or the solidification of molten rocks;
(vii) direct ingress of intensely hot magmatic gases pressuring their way through bedrock faults into the aquifer.

This latter may well be the most significant of all the factors. It must be clarified here that the term 'aquifer' is applied not merely to water-bearing formations as is normally the practice, but also to *steam-bearing* permeable zones which occur in hyperthermal fields. Three distinct types of ground water are involved. The first is of course that deriving from precipitation on the terrestrial surface, i.e. infiltrated meteoric water. The second is magmatic water, namely water origination in released vapours from the water of crystallisation when magmatic matter completely solidifies on cooling down. The third is connate water which can be described as water associated with the originating of a rock formation, e.g. water of crystallisation released from some rocks when their stability has been disturbed as a result of physical or chemical changes.

It may be added that magmatic water is sometimes termed juvenile water, a term including water deriving from volcanoes. As might be expected, waters of magmatic origin differ from meteoric water in the stable isotope contents. Thus, the ratio of hydrogen to deuterium (H/D) in precipitation is about 6800:1, but in magmatic steam (or juvenile steam, as it may be called alternatively), the H/D ratio is about 6400:1. As a result of this difference, it is possible to ascertain the relative proportions in a mixture of meteoric and magmatic waters. Actually, the magmatic water content of known hyperthermal fields is small, probably never exceeding 10%. Nearly all of the water involved in the ground water circulation system, therefore, is meteoric in origin and penetrates from the surface through the permeable formations of the aquifer *down* to considerable depth at which heating takes place as a consequence mainly of conduction through the bedrock from underlying magma. To a lesser extent, small amounts of magmatic vapours may *upwardly* infiltrate and these give rise to the magmatic water component. In the aquifer itself, convection currents flow and, while ascending to the underside of the cap rock, hotter water from the depths tends to boil and release steam. This may either accumulate (under certain conditions) or migrate along the underside of the cap rock to reach cooler regions where condensation occurs and it rejoins the convection water stream (under other conditions). Several 'circulation cells' of this type may occur within a particular aquifer. If the aquifer is dome-shaped, hot water may accumulate below and steam above. Under these conditions, the geothermal field would prove to be a dry one unless deep drilling is carried out in order to liberate boiling water.

Surface manifestations appear where the overlying cap rock is fractured through faulting and geothermal fluids penetrate to ground level.

The writer has described such typical hyperthermal fields as The Geysers, Ca, USA, Larderello, Italy and Wairakei, New Zealand in his book on geothermal resources.[1]

As regards the first of these, The Geysers, *Geotimes* reported (August, 1979) that a body of magma more than 5 km deep is likely to be the heat source. It lies directly under Mt Hannah and was detected by studies of recorded seismic waves travelling through the magma chamber from distant earthquakes. This ties in with a suspicion of Roger Chapman in 1966 based upon gravity work demonstrating a mass deficiency under the mountain. It is believed that the field observations at The Geysers, the first delineation of a magma body in a geothermal region which is commercially productive, may be of great significance. It seems that waves traversing that zone underlying the steam-producing region of The Geysers and the volcanic area to the north and east of it underwent considerable slow-down (about 15%) at a depth of 15 to 20 km. This accords with the known fact that molten rock can cause this effect. That zone underlying the volcanic area is no doubt partially molten and under the geothermal production zone probably occurs a highly fractured steam reservoir overlying magma. This latter fractured portion could also slow down seismic waves as noted.

10.5.   HEATING OF GROUND WATER AT DEPTH

If there were no outside factors to consider, heat emanating from magmatic sources would heat water in an aquifer so that basal temperatures would gradually rise until boiling point is reached and steam is emitted. This would then ascend into higher and therefore cooler regions and condense, thus raising the temperature of the region and causing boiling. The hydrostatic pressure here is less than that of the basal region, however, consequently boiling would commence at a slightly *lower* temperature. Steam so formed would ascend, of course, into a yet higher region and again condense and again cause boiling at a still lower temperature. In fact, the process would proceed until all the water is boiling. The temperature at every level would be the boiling point for the hydrostatic pressure at that particular level. A simple depth/temperature relationship will be affected, however, by just those outside factors alluded to above. Principal among these is the cooling effect of ground water near the surface. Descending convection currents would be at temperatures below those indicated by the depth/boiling point relationship because they would not descend unless a marked cooling had occurred. Centrally in a geothermal field, a heated water plume probably rises vertically at a point where two convection currents become contiguous.

10.6.   EFFECTS OF EXPLOITATION OF 'WET' GEOTHERMAL FIELDS

Obviously, as exploitation proceeds, pressures and water levels in the relevant aquifer will decline so that the mass rate of fluid recharge will increase due to the greater head differential from outside the field. Most of the inflowing fluid derives from cooler ground water outside the confines of the field. Clearly, these waters would draw in heat, but nevertheless the field itself would show a slow and steady diminution of temperature. Of course, in nature the actual periphery of the field will not be sharply defined and it is to be expected that a zone of *warm* water will exist between the hot waters of the actual field and the cold waters beyond it. An additional point is that hot waters may flow in *from depth* and partly replenish the depleted fluids within the aquifer and if this takes place, then the *heat* inflow might well also show an increase.

In fact, this phenomenon has been observed at Wairakei in New Zealand where, after a quarter of a century of drilling and exploitation, heat is now flowing *in* at a rate of about 70% of the extraction rate so that the fluid inflow is practically equal to the fluid withdrawal.[2] Initially, on exploitation, pressures fell rapidly, but later stabilised. Of course, if exploitation continues at a higher rate than the inflow of heat, the permissible rate of extraction must ultimately suffer. This position will be attained gradually and be preceded by falling temperatures as a result of the extraction of stored heat from the aquifer rocks by inflowing cool waters from outside. These rocks will then cool. In 1968, the draw-off at Wairakei was intentionally reduced to approximately a third of the normal rate for a quarter of a year so as to observe whether the field would show any sign of recovery and there was, in fact, an immediate small rise in field pressures.

10.7. HOT WATER CONTROL

Hot water is extracted from geothermal fields of the 'wet' kind and raises two major problems, namely (a) disposal when unwanted, (b) control when piped.

Considering these in turn, the first case is found where the economics of extracting inherent energy from hot water are insufficiently attractive to justify effecting it and hence the water is rejected to waste. At constant pressure, the water/steam ratio remains quite steady, but is still subject to short term fluctuations which can be coped with by a water collection drum. However, a cheap means of disposal from such a drum is required and this rules out using float-controlled discharge valves which are expensive and can stick. In various wet fields, the matter has been resolved by discharging the hot water through bell-mouthed holes of a convenient size. As regards control when piped, this brings to mind the very dangerous explosive potential of superheated water. Consequently, great care must be exercised and additional effort is needed in order to ensure that supply and demand of the hot water are continuously in accord. The optimal solution would be a submersible pump capable of transmitting superheated water at pressures exceeding saturation pressure corresponding with the temperature. Slightly pressurised water at 200 °C has been transmitted successfully over a length of a mile in an experimental installation at Wairakei and power was thereby extracted. Lower temperature waters, i.e. those at or below boiling point, have been transmitted for years in Iceland for space heating.

The major problem with the transmission of the very hot waters is to ensure that boiling does not occur during this. If it does, pockets of steam may form and later collapse which could produce undesirable stresses which themselves could result in a burst pipeline. Superheated water is explosive and far more dangerous than steam at the same temperature. Thus, hot water at 200 °C has an isentropic heat drop to atmospheric pressure of only some 11 % that of steam at the same temperature, but its density is greater by a factor of 110. Consequently, a pipeline containing such water has far higher potential for doing mechanical work than if it contained steam at the same temperature and therefore a far higher explosive potential also. Prevention of boiling in a hot water pipe may be effected by making sure that everywhere the hydraulic pressure is greater than the vapour pressure.

10.8. CONDITIONS IN A VERY DEEP, HYDROTHERMAL SYSTEM

Probably there is no such animal because it is difficult to imagine a formation the strata of which could retain their permeability sufficiently to act as an aquifer when the increase in lithostatic pressure is taken into account. Thus, although under enormous hydrostatic pressure, the boiling point of water rises to attain the critical temperature of 374 °C, this can only be envisaged at a depth of approximately 3500 m and here the above observation applies, i.e. permeability would be lost because of lithostatic pressure. Where such a deep aquifer could exist, a strange situation would exist, namely a deep layer of boiling water floating on a base of high pressure superheated steam.[2]

10.9. GEOPRESSURISED FIELDS

These occur in non-thermal areas where the geothermal gradient is more normal. Their increased temperatures result from great depth of up to 6000 m and these range from under boiling point to over 150 °C. Such fields, for instance those in Hungary or on the Gulf Coast, USA, are filled with pressurised hot water of 'connate' origin at pressures ranging from 40 % to 90 % in excess of hydrostatic pressure corresponding to the depth. These pressures probably result from gradual subsidence through faults leading to the final isolation of entrapped water pockets contained in alternating layers of sandstone and shale. The entrapped water supports much of the weight of superincumbent beds and prevents complete compaction of the formation. Pore pressures in the pockets will range between the hydrostatic and the lithostatic pressures. A well in the Gulf of Mexico region of 4900 m depth with a bottom reservoir pressure of 871 atm can produce a net wellhead pressure of approximately 439 atm, i.e. 6450 psi at no flow, an excess pressure of about 95 % of the hydrostatic value. Geopressurised fields yield the heat energy of the pressurised hot water and in addition give hydraulic energy as a result of the pressure in excess of the vapour pressure which can be utilised in order to drive a water turbine. Also, the fluids may contain large quantities of dissolved natural gas possibly contributing extra heat.[2]

10.10. DRILLING

This is effected by techniques basically similar to those utilised in the petroleum industry and sometimes a deviated borehole is needed, i.e. one which does not descend vertically. *Aiming* a borehole in such a manner is useful when a bore out of control has to be sealed and also where economising of surface pipework can be effected thereby. Associated with this is the possibility of reaching a suitable aquifer without interfering at the surface with a beauty spot or an unstable or expensive terrain.

A particularly important application is that in which deviated drilling can bring in to a rather limited area of collection the potential of a widespread aquifer. The most significant event to avoid in drilling activities is the blow-out of steam, but there are other possible accidents such as sticking of drill piping or casing collapse which have to be avoided also. Precautionary measures can include care in bit selection, proper cooling procedures during drilling, the use of consolidation grouting around cellars and evasion of thermal shock by heating or cooling bores slowly when commencing or during servicing.

A famous accident occurred in the Cerro Prieto field in Baja California, Mexico, in 1967 when a wellhead pipe fractured below the shut-off valve. Huge amounts of steam and boiling water escaped into the air and the remedial work had to be carried out under dangerous conditions.

In 'wet' hydrothermal systems, boreholes will give steam/water mixtures and of course saturated conditions exist. Here, wellhead pressure and temperature are interdependent as are also fluid enthalpy and degree of 'wetness'. The mass flow of the steam and hot water differ from one boring to another and also from one field to another and can only be determined by direct measurement.

When a borehole is closed, there is a cut-off of water and steam flow and that pressure registered instantaneously at the instant of closure is termed the shut-in pressure.

This may decline as the fluid in the borehole cools. Taking into account the characteristics of both the steam and the hot water, it is easy to determine the total fluid flow (excluding non-condensible gases) by summing the two and the enthalpy may also be derived from appropriate tables showing this.

Some general conclusions which may be drawn are as follows. Firstly, there is, as might well be anticipated, a great variety of bore characteristics over a field and between fields. Secondly, the fluid enthalpy has often been found to be quite constant over a wide range of pressures as, for instance, at

Otake in Japan. Thirdly, enthalpy may rise (as at Broadlands in New Zealand) or fall (as at Cerro Prieto in Baja California) and if the former or the latter is the case, it is associated with *increasing* wellhead pressure. Fourthly, increasing wellhead pressures cause increasing wetness.

10.11. DISCHARGE

Where a well discharges into the atmosphere through an open-ended pipe, superheated steam emerges usually in a parallel jet characterised by a transparent interval between the end of the pipe and the point of initial condensation of the steam into an opaque stream of droplets of water. Later, air friction dissipates the kinetic energy of the jet and the condensed steam creates a rising and billowing cloud. Dry saturated steam has a short transparent zone and wet steam emits a tulip-shaped discharge. This latter results from the evaporative 'explosion' of the particles of water as these flash (due to the fall of pressure to atmospheric level).

10.12. THE VELOCITY OF FLUIDS AT WELLHEADS

If a dry field is involved, where steam enters the lower and uncased part of a bore at several levels, the velocity of the steam will accelerate as it rises, primarily because of the falling pressure and increasing specific volume of the steam as it ascends. At the wellhead, it is simple to calculate the average steam velocity if mass flow, pressure and temperature are known. The last two factors enable specific volume to be determined and the mass flow can then be converted to volumetric flow which, divided by the bore's areal cross section, will yield the average steam velocity.

REFERENCES

1. BOWEN, R., 1979. *Geothermal Resources.* Applied Science Publishers, London.
2. ARMSTEAD, H. CHRISTOPHER H., 1978. *Geothermal Energy.* E. & F. N. Spon, London.

CHAPTER 11

Ground Water and the Law

In normal practice, the insertion of interpreted technical geological information on specification drawings or on maps or in reports, etc., can have serious legal consequences in the event that something goes wrong. Therefore, the geologist who prepares documents of this type must take very great care to show only those conditions actually encountered in exploration or other appropriate procedures. Where rock strata are concerned, for instance, attempts to extend borehole data by interpretation of contacts between formations and depths to bedrock, etc., can be inaccurate and the contractor involved can establish thereby a valid basis for a legal claim. In fact, he has little option but to press this where damages have been sustained. Sometimes it makes the geologist wonder whether it is not safer merely to present subsurface exploratory information in the form of precise replicas of the original borehole logs rather than to submit these drawn on a profile, as is the customary practice. It is interesting to note that terminology may not be a legal protection as, for instance, where the word 'assumed' is employed, as in the case where such a bedrock surface may be indicated by simply connecting the points at the summit of bedrock in a series of boreholes with a curved or straight line. Obviously, this affects ground water work as well. Accuracy in presentation of ground water maps is mandatory since adverse water conditions are both deleterious and expensive to a contractor when unforeseen. Consequently, certain precautions are advisable. One is to insert the water level on each borehole log and append the date of measurement to it. This guards against the possibility that substantial fluctuation may occur and result in the water table rising prior to the constructional activity. Another is to ensure that reference is made to water in all logs. If on some, the water table is stated and on others, it is not, the contractor may conclude erroneously that in these latter water is not present. Later he may find that it is and then he will have a claim for any additional costs thereby incurred. Consequently, if water really is not encountered in a borehole, this fact should be stated on the relevant log. Actually, the factual data from all the exploratory work should be given in the geological reporting and naturally, logs should be given for all boreholes. If, in an area where boreholes were drilled, logs were omitted either deliberately or carelessly, later difficulties being met by a contractor, such omission may constitute grounds for a valid claim against the geologist. Omission of data may sail close to the wind of negligence and/or misrepresentation.

The above-mentioned considerations become important in matters relating to land use. In planning for the optimal employment of land, water enters the picture. For instance, in 1966 San Antonio Texas entered into a land use mapping programme in association with the United States Soil Conservation Service as a result of which soil maps and a soils handbook were produced. Consequently, various sites were classified for recreational, residential and other purposes and among the beneficiaries was the City Water Board. Nevertheless, not enough data were provided in respect of such matters as hydrologic factors and the subsurface conditions below a depth of 10 ft.

This emphasises the significance of C. L. McGuiness's call for hydrologically sound statutes.[1]

In normal legal practice, a right to take possession of water which derives from a natural supply source and apply it to a beneficial use can be granted and constitutes a water right.

In the USA, there are two main systems followed, namely a common law one of riparian rights and one of prior appropriation. The former is grounded in land ownership near a natural water supply. As regards ground water, this refers to the ownership of land overlying a water-bearing formation and the term *land-ownership right* is applicable.

The matter of prior appropriation refers to cases where earlier rights override later ones. The essential difference between the two approaches is that the first involves spatial position and the second involves chronological position.

11.1.   THE OWNERSHIP OF LAND

This concept originated in the UK in the early nineteenth century and W. A. Hutchins listed the pragmatic arguments in favour of it as follows:

(a)   the origin of the relevant waters were unknown and hence not subject to law;

(b)   recognition of correlative rights, i.e. of adjacent landowners, would interfere with important public projects.[2]

This English 'rule of *unlimited* use' proved inappropriate in the USA, especially in the west. Stemming from a law suit (*Basset* v. *Salisbury Manufacturing Co*, 43 N.H. 569, 82 Am. Dec. 179) in 1862 arose the principle that right of use of percolating water will be *limited* by the corresponding use of a neighbour, a principle which recognises the rights of others in the matter.

Later, this new idea became known as the American rule of reasonable use.

Later, actually in 1903, a modification arose, the California rule which states that the rights of landowners over a common ground water basin are coequal. Of course, this means that no owner can use more than his or her share if by so doing the rights of others are adversely affected. Obviously in conditions of inadequate supply, reasonable amounts must be employed, i.e. reasonable shares, *not* amounts sufficient for all reasonable uses.

11.2.   PRIOR APPROPRIATION

This depends upon the concept that a landowner does not enjoy any inherent right to water from sources on or sources contiguous to or sources underneath his or her land, but rather that the rights to such sources shall be grounded upon the chronological priority of beneficial utilisation and can be lost after such beneficial utilisation stops. The origin of this approach is California where miners used stream water in placer mining on public land. The Supreme Court of that state recognised the doctrine in 1855 and Congressional Acts in 1866 and 1870 recognised the right to appropriate water on public land, even extending protection to land which later passed into private hands.

Additionally, the Desert Land Act, 1877, recognised the doctrine. In fact, all western states of the USA now acknowledge it to a certain extent. Summarising, the doctrine may be expressed as conferring initial right upon whoever first beneficially utilises water and a consequence is that under drought or shortfall conditions, later appropriators must stop usage in reverse order of priority. Of course, there are no rights at all for the non-beneficial usage of water.

The doctrine has tended to gain strength as against that of the ownership of land because it is thought to have less defects and also could lead to more development and greater protection of vested rights, see for instance the opinion of the National Resources Planning Board in 1943.[3]

11.3. ADVERSE USAGE

Certain US states permit claimants to prescriptive rights, i.e. to loss of rights by prior appropriators or landowners if they use water adversely, under certain legally specified conditions.

11.4. GROUND WATER IN LAW

Much of the difficulty in earlier legal interpretation relates to the fact that in the past, ground water was not properly understood, e.g. in *Roath* v. *Driscoll* 20 Conn 533 in 1850, where it was referred to as moving through factors beyond apprehension.

At that time and later, attempts were made to differentiate between water courses and percolating waters. The former category was defined as natural streams on the surface or subterranean water flowing along channels and possessing definite points of origin. The latter category referred to waters moving downwards and *not* constituting part of a subterranean water stream. Obviously, ground water law must apply to water in the zone of saturation.[1]

In the USA, there seems to be general agreement that the legal control of ground water ought to be derived from the state (states' rights) rather than from the federal government level, but this results in inconsistency between the laws of different states and raises difficulties in the matter of the control of waters shared jointly between states. Climate plays an important part in the laws about water rights between states. In thirty-one eastern states, there is usually a water surplus and the precipitation is normally quite sufficient to provide an adequate water supply. This is probably the reason for the general predominance in them of the land ownership approach as mentioned earlier. The Rocky Mountain states are arid with insufficient rainfall, and irrigation water must be imported except in the actual mountainous areas which provide some water. Here, the prior appropriation approach prevails. In the case of the Pacific Coast states and those of the Great Plains (Montana to Texas), both approaches are to be found and this results from the fact that the former contain *both* arid and humid regions while the latter have a semi-arid climate of type intermediate between those of the arid west and the humid east of the continent.

11.5. OVERDRAFT

Areas where this phenomenon occurs are peculiarly open to difficulties. In the cases where the annual withdrawal of water is in excess of replenishment, the extra water used must deplete the storage, S. As water is a renewable natural resource, mining of it is often thought of as economically justifiable. With this philosophy, it was possible to establish an economy otherwise impossible by exploitation of ground water in the south-west of the USA, certainly, but on the other hand, conservationists would argue that mining is undesirable. Often, of course, there is no option but to mine water in the way outlined. David K. Todd has opined that it is better to continue a water right to the point of exhaustion of the water source rather than to restrict the withdrawals so as indefinitely to extend the availability of the water.[4]

As might well be expected, the matter of controlling ground water in overdraft conditions is complex. It may be handled by the courts or by landowner associations or by state administrative agencies in the USA. Actually, many law suits have originated in such conditions, perhaps due to the fact that there is such a plethora of differing approaches to the problem. Ideally, any regulations aimed at governing pumpage from a ground water basin ought to be preceded by discussions involving every interested party, but this is not always the case. Probably it is better to avoid overdraft conditions altogether rather than to attempt to initiate remedial measures or control, i.e. essentially ration, usage. The way to effect this is to limit pumping drafts and also to restrict the number of years through which pumping is permitted to go on. Obviously, police powers must be invoked and they imply that the prior appropriation approach to water rights is to be regarded as a chronological function rather than depending upon the ownership of land. David K. Todd has cited a famous instance of control started by the action of water users and this may be quoted here.[4] The case in question arose in Raymond Basin (San Gabriel Valley) in southern California. It commenced because an auxiliary water supply, i.e. Metropolitan Water District water conveyed by conduit from the Colorado River, was available—if it had not been, the issue would have been too uncertain to proceed. One of the water users was the City of Pasadena and it initiated an action in 1938 for adjudication of all the subterranean water rights in the basin after city engineers decided that the draft greatly exceeded the recharge to the Raymond Basin. A total of no less than thirty-one parties became involved in the suit and in 1939, after a petition brought by a number of these parties, the court referred the matter to the State

Division of Water Resources in order to obtain a technical report on the actual physical situation which existed. This reported in 1943 that recharge was, in fact, approximately 70% of draft and the final settlement was given in 1949 by the Supreme Court of California. It ruled that the pumping activities of all the parties concerned were to be proportionately reduced in order to ensure that the total annual pumpage should not be in excess of the safe yield. An official, a watermaster, was appointed in order to monitor this. Since those parties possessing other sources of water (e.g. the City of Pasadena) were allowed to sell annually all or part of the water from the basin to which they had rights to parties without access to other sources, the reduction in usage was effected quite amicably. The water so sold could be pumped by the purchaser from his own wells. Later on, a law was enacted to encourage the development of substitute water supplies other than ground water and this seems to be an eminently sensible idea in areas liable to overdraft problems.

A complication can arise in the event that surface water is utilised in order to supplement ground water, for instance to overcome overdraft conditions. The title to using such water can be based on different grounds from those which apply to natural ground water itself. It may be invested in the overlying landowner or in several such landowners or even in a state in the USA. Where no claim of ownership is made by whoever was responsible for injecting such surface water, the position is that the overlying owner may claim it. The introduced supply is then regarded as abandoned water mixing with natural ground water. However, the actual injection of such recharge water may be expensive and involve physical works and where this is the case, the individual landowners may not be able to defray the necessary costs. Either an association of these or the state or some other body may then step in and effect the required financing and they will retain the title to the supplementary water. This has happened in a number of states in the USA where the recharging of ground water has been considered as beneficial. The US Bureau of Reclamation is one agency which may reserve rights to all return flows and wastage from project water which has been delivered to contracting regions. Any unappropriated ground water will belong usually to the state wherein it is found and where a state acquires surface water and introduces it underground on lands not actually owned by the state itself, it is considered as acting for the public interest and as a non-landowning agency.

The general regulations which apply in most of the US states in order that ground water may be developed optimally in the public interest include a number of obvious requirements. One is that drillers must be licensed. Also, they must report—on prescribed forms—facts relating to the installation or deepening or reperforating of a well. Alternatively, well drilling permits may be a necessary prerequisite to such drilling activities. Geologic logs of the usual type must be kept and refer to such factors as depth, details of strata encountered and their structure and they must be kept not only for new wells, but also for wells undergoing deepening. Any artesian wells characterised by flowing water must be capped or otherwise regulated as a conservation measure. Any abandoned wells must be suitably sealed in order to obviate waste or contamination or accidents. Any water which is pumped in order to cool or for use in air conditioning must be recycled back to the aquifer by means of recharge wells. Alternatively, a sewer tax may be levied on ground water which is wasted into sewers. Disposal of pollutants is usually subject to strict regulation because their introduction would be degradative to the ground water system, for instance if brine or industrial waste were to be added to it.

11.6. THE LEGAL SITUATION IN THE UNITED KINGDOM

In 1963, a Water Resources Act became law and was intended to provide for the establishment of river authorities and a Water Resources Board as well as providing for the transfer to river authorities of functions previously exercised by river boards and other bodies. The meaning of the term 'water resources' was given as: water for the time being contained in any source of supply in (an) area and this source of supply includes inland waters and any water in underground strata. No distinction appears between water in the zone of aeration and true ground water. The sole clarification is that water in underground strata is stated as comprising:

(a) water for the time being contained in a well, borehole or similar work including any adit or passage constructed in order to facilitate collection of water in the well, borehole, etc.; and

(b) water for the time being contained in any excavation into such underground strata where the level of the water is a function of the entry of water from these same strata, i.e. depends wholly or mainly upon such an entry taking place.

Conservation, augmentation or redistribution of water are primary purposes of the Water Resources Board.

A river authority is entitled, after consultation with the Board, to propose the construction of wells, etc., in order to:

(a) ascertain the presence of water in underground strata; and
(b) ascertain the effects likely to arise because of the abstraction of such water.

A license to abstract water can be granted by the Board, in the case of statutory users subject to:

(a) seasons;
(b) emergencies such as water deficiency;
(c) the provision of equipment in regard to future requirements.

Land may be acquired by a river authority in order to protect ground water against pollution and this also applies to surface water. Discharges into underground strata are controlled so as to prevent the introduction of trade effluent or sewage effluent or poisonous, noxious or polluting matter.

Hydrometric schemes of river authorities should report periodically on:

(a) rainfall,
(b) evaporation,
(c) flow, level or volume of inland waters in their areas;
(d) other matters relevant to the question of water resources.

Each river authority is required to keep under review any statement of minimum acceptable flows relating to inland waters in their area.

Control of abstraction and impounding is vested in licensing under the Act by the appropriate river authority area. With regard to abstraction from underground strata, any person who is the occupier of land consisting of or comprising those underground strata shall be entitled to apply for such a licence.

A later piece of legislation may now be cited and this is the Water Act of 1973. This was intended to make provision for a national policy for water including such matters as conservation, augmentation, distribution and proper usage of water resources and also the provision of water supplies. Other relevant points covered were:

(a) sewage and its treatment and disposal, also the 'wholesomeness' of rivers, its restoration and maintenance in them and other inland waters;
(b) usage of such inland waters in recreation and the enhancement and preservation of amenity in connection with inland waters;
(c) usage of inland waters for navigation.

Water authorities were also to be established on a regional basis. A large number of previous pieces of legislation were affected by this and include:

(a) The Water Act, 1948;
(b) The Rivers (Prevention of Pollution) Act, 1951;
(c) Rural Water Supplies and Sewerage Act, 1955;
(d) Highways Act, 1959;
(e) The Public Health Act, 1961;
(f) Land Drainage Act, 1961;
(g) Harbours Act, 1964;
(h) New Towns Act, 1965;
(i) Sea Fisheries Regulation Act, 1966;
(j) Countryside Act, 1968;
(k) Agriculture Act, 1970;
(l) Town and Country Planning Act, 1971;
(m) Salmon and Freshwater Fisheries Act, 1972;
(n) Local Government Act, 1972.

REFERENCES

1. McGuiness, C. L., 1951. *Water Law with Special Reference to Ground Water.* US Geol. Surv., Circ. 117, 30 pp., Washington, D.C.
2. Hutchins, W. A., 1942. *Selected Problems in the Law of Water Rights in the West.* US Dept. Agri., Misc. Publ. 418, 513 pp., Washington, D.C.
3. Nat. Res. Planning Board, 1943. *State Water Law in the Development of the West.* Water Resources Committee, Sub-Committee on State Water Law, Washington, D.C.
4. Todd, D. K., 1959. *Ground Water Hydrology.* John Wiley, New York and London, p. 303.

CHAPTER 12

Models

The distribution and flow of ground water can be studied using model techniques and these can include sand, electric, viscous fluid, membrane, etc. As regards surface water, this must also be considered because in the next chapter, water balances will be discussed and these necessarily include the latter as well as subterranean water. In dealing with inland waters, river basins constitute a type of logical regional unit for hydrological studies and a basin cycle can be expressed in terms of its operation as:

precipitation = basin channel runoff − evapotranspiration − storage changes

Components of such a basin hydrological cycle can be studied in five major ways, namely:

(a)   using natural analogues;
(b)   using hardware models;
(c)   using synthetic systems;
(d)   using partial systems;
(e)   using a 'black box' approach.[1]

Some reference to these may be useful.

12.1.   NATURAL ANALOGUES AND HARDWARE MODELS

A natural analogue is an analogous natural system which is simpler and more easily observed than the original. Representative and experimental basins provide natural analogues of this type as discussed by UNESCO.[2]

As there may be insufficient accord between the natural analogue and the original basin, hardware models may be employed. In these, important structural elements of the basin are physically constructed either as scale models using real materials such as sand and water or analogue mod involving a change in the representational media, for instance from water flow to electric flow. As noted above, a sand model may be used also to represent an aquifer. Such models have been made in many different shapes in watertight boxes. Unconfined aquifers can be represented with the water table acting as the upper boundary while confined ones are made by applying an impermeable cover enabling pressure to be applied. Piezometers may be inserted into such models in order to identify the water table or the piezometric level whichever type of aquifer is being modelled, but they must be small so as not to modify flow patterns too much. These can be revealed by using chemical dyes such as potassium dichromate. With ground water studies, electric models can be employed. The flow of an electric current depends upon Ohm's law and may be expressed

$$I = \sigma_0 \frac{dE}{dx}$$

where I is the electric current per unit area through a material possessing a specific conductivity σ_0 and dE/dx is the voltage gradient. The above equation accords both with the Laplace equation and analogously with Darcy's law. In practice, an electric field is produced by an applied voltage in a model which reproduces ground water boundaries and this is similar to ground water flow in the prototype. As implied, there is a correspondence between head and voltage, hydraulic gradient and voltage gradient, permeability and specific conductivity, equipotential flow lines and equipotential lines of current, and flow lines and lines of current flow.[3] Electric models are limited to steady flows and simple ones presuppose homogeneous and isotropic aquifers; solid and liquid and even gelatin conductors have been utilised. A limitation is that an analogous force of gravity is not set up so that a water table is difficult to produce. This reflects the difficulties indicated by J. Amorocho and W. E. Hart in attempting to simulate natural basin behaviour from a hardware model.[4] As they pointed out, it is really impossible to establish *complete* dynamic similitude between model and prototype; additionally it is not feasible to operate the many simulated variables over a range wide enough for adequate simulation. Obviously, the electronic computer alone can now be considered as an acceptable hardware model.

12.2. SYNTHETIC SYSTEMS

Use of overall synthetic systems has been considered as the best approach in some problems, for instance understanding a basin hydrological cycle as was stated by J. E. Nash.[5] Analysis of these is effected by computers. Inputs of various kinds can be introduced. For example, precipitation can be fed in and permitted mathematically to filter through the system, contributing to such phenomena as storage changes and evapotranspiration. In the case of ground water systems, parameters can be varied at will so as to enable forecasting of the results of gradual man-made or other changes to the aquifer to be effected.

12.3. PARTIAL SYSTEMS AND THE 'BLACK BOX'

A partial system approach may be considered as a simplification to be undertaken where very detailed analysis is unnecessary. For instance, in considering precipitation, only that proportion of it which infiltrates may be germane. The application of the 'black box' approach, for instance to a basin cycle, involves considering this as such a black box where no detailed knowledge is assumed as regards the components or relationships within the cycle and interest may be totally directed at input and output and the establishment of a direct link between them. As might be expected, there has not been too much progress using this method.

12.4. VISCOUS FLUID MODELS

The flow of ground water may be simulated by effecting the flow of a viscous liquid between two closely spaced and parallel plates, a fact known since the nineteenth century. Where the flow is laminar, the flow lines constitute a two-dimensional potential flow field. Following the Navier–Stokes equations of motion and for steady flow with the Dupuit assumptions, the mean velocity of flow in the model is given by

$$v_m = \frac{b^2 \rho_m g}{3\mu_m} \frac{dh}{dx}$$

where b is the half-width of the channel, ρ_m and μ_m are the model fluid density and viscosity respectively, g is the acceleration due to gravity and dh/dx is the surface slope.[3] On analogy with Darcy's law, the plate spacing and fluid can be selected so as to correspond to a desired permeability. The velocity ratio

$$v_r = \frac{v_m}{v_p}$$

and this plus a given scale factor enables a time ratio to be determined:

$$T_r = \frac{L_r}{v_r}$$

where L is the length ratio.

Glass or plastic may be utilised to make the plates or sheets and either oil or some other fluid of suitable viscosity can be utilised, added dye being useful in facilitating the revelation of the flow lines. Steady and unsteady flows in confined and unconfined aquifers can be studied with the aid of such models.

12.5. MEMBRANE MODELS

In 1952, V. E. Hansen pointed out that complicated well problems may be solved by application of the membrane analogy.[6] In the case of small slopes, the surface of a membrane of rubber can be expressed in cylindrical coordinates as

$$\frac{d^2z}{dr^2} + \frac{1}{r}\frac{dz}{dr} = -\frac{W_m}{T_m}$$

where dz is the deflection at a radial distance dr from a central point of deflection, W_m is the weight of the membrane per unit area and T_m is a uniform membrane tension. Then the Laplace equation in cylindrical coordinates is expressible as[3]

$$\frac{\partial^2 h}{\partial r^2} + \frac{1}{r}\frac{\partial h}{\partial r} + \frac{1}{r^2}\frac{\partial^2 h}{\partial \theta^2} + \frac{\partial^2 h}{\partial z^2} = 0$$

in which h is the hydraulic head, r the radial distance, θ the angular coordinate and z the vertical coordinate. In the case of steady axially symmetrical flow in an incompressible fluid, it becomes[3]

$$\frac{d^2 h}{dr^2} + \frac{1}{r}\frac{dh}{dr} = 0$$

and this is applicable to well flow in an ideal confined aquifer as well as being a reasonable approximation in the case of an unconfined aquifer where a small drawdown is involved.

In actual studies, a rubber membrane is clamped under uniform tension over a circular boundary positioned horizontally. A central probe can be used to deflect the membrane and this probe represents a well. Measured deflections approximate the theoretical semilogarithmic drawdown relationship. Modifications have been introduced involving a part membrane, part electrical model.

The membrane model can be employed usefully in situations involving multiple well systems.

12.6.   THE DIGITAL COMPUTER

Computers have been alluded to above in section 12.1 and they constitute valuable tools for investigation of the behaviour of various hydrological systems. Digital computer programmes can reproduce components of these systems and of course parameters in the programmes can be altered in order to represent any required set of circumstances. Also, time scales can be compressed greatly.

In 1978, E. J. Reardon and P. Fritz published details of an appropriate isotope subroutine written for WATEQF, a Fortran IV version of the water analysis treatment programme WATEQ, translated and modified from an original version and aimed at computer modelling of ground water carbon-13 and radiocarbon compositions.[7] This is capable of performing a series of simulations on water samples where carbon-13 and radiocarbon data are available by assuming various initial pH-log(P_{CO_3}) values under open-system conditions and computing the $\delta^{13}C$ of the carbon dioxide gas phase to be compared with the actual water sample's value and an age for each simulation applied. Some of the models use total calcium and magnesium as a measure of whole rock carbonate dissolved under closed-system conditions while others make corrections for gypsum dissolution and ion-exchange reactions.

Mixed integer programming was used by P. G. O'Neil in 1972 to select and schedule for construction the minimum present cost configuration of water supply projects to meet future demand in south-east England.[8] The same technique was also utilised by D. W. Moody in a Water Resources Planning Model for Puerto Rico.[9]

REFERENCES

1. More, Rosemary, J., 1969. The basin hydrological cycle. In *Introduction to Physical Hydrology*, ed. Richard J. Chorley. Methuen, pp. 27–36.
2. Unesco, 1964. Document NS/188. IHD Inter-governmental meeting of Experts. Final Report.

3. TODD, D. K., 1959. *Ground Water Hydrology*. John Wiley, New York and London, p. 310.
4. AMOROCHO, J. and HART, W. E., 1965. The use of laboratory catchments in the study of hydrological systems. *J. Hydrol.*, **3**, 106–123.
5. NASH, J. E., 1967. The role of parametric hydrology. *J. Inst. Water Engrs*, **21** (5), 435–456.
6. HANSEN, V. E., 1952. Complicated well problems solved by the membrane analogy. *Trans. Am. Geophys. Union*, **33**, 912–916.
7. REARDON, E. J. and FRITZ, P., 1978. Computer modelling of ground water ^{13}C and ^{14}C isotope compositions. *J. Hydrol.*, **36**, 201–224.
8. O'NEIL, P. G., 1972. A mathematical programming model for planning a regional water resources system. *J. Inst. Water Engrs*, **26**, 1, 47–61.
9. MOODY, D. W., 1976. Application of multiregional planning models to the scheduling of large scale water resource systems development. *J. Hydrol.*, **28**, 101–126.

CHAPTER 13

Water Balances

13.1. INTRODUCTION

There is no doubt that the determination of water balance in a region is a
most important, perhaps *the* most important, objective of hydrologic
studies and ideally the determination of this on a planetary scale would be
invaluable and, in fact, constituted one of the aspects of the International
Hydrological Decade activities of UNESCO and other agencies. Ground
water studies are effected in order to ascertain the quantity of water
available for development in a region and this can be done only after
identification of the various physical features of the hydrologic system
involved, their hydraulic characteristics and their hydraulic inter-
relationships. Clearly, after the ground water system is fully understood,
the results can be combined with data regarding the amounts of water
transiting the stream network in the relevant region as well as precipitation
in it in order to furnish the basis of a water balance or water budget analysis.

13.2. BASIC CONSIDERATIONS

The equation of hydrologic equilibrium has been stated earlier (see
Chapter 1, section 1.9) but may be repeated here, again in its simplest form:

$$I = O \pm \Delta S$$

where I is inflow, O outflow and ΔS change in storage.

Obviously, this is grounded in the premise that a balance exists between
the amount of water which enters an area, changes in the amount of water in
storage in the area and the water which leaves the area. Clearly, the items in

the equation can include a number of factors of which the most significant may be listed:

(a) inflow: surficial, subsurface, precipitation, imported water;
(b) outflow: surficial, subsurface, consumptive usage (including evapotranspirative losses), exported water;
(c) storage: change in surface storage, change in ground water storage, change in soil moisture.

While some of these factors can easily be measured with a high degree of precision, this is not always the case. For instance, while the quantity of imported or exported water in a region can be determined quite simply by using a suitable meter on pipelines (where pipeline transportation is involved), consumptive usage is very hard indeed to measure. Often, too, evaporation is extremely difficult to estimate although transpiration is not.

All of the inflow, outflow and storage characteristics noted include all the parts to be included in a water balance analysis and as was indicated by the American Society of Civil Engineers' 1961 Manual of Engineering Practice, section on ground water basin management, this can be highly complex.[1]

Probably this is the reason why areas have often been selected for water balance analyses which involve as few factors as feasible. For instance, the factor subsurface outflow can be eliminated in cases where outflow is measured at a point where impermeable strata direct all outflow to the surface. Again, storage can be neglected if the balance is determined for any time period during which no significant change in this is believed to occur. In view of this, it is possible to utilise a simplified version of the equation of hydrologic equilibrium in appropriate situations and this may be given as

$$P = O + ET$$

where P is the precipitation, O the total outflow, and ET evapotranspirative losses. In such situations, the following steps may be taken in order to obtain relevant information regarding these parameters.

13.3. ANALYSES OF PRECIPITATION

Firstly, the quantity of precipitation falling in a study area has to be determined. Generally speaking, there are insufficient precipitation stations for all the effects of physiography, etc., to be monitored and thus to illustrate the reasons behind variation in the amounts of this from place to place. Thus the matter is not as simple as it appears at first sight.

In flat regions, for instance the Gulf Coastal Plain of the USA, it is possible to approach the problem by determining the weighted average precipitation using the Thiessen method in which the precipitation stations within and near to the area under study are plotted on a map and connected by lines drawn between adjacent ones. Next, perpendicular bisectors are drawn on these connecting lines and by joining these bisectors, polygons are made, each one centred on a precipitation station. The area of each polygon is determined and afterwards the precipitation recorded from the central station is applied to the entire area of the polygon. Obviously, where high relief is involved, the method cannot be used satisfactorily. Here, the isohyetal approach must be employed. In this, the precipitation stations in and round the area are plotted and utilised, taking the precipitation at each station during the water balance period, as a base for drawing lines of equal precipitation (precipitation contours, as it were), i.e. isohyets. The average weighted precipitation may be determined by measuring the areas *between* isohyets and then giving to each area the mean value of the boundary lines.

13.4.   ANALYSES OF OUTFLOW

Total outflow comprises two components, namely water which moved over the surface of the land and water which, after infiltration, moved through the zone of saturation so that

$$O = O_s - O_g$$

in which O_s is the overland runoff and O_g is the ground water discharge. Usually it is the practice to select the downstream area of any region in which a water balance analysis is to be effected so that this coincides with the location of a continuous stream-gauging station. Clearly, if the stream channel at the station happens to be underlain by impermeable rocks, then the discharge record will show the total outflow from the area. On the other hand, it is a different matter where permeable rocks underlie the stream channel; then the water leaving the area as underflow must be calculated using Darcy's law.

It is necessary to separate ground water discharge from total outflow. In doing this it is taken for granted that:

(a)   during good weather periods, all the flow in many streams consists of water which has been discharged from the ground water system;

(b)   ground water discharge is proportional to ground water level.

Ground water level can be ascertained by making measurements in observation wells and the number of these must suffice to show the *mean* ground water level for an area. Of course, such measurements may be carried out in a number of ways—at regular intervals, for instance, or by using continuous recorders. A composite hydrograph for the area can be constructed using these measurements. Where observation wells are regularly distributed over the area, the composite hydrograph may be made by referring water levels to a datum such as mean sea level, adding simultaneous measurements at each well together and dividing this total by the number of wells, subsequently plotting the resultant values on a suitable hydrograph paper. Matters become more complicated where such wells are *not* regularly spaced, but the procedure is to estimate the size of the various subsidiary areas represented by each well and then use this information in order to find out the relative weighting given to each observation well in preparing a composite hydrograph.

Mean diurnal streamflow at the outflow gauging station is plotted on graph paper plus a bar graph of diurnal precipitation at a representative station within the area. Examination of the precipitation graph ought to show several periods of a number of days duration during which no precipitation at all fell in the area. At the same periods, the streamflow hydrograph should demonstrate a gradually diminishing flow. When these practically rainless periods commence, it may be assumed that streamflow comprises both ground water discharge and overland runoff. Overland flow will become quite negligible after rain ceases to fall and from then until the *next* rain the streamflow will consist only of ground water discharge added to which is water obtained from channel storage as the stream stage goes down. This latter, i.e. channel storage, may be ignored if the stream stage is declining slowly and it may then be assumed that *all* the streamflow is composed of ground water discharge. Next, a ground water rating curve may be drawn and to effect this, the streamflow is recorded at the end of each 'rainless' period and the simultaneous ground water stage is shown on the composite hydrograph. The streamflow is normally represented on the x-axis of arithmetic graph paper and the ground water stage is shown on the y-axis. All this presupposes, of course, that there are no bodies of water in the basin other than the stream, i.e. no paludal regions or lakes, etc. The relationship between ground water stage and base streamflow becomes more complex where large amounts of water are directly discharged from the zone of saturation by evapotranspiration.

When the ground water rating curve is complete, cf. Fig. 13.1, reference may be made to the composite hydrograph of ground water levels. Using

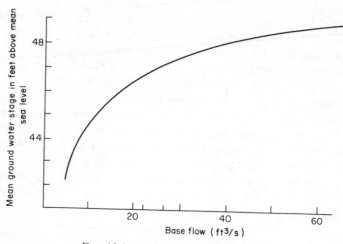

FIG. 13.1. Example of rating curve.

stages from this hydrograph, ground water discharge may be determined from the rating curve and may be plotted on the streamflow hydrograph. Now, the separation of the total outflow hydrograph into its constituent parts, namely overland runoff and ground water discharge, has been accomplished.

13.5. ANALYSES OF EVAPOTRANSPIRATION

This phenomenon involves both the evaporation of moisture from exposed surfaces and the transpiration of moisture by plants. Usually, it is very difficult to separate these and so they are treated together as evapotranspiration. It may refer to surficial evapotranspiration or evapotranspiration from the zone of saturation, the former including both the surface and also the soil zone.

The relationship may be given thus:

$$ET = ET_s + ET_g$$

where ET_s is evapotranspiration from the surface and from the soil zone and ET_g is evapotranspiration from the zone of saturation.

Losses due to evapotranspiration may arise from a variety of factors such as the temperature of the atmosphere, the duration of sunshine, relative humidity and wind velocity. C. W. Thornthwaite produced an empirical formula for evapotranspiration in 1948.[2] It was based upon lysimeter experiments in the USA. If t_n is taken as being the average monthly temperature of the consecutive months of the year in °C (where $n = 1, 2, \ldots, 12$) and j is the monthly heat index, then

$$j = \left(\frac{t_n}{5}\right)^{1 \cdot 514}$$

and the yearly heat index, J, is given by

$$J = \Sigma_1^{12} j \qquad \text{(for the 12 months)}$$

The potential evapotranspiration for any month with average temperature $t°$ is then given as PE_x by

$$PE_x = 16\left(\frac{10t}{J}\right)^a \quad \text{mm per month}$$

where

$$a = (675 \times 10^{-9})J^3 - (771 \times 10^{-7})J^2 + (179 \times 10^{-4})J + 0 \cdot 492$$

Of course PE_x is a *theoretical* standard monthly value based upon 30 days and 12 hours of sunshine per day. The *actual PE* for the particular month with average temperature $t°$ is given by

$$PE = PE_x \frac{DT}{360} \quad \text{mm}$$

where D is the number of days in the particular month, T the average number of hours between sunrise and sunset in the month.

The method has been thoroughly tested by Serra who showed that the initial and penultimate equations may be simplified thus:

$$j = 0 \cdot 09 t_n^{\frac{3}{2}}$$
$$a = 0 \cdot 016 J + 0 \cdot 5$$

It must be emphasised that the method is an empirical one and also it is complex, requiring the use of a nomogram for its solution. Thornthwaite published just such a nomogram.

Evaporation may be directly measured by pans. In the UK, the standard pan is 6 ft square and 2 ft deep, filled to a depth of 1 ft 9 in and so set in the ground that the rim projects 3 in above the surrounding ground. In the USA, the Class A pan is circular, 4 ft in diameter and 10 in deep, filled to a depth of 7 in and set on a timber grillage with the bottom of the pan 6 in above ground level.

TABLE 13.1

ANGOT'S VALUES OF SHORT WAVE RADIATION FLUX (R_A) AT THE OUTER LIMITS OF THE ATMOSPHERE IN GRAMME-CALORIES PER SQUARE CENTIMETRE DAILY AS A FUNCTION OF LATITUDE AND MONTH OF THE YEAR

Lat.	Jan.	Feb.	Mar.	Apr.	May	June	Jly	Aug.	Sep.	Oct.	Nov.	Dec.	Year
N90	0	0	55	518	903	1 077	944	605	136	0	0	0	3 540
80	0	3	143	518	875	1 060	930	600	219	17	0	0	3 660
60	86	234	424	687	866	983	892	714	494	258	113	55	4 850
40	358	538	663	847	930	1 001	941	843	719	528	397	318	6 750
20	631	795	821	914	912	947	912	887	856	740	666	599	8 070
Eqr	844	963	878	876	803	803	792	820	891	866	873	829	8 540
20	970	1 020	832	737	608	580	588	680	820	892	986	978	8 070
40	998	963	686	515	358	308	333	453	648	817	994	1 033	6 750
60	947	802	459	240	95	50	77	187	403	648	920	1 013	4 850
80	981	649	181	9	0	0	0	0	113	459	917	1 094	3 660
S90	995	656	92	0	0	0	0	0	30	447	932	1 110	3 540

Another kind of pan, the Peirera pan, is sometimes utilised in Great Britain and this resembles the Class A pan in being circular, but is deeper and sunk into the ground with a 3 in air space around it.

Of course, as such pans are much smaller than natural water bodies and, being situated near the surface of the ground, allow proportionately much greater quantities of advected heat from the atmosphere to be absorbed by the water in them, evaporation measured in them is too high and an appropriate pan correction must be applied. This is in the form of a pan coefficient which may range from 0·65 to more than unity; in the UK, most pans are of the standard kind and carry a pan coefficient of about 0·92. US Weather Bureau Pan, A Class, has one of about 0·75. Of course, wide variations exist.

In estimating evaporation from large open bodies of water, Penman's theory may be applied.

13.5.1. Penman's Theory

Devised by H. L. Penman in 1948, this contains a formula for estimating evaporation from weather data and it is based on two requisites, namely:

(a) there must be a supply of energy to provide latent heat of vaporisation,
(b) there must be a mechanism for removing vapour, once it is produced.[3]

In the daylight, short wave radiation is incident upon the surface of the planet and the quantity at any one locality will depend upon latitude, season, cloud cover and time of day. If a cloudless and transparent atmosphere existed, the total radiation which might be expected has been given in tabular form by Angot (see Table 13.1).

If R_C is the short wave radiation actually received on the planetary surface and n/D the ratio of actual to possible hours of sunshine, then, for southern England,

$$R_C = R_A(0·18 + 0·55\,n/D)$$

and, for Virginia, USA,

$$R_C = R_A(0·22 + 0·54\,n/D)$$

and, for Canberra, Australia,

$$R_C = R_A(0·25 + 0·54\,n/D)$$

From this, it is apparent that even when there is total cloud cover, i.e. n/D = 0, one-fifth of solar radiation penetrates to the Earth's surface. When there are no clouds, at least three-quarters of the solar radiation gets through.

An empirical equation for evaporation when both water surface and atmosphere are at the same temperature is:

$$E = C(e_s - e)f(u)$$

where E is the open water evaporation per unit time in mm/d, C the empirical constant, e_s the saturation vapour pressure of the air at $t \,°C$ in mm Hg, e the actual vapour pressure in the air above (mm Hg), and u the wind speed at a standard elevation (m). A generally valid equation for the case is:

$$E = 0.35(e_s - e)(0.5 + 0.54\,u')$$

where E is again open water evaporation per unit time in mm/d, e_s and e have the same significance as above, and u' denotes wind speed in m/s at a height of 2 m. When the air and water surface temperatures are different (the usual case),

$$E_o = C(e_s' - e)f(u)$$

where E_o is the evaporation of the water body in mm daily, other symbols having the previous values. However, e_s' denotes the saturation vapour pressure of the boundary layer of air between air and water. The temperature of this is practically impossible to measure.

Some of the incident short wave radiation is reflected by an amount depending upon the reflection coefficient for the surface, r.

Assuming that R_I is the net quantity of radiation absorbed, then:

$$R_I = R_C(1 - r) = R_A(1 - r)(0.18 + 0.55\,n/D)$$

Some of the R_I is reradiated by the Earth as long wave radiation and this is particularly so at night when the air is dry and the sky clear and the net outward flow is empirically expressible thus:

$$R_B = \sigma Ta^4(0.47 - 0.077\sqrt{e})(0.20 + 0.80\,n/D)$$

where R_B is the outward flow, σ is the Lummer and Pringsheim constant $(117.74 \times 10^{-9} \,\text{gcal/cm}^2/\text{d})$, Ta is the absolute Earth temperature $(t \,°C - 273)$, e is the actual vapour pressure of air in mm Hg, and n/D is the ratio of actual to possible hours of sunshine.

The net amount of energy remaining at a free water surface ($r = 0.06$) is:

$$H = R_1 - R_B$$
$$= R_C - rR_C - R_B$$
$$= R_C(1 - r) - R_B$$
$$= R_A(0.18 + 0.55 n/D)(1 - 0.06) - R_B$$

so that

$$H = R_A(0.18 + 0.55 n/D)(1 - 0.06)$$
$$- (117.74 \times 10^{-9})Ta^4(0.47 - 0.077\sqrt{e})(0.20 + 0.80 n/D)$$

the heat being used up in four different ways,

$$H = E_o + K + S + C$$

where E_o = heat available for evaporation from open water
K = convective heat transfer from the surface
S = increase in heat of the water mass (storage)
C = increase in heat of the environment (negative advected heat)

13.5.2. Vapour Removal (Discussion from E. M. Wilson[4])

In the evaporation equation already quoted, namely

$$E_o = C(e'_s - e)f(u)$$

it has been noted that e'_s is impossible to evaluate if the air and water temperatures are different. Penman assumed that the transport of vapour and the transport of heat by eddy diffusion are controlled by essentially the same mechanism, i.e. atmospheric turbulence, the former governed by $(e'_s - e)$, the latter by $(t'_s - t)$, so that it is possible to state that

$$\frac{K}{E_o} = \beta = \frac{\gamma(t'_s - t)}{e'_s - e}$$

where γ is the psychrometer constant, 0.66 if t is °C + e in mbar.
Since

$$H = E_o + K = E_o(1 + \beta)$$

then

$$E_o = H/\{1 + (\gamma/\Delta)(e'_s - e_s)/(e'_s - e)\}$$

Wilson eliminated e_s.
Since

$$e'_s - e_s = (e'_s - e) - (e_s - e)$$

and from the empirical equation

$$E = C(e_s - e)f(u)$$

and

$$E_o = C(e'_s - e)f(u)$$

or restated, they become

$$E = Cf(u)(e_s - e) \qquad \text{and} \qquad E_o = Cf(u)(e'_s - e)$$

and therefore

$$\frac{E}{E_o} = \frac{e_s - e}{e'_s - e}$$

where E is the evaporation in terms of energy for the case in which air and water have equal temperatures.

By substitution, the following equation may be derived:

$$E_o = H/\{1 + (\gamma/\Delta)[(e'_s - e) - (e_s - e)])/(e'_s - e)\}$$

and

$$E_o = \frac{H}{1 + (\gamma/\Delta)(1 - E/E_o)}$$

and

$$E_o = \frac{\Delta H + \gamma E}{\Delta + \gamma}$$

Δ has values which may be obtained from the saturation vapour pressure curve, for instance:

$t =$	$\Delta =$
0 °C	0·36
10	0·61
20	1·07
30	1·80

E_o is computed from standard meteorological data regarding mean air temperature, relative humidity, wind velocity at a standard height and hours of sunshine. The formula has been subjected to a great deal of checking and has proved to be generally applicable.

There is a nomogram which eliminates computational work in solving the equation (originally devised by P. J. Rijkoort of the Royal

Meteorological Institute, Holland) and this is given by E. M. Wilson.[4] The value of R_C used is slightly different from Penman's:

$$R_C = R_A(0.20 + 0.48\,n/D)$$

instead of his

$$R_C = R_A(0.18 + 0.55\,n/D)$$

but the difference is less than the probable margin of error in cloud cover estimation and can be ignored.

13.6. GLOBAL WATER BALANCE

The above discussion of the precipitation and outflow analyses showed that the methodology described can be utilised in order to generate values of these factors for various periods, weeks, months or longer. Nevertheless, it is very difficult to balance the water budget unless changes in surface storage, soil moisture and ground water storage are measured. Naturally, a large number of data-collecting stations are necessary to determine these parameters and, due to costs, not enough are usually available. Consequently, many water balance studies are limited to annual estimates. To refer to the planetary water balance, therefore, may be inadvisable, but is certainly interesting.

Studies of the global water balance have been carried out by a number of people, among them M. I. Budyko in the USSR.[5] His approach, necessarily crude, involved precipitation, P, evaporation, E, and runoff, r, as well as water exchange between oceans, ΔW:

$$P + r = E \pm \Delta W$$

Some computations may be cited (see Tables 13.2 and 13.3).

TABLE 13.2
THE WATER BALANCE OF THE OCEANS (cm/y)

Ocean	Precipitation	Runoff from adjoining land areas	Evaporation	Water exchange with other oceans
Atlantic	78	20	104	−6
Arctic	24	23	12	35
Pacific	121	6	114	13
Indian	101	7	138	−30

TABLE 13.3
THE WATER BALANCE OF THE CONTINENTS (cm/y)

Continent	Precipitation	Evaporation	Runoff
Africa	67	51	16
Asia	61	39	22
Australia	47	41	6
Europe	60	36	24
N. America	67	40	27
S. America	135	86	49

The inference from the above is that precipitation and evaporation for the Earth are of the order of 100 cm/y and the global water balance may be something like that shown in Table 13.4. Obviously, all this must be regarded with some suspicion as indeed is the case for all estimates of this type at the present time. One thing is certain, however, and that is that the circulation of water in the atmosphere and oceans is closely related to the global energy budget. The yearly input of solar radiation into the terrestrial atmosphere and the loss of terrestrial radiation cause a positive energy budget to arise in low latitudes, the converse, i.e. a negative energy budget, being the case in middle and higher latitudes, and for yearly averages, the budget is balanced at some 35° latitude. In order that the higher latitudes should not get progressively colder and the lower ones progressively hotter, heat transport in a polar direction must take place. This actually happens and in various ways, for instance as warm water in oceanic currents and in the atmosphere. In fact, approximately four-fifths of the pole-directed heat transport is believed to occur in the atmosphere. Nevertheless, oceanic currents too are significant, particularly those like the Gulf Stream which ameliorates the British climate! There are several others, e.g. the Brazil current and the equatorial currents.

A fact of extreme importance is that the slightest change in any climatic parameter can have tremendous repercussions. This is because of the

TABLE 13.4
THE GLOBAL WATER BALANCE (cm/y)[6]

Units	Precipitation	Evaporation	Runoff
Oceans	112	125	−13
Continents	72	41	31
Earth	100	100	0

interdependence of the constituents of the hydrologic cycle. Thus, for instance, a 1 % increase in evaporation from the tropical oceans would cool a 200 m layer by 3 °C in half a century.[7] In this connection, it is estimated that at the maximum of the Quaternary glaciation (Illinoian, say or Riss), ice affected an area three times greater than now and the mass of ice exceeded today's by a factor of five. Consequently, a eustatic depression of sea level occurred and is thought to have amounted to 453 ft in the Illinoian, for example. A possible consequence of this is a decrease in both evaporation and precipitation because a larger area of land is exposed. On the other hand, a eustatic elevation of sea level probably promotes a warm interglacial condition accompanied by an increase in both evaporation and precipitation. It seems very probable that important changes in the precipitation–evaporation cycle occurred due to the planetary surficial cooling occasioned by the glacial phases of the last ice age of the Pleistocene. H. Flohn in 1953 provided a model of the alteration of the moisture budget zones under glacial conditions compared with the present situation but there is always need for the extension of work like this.[8]

13.7. THE UTILISATION OF ENVIRONMENTAL ISOTOPES IN WATER BALANCE STUDIES[9]

This may be done in more restricted studies, for instance in regard to a river basin. The relevant part of the hydrologic cycle is that encompassing:

(a) deposition of water on the basin's surface;
(b) departure of water by runoff and infiltration;
(c) loss of water by evapotranspiration.

Restating the fundamental balance equation for any hydrologic system gives

$$\Sigma \, \Delta V_i = \Sigma I \Delta t - \Sigma O \, \Delta t$$

where ΔV_i are changes of storage in surficial and subsurface reservoirs during Δt, I's are inputs to the system, for instance precipitation, and O's are outputs from the system at the outlet such as runoff.

Ground water storage is difficult to determine conventionally and isotopic techniques using environmental isotopes can be of great assistance in its evaluation. Turnover and replenishment rates can be estimated also. Of course, not only the active storage (which is subject to considerable fluctuations) may be involved, but in addition that portion of the ground water which occurs below the horizon of a ground water outlet. If ground water reservoir volumes are estimated, for instance by using the tritium contents of springs, they are usually greater than the volumes which may be estimated using recession curves.

13.7.1. Nuclear Techniques

In the case where the number of unknowns in the water balance equation is greater than one, extra equations become necessary if the value of the unknowns is to be calculated. Then balance equations can be written for different isotopic species of water such as HTO, HDO and H_2O. Such environmental isotopic water tracers are of great value because they cannot be lost due to adsorption and preferential biological uptake. The equations in question will be of the following type:

$$\Sigma C_i \Delta V_i - \Sigma V_i \Delta C_i = \Sigma C_i I \Delta t - \Sigma C_o O \Delta t$$

where ΔV_i is the alteration in storage, C_i the mean isotope concentration in the storage, ΔC_i the change of concentration during the period, V the mean storage and C_i and C_o the isotopic concentrations in the inflow and outflow components respectively. In order to use the equations, systematic measurement of the concentrations of the environmental tracers in the respective constituents of the flow and in the surficial, soil and ground water reservoirs in the system must be carried out. Obviously this becomes simpler in a system in which some of the terms of the equations may be neglected; for instance, in a basin overlying impermeable strata, it is permissible to leave out ground water storage because there will be none.

One of the important matters to be determined in using such isotope balance equations in water balance studies is the estimation of the isotopic composition of evaporated water and this is extremely difficult to do. Tritium usage is also a problem because of the thermonuclear pulses injecting this radioisotope into the hydrologic system since 1953. The general form of tritium concentration in the output of a hydrologic system is expressible as:

$$g(t) = \int c(t - T) e^{-\lambda T} f(T) \, dT$$

where $g(t)$ is the tritium output function, $c(t - T)$ is the tritium input function, λ is the radioactive decay constant for tritium and $f(T)$ is the system response function of the system.

Utilisation of this relation and combination with an appropriate model enables several tritium output curves to be developed for different parameters' values, i.e. various values of the parameters existing in the system response function (time distribution) of the particular hydrologic system being considered. Comparison of these curves with the *actual* tritium–time variation in the mass output of the system will enable determination of the parameter(s) to be made and will lead to an estimate of the turnover or transit time of the system under consideration. When the volume of the reservoir in question is known, then it is possible to estimate the mean flow or recharge to the system, i.e. the fundamental component of the water balance equation.

13.7.2. Applications

Obviously use of this approach necessitates regular sampling of the components of the water balance equation. In order to obtain reasonable statistical accuracy, concentration values with relatively small errors must be available. In using the radioisotope tritium, the experimental $g(t)$ curve must be determined over a period of at least several years. This obviously entails regular sampling of the precipitation, the stream flow and the ground water.

The first employment of environmental isotopes in water balance work was that of F. Begemann and W. F. Libby in 1957 and they developed one for the upper Mississippi River valley based upon tritium.[10] It was assumed that complete mixing of precipitation tritium with ground water occurred and an estimate of the storage in the basin was made. However, subsequent studies have been made, among them that of R. M Brown on the Ottawa River basin.[11] He developed the isotope-balance equation so as to account for the variation of tritium in river water as a function of tritium in precipitation and the storage of the river in the basin. E. Eriksson also utilised the Ottawa River data and introduced the concept of transit time distribution in the basin.[12] He concluded that some of the precipitation runs off within a year and a half while there is a delay of about three years in some parts of the basin attributable to the extensive lake system in the upper part of it.

R. M. Brown also made a study of the distribution of hydrogen isotopes in Canadian waters.[13] He found that geographically tritium and deuterium concentrations in natural waters vary inversely. Turnover characteristics were elucidated by data on the drainage of tritium from the systems examined.

An environmental isotope balance of Lake Tiberias in Israel was derived by J. R. Gat.[14] This water body had been monitored for more than a decade prior to 1970 when the paper was produced and is fresh water and lies in the northern part of the Jordan Rift Valley. Apart from the Jordan River, the water sources are precipitation and runoff, smaller rivulets and sublacustrine saline springs and seepages. It shows a thermally controlled seasonal stratification which disappears late in winter. The tritium balance and the hydrologic balance in a mixed lake were given by Gat as:

$$\frac{d(VT)_L}{dt} = \sum_i I_i T_i - OT_L - \lambda(VT)_L - u(\beta T_L - hT_a)$$

$$\frac{dV_L}{dt} = \sum_i I_i - (E + O)$$

where V_L is the volume of the lake, T_L its tritium content, I_i the inflow rate of water, and T_i the respective tritium content of the waters entering from different paths, E and O being the evaporation and liquid outflow rates respectively; β is the tritium fractionation factor for the liquid–vapour transition, λ the tritium decay rate, and T_A is the tritium concentration in atmospheric water vapour; u is the exchange rate of surface air with the atmosphere, a function of the wind stress at the surface; h is the atmospheric vapour content normalised to that of saturated vapour at the temperature of the lake surface. The last term of the first equation gives the tritium flux into the atmosphere.

Using the above equations and their derivatives as the basis for a tritium balance calculation, Lake Tiberias can serve as a model for a semi-arid lake zone. The applicability of the first equation was confirmed and it is possible to assess water residence time within 10 or 20%. As regards the oxygen-18 and deuterium balance, it was found that a seasonal cycle of depletion during the rainy season and enrichment during summer was underlain by long term drifts which are related to the changes in the throughflow rates of fresh water in the lake reflecting alternating periods of drought or floods. The stratification of the lake is admirably shown in the depth profiles of the stable isotope concentration, with the hypolimnion close in composition to the mixed spring lake. The stable isotope inventory of the lake was expressed by Gat as:

$$d\delta_L/dt = \frac{1}{V}\left[\sum I_i \delta_i - E\delta_E - \left(O + \frac{dV}{dt}\right)\delta_L\right]$$

all symbols having the same meanings as before and with δ_i, δ_E and δ_L being the isotopic content of inflow, evaporative flux and the lake.

Such an equation will be applicable both to the oxygen-18 and the deuterium balance. As opposed to tritium, there is no systematic secular change in the δ values of both the inflow and the lake, although they do vary seasonally and in response to hydrological imbalances.

Of course, quantitatively to utilise the above equation, it is necessary to have representative δ values for all the inflow routes, i.e. ground waters, river flow and precipitation. An advantage is that these are known much better than the corresponding tritium data. Again unlike tritium, the isotopic fractionation which accompanies evaporation plays a very important part in the balance of oxygen-18 and deuterium and therefore requires close attention and study. The oxygen-18 concentration in the upper water mass was found to undergo a yearly cycle of average amplitude of $\Delta\delta^{18}O = 0.5\%$. The hypolimnion follows the change at a greatly reduced amplitude. Deuterium concentrations change in a similar manner and obey the relationship

$$\Delta\delta D = 5.3 \times \Delta\delta^{18}O$$

The mean annual isotope composition shifts up to $\pm 1.5\%$ for ^{18}O as a result of hydrological imbalances between water gains and losses.

Detailed balance calculations based on available climatic and hydrologic information were made and their reliability was discussed.

The effects of vertical stratification and the size of separation coefficients were examined and it was demonstrated that controlled evaporation experiments using thermostatted pans gave more useful data on the exchange fluxes both of tritium and the stable isotopes than calculations grounded in time-averaged humidity information. Another interesting water balance study effected in Lake Neusiedl in Austria by U. Zimmermann and D. H. Ehhalt may be mentioned.[15] This is a lake with an area of about $250 \, km^2$ and it is located near Vienna. It is very shallow with an average depth of only 1 m. The water balance equation utilised was:

$$dV = (J + P - O - E)\,dt$$

where dV is the change in the volume of the lake in the time dt, J is the inflow rate from rivers and ground water, P is the precipitation rate over the lake, O is the outflow rate and E is the evaporation rate.

The necessary modification using isotope contents is given by:

$$d(V\delta_l) = V\,d\delta_l + \delta_l\,dV = (J\delta_J + P\delta_P - O\delta_O - E\delta_E)\,dt$$

where δ_l is the isotope content of the lake water and $d\delta_l$ its change through time dt. This equation applies equally to oxygen-18 and deuterium, but Zimmermann and Ehhalt noted that one alone should be utilised because when both are, much larger errors arise. Combination of the above two equations makes it possible to eliminate the factor J and estimates the evaporation rate as:

$$E = \frac{P(\delta_P - \delta_J) - O(\delta_J - \delta_O) - dV(\delta_J - \delta_I) - V \times d\delta_I}{\delta_E - \delta_J}$$

this being valid only on a short time scale.

The isotopic content of the evaporating moisture, δ_E, is determined by isotope separation effects during the evaporation process and by isotope exchange. δ_E is calculable using the following equation:

$$\delta_E = \frac{\alpha + \delta_I - h\delta_A - \varepsilon^+ - \varepsilon_K}{1 - h - \varepsilon_K}$$

where

$$\alpha^+ = 1 - \varepsilon^+ = R_V/R_L$$

(equilibrium isotope fractionation factor), R_V is the isotope ratio of the vapour and R_L that of the liquid, ε_K the kinetic separation, h the relative humidity with respect to the lake temperature, δ_A the isotope composition of the atmospheric water vapour.

This equation depends upon the assumption that immediately at the water surface, the water vapour is in equilibrium with the lake water. Also, complete mixing of the lake is assumed and a further assumption is that the isotopic composition and the concentration of atmospheric water vapour are not influenced by the evaporation. Difficulties arose at Lake Neusiedl because its surface is half covered with reeds and hence it was difficult to calculate δ. Separate calculations had to be made for the reed-covered 45% and the open 55% and the isotope composition of the total evapotranspirating moisture from the lake, E, is then given by the weighted mean:

$$\delta_E = \frac{E_F}{E} \delta E_F + \frac{E_R}{E} \delta E_R + \frac{T}{E} \delta_T$$

where $E = E_F + E_R + T$,

E_F = evaporation rate of the free water surface

E_R = evaporation rate of the reed-covered surface

T = transpiration rate of the reeds

δE_F = isotope content of the evaporating moisture from the free water surface

δE_R = isotope content of the evaporating moisture from the reed-covered surface

δ_T = isotope content of the transpired water

The data obtained from pan evaporation for the summer of 1968 permitted the estimation of weighting factors as:

$$E_F/E = 0{\cdot}5$$
$$E_R/E = 0{\cdot}2$$
$$T/E = 0{\cdot}3$$

The results of the whole exercise were rather disappointing because the authors showed that even where all isotope data are determined with good accuracy, it can be difficult to determine the evaporation rate of a lake with an accuracy better than 50%.

13.7.2.1. *The Case of Lake Chala*

Bryan R. Payne has described this in 1970 and it is so interesting as a water balance study using environmental isotopes and artificially injected tritium that it may be cited here[16] in greater detail than it was in Chapter 3 above. It was begun as a feasibility study aimed at utilising water from this lake in order to expand the Taveta irrigation scheme in Kenya. Isotope investigations were started so as to determine the relationship of the lake to springs in the area and establish the turnover time of the lake water.

The lake is 840 m up the south-eastern slope of Mt Kilimanjaro and is a volcanic crater lake $4{\cdot}2\,km^2$ in area with a volume around $3 \times 10^8\,m^3$ and a maximum depth of 100 m. It has no surface inflow or outflow and was formerly thought to feed the Njoro Kubwa and other springs on the west bank of the Lumi River. This discharges into Lake Jipe through the Lumi Delta Swamp and thereafter into the Ruvu River in Tanzania.

Geologically, the region is extrusive volcanic rock terminating against basement igneous and metamorphic rocks lying approximately $3{\cdot}2\,km$ east of the lake. The 12 year precipitation in the area of the irrigation scheme is 575 mm. Evaporation data were derived from a pan at the lake and the readings differed from those at Taveta by a factor of $0{\cdot}9$.

Tritium was introduced into the lake and of course its concentration decreased with time due to the radioactive decay of the radioisotope, the dilution effect of inflowing water with a lower concentration, removal by subsurface loss and exchange with atmospheric water vapour.

The radioactive decay is resolved by normalising the lake values to the time of the actual injection. The relationship between the other factors can be shown after establishing a tritium balance for the system thus:[16]

$$V\,dC_L - C_L\,dV = IC_i\,dt - PC_P\,dt - \frac{EC_a h}{(1-h)}\,dt - \frac{EC_L}{\alpha(1-h)}\,dt - C_L O\,dt$$

where

$$V = \text{volume of the lake}$$
$$I = \text{inflow to lake per unit time}$$
$$P = \text{precipitation falling on the lake per unit time}$$
$$O = \text{subsurface outflow from the lake per unit time}$$
$$E = \text{evaporation from the lake per unit time}$$
$$h = \text{relative humidity}$$
$$\alpha = \text{fractionation factor for tritium}$$
$$C_L, C_i, C_P \text{ and } C_a = \text{tritium concentration of lake, inflow, precipitation and atmospheric water vapour.}$$

Sampling established that the tritium concentration in the lake was homogeneous and the initial concentration was computed as 1600 TU (1900 C_i were introduced). Over a 5-year period, annual subsurface inflow and outflow were estimated as $12.5 \times 10^6 \, \text{m}^3$ and $8.2 \times 10^6 \, \text{m}^3$, respectively. It was concluded that environmental tritium cannot be used for such a balance estimation.

The relation of the lake to springs in the area based on ^{18}O and D measurements demonstrated that none of the springs derives a major component of its discharge from the lake. The contribution of Lake Chala cannot exceed about 6% of the individual discharges of the springs.

However, tritium concentrations at two springs indicated a probability of partial recharge by lake water.

13.7.2.2. *Usage of Stable Isotopes in the Water Balance of Lakes*

This subject was discussed by T. Dincer in 1968 and he showed how natural concentrations of stable isotopes of hydrogen and oxygen, i.e. deuterium and oxygen-18, may be utilised in determining the water balance of lakes located in a subhumid climatic regimen of south-western Turkey.[17]

13.8. WATER BALANCE FOR A PERIOD AND A VOLUME OF SOIL

Expressed mathematically, the appropriate equation may be given as:

$$P = S + iD + iM + GW + SE\,dt$$

where S is the surface drainage or runoff from the area, iD is the increase in surface water detention, iM is the increase in moisture in the soil, E is the evaporation or evapotranspiration and GW is the percolation into the ground beyond the depth to which M is considered, to form ground water storage, and P is the rainfall (precipitation) received in the relevant area in time dt. All these components are subject to variation from moment to moment depending upon other factors. There will be continuous re-distribution between the values of each factor as water moves. The equation demonstrates how complex it is to estimate the quantity of ground water resulting from a known quantity of rainfall.

REFERENCES

1. AMERICAN SOCIETY OF CIVIL ENGINEERS, 1961. Ground water basin management. *Manual of Engineering Practice*, No. 40.
2. THORNTHWAITE, C. W., 1948. An approach towards a rational classification of climate. *Geog. Rev.*, **38**, 55.
3. PENMAN, H. L., 1948. Natural evaporation from open water, bare soil and grass. *Proc. Roy. Soc. (London)*, A, **193**, 170.
4. WILSON, E. M., 1974. *Engineering Hydrology*, 2nd ed. Macmillan, London and Basingstoke.
5. BUDYKO, M. I., 1956. *The Heat Balance of the Surface of the Earth*. Leningrad, translated by N. A. Stepanova, Washington, D.C.
6. BUDYKO, M. I., 1962. The heat balance of the surface of the Earth. *Soviet Geog.*, **3**, 5, 3–16.
7. MALKUS, J. S., 1962. Inter-change of properties between sea and air. Large scale interactions. In *The Sea*, Vol. 1, ed. M. N. Hill. John Wiley, New York and London, pp. 88–294.
8. FLOHN, H., 1953. Studen über die atmosphärische Zirkulation in der letzten Eiszeit. *Erdkunde*, **7**, 266–275.
9. DINCER, T., 1968. The use of environmental isotopes in water balance studies. V.4 section in *Guidebook on Nuclear Techniques in Hydrology*. Technical Reports Series No. 91, International Atomic Energy Agency, Vienna.
10. BEGEMANN, F. and LIBBY, W. F., 1957. Continental water balance, groundwater inventory and storage time, surface ocean mixing rates and worldwide water circulation patterns from cosmic ray and bomb tritium. *Geochim. et Cosmochim. Acta*, **12**, 277–296.
11. BROWN, R. M., 1961. Hydrology of tritium in the Ottawa Valley. *Geochim. et Cosmochim. Acta*, **21**, 199–316.
12. ERIKSSON, E., 1963. Atmospheric tritium as a tool for the study of certain hydrologic aspects of river basins. *Tellus*, **15**, 3.
13. BROWN, R. M., 1970. Distribution of hydrogen isotopes in Canadian waters. *Isotope Hydrology*. Symp. 9-13/3/70. International Atomic Energy Agency, Vienna, 3–22.
14. GAT, J. R., 1970. Environmental isotope balance of Lake Tiberias. Symp. 9-13/3/70. International Atomic Energy Agency, Vienna, 109–127.
15. ZIMMERMANN, U. and EHHALT, D. H., 1970. Stable isotopes in study of water balance of Lake Neusiedl. Symp. 9-13/3/70. International Atomic Energy Agency, Vienna, 129–138.
16. PAYNE, B. R., 1970. Water balance of Lake Chala and its relation to groundwater from tritium and stable isotope data. *J. Hydrol.*, **11**, 47–58.
17. DINCER, T., 1968. The use of oxygen-18 and deuterium concentrations in the water balance of lakes. *Water Res. Res.*, *Bull.*, **4**, 6, 1289–1306.

APPENDIX

This Appendix comprises several sections containing material considered to be important in relation to ground water work.

It begins with a dictionary of water terms especially orientated towards ground water and for much of this, the author is indebted to A. Nelson and K. D. Nelson's excellent *Dictionary of Water and Water Engineering*. Over 230 entries make the contents useful.

Following this a table showing the analysis of water quality with reference to its chemistry and here are listed almost all the significant properties of water correlated with characteristic elements, compounds and factors such as pH, alkalinity and radioactivity.

Finally there is an index of relevant organisations. These are of course those with particular pertinency to ground water work and water work in general. One or two may appear slightly esoteric, but nevertheless merit a place. An example is the British Non-ferrous Metals Research Association from which many water engineers have derived valuable assistance in the investigation of corrosion problems.

1. Dictionary of Water Terms

Absolute drought: Usually applied to periods of fifteen consecutive days or more characterised by less than 0·25 mm rainfall daily.

Absorption (water): The imbibing of water by a soil or rock, a quantity expressed in percentage terms of the original dry weight.

Acidification: Using acid (normally hydrochloric) to increase water supply from a borehole failing due to encrustation on screens and slotted pipes.

Acre: A unit of area equal to 4840 yd^2 (or 0·405 hectare).

Acre foot: That volume of water which will cover 1 acre to a depth of 1 ft. Equal to 1233·5 m^3.

Adit: A rectangular heading or tunnel either horizontal or inclined for tapping ground water. Often driven from a shaft and may be lined or unlined.

Adsorbed water: That water which is retained in a mass of soil by physicochemical forces.

Aeration, zone of: Subsurface between the surface and the water table divisible into a belt of soil water, an intermediate region and a lowermost capillary fringe.

Air-lift pump: A piece of equipment capable of lifting water in a well and comprising an air compressor at the surface and two pipes hanging down vertically with one inside the other. The smaller pipe delivers compressed air to the depth of occurrence of water where a nozzle discharges it into the free water and, by aeration, causes its density to drop. Thereafter, the water/air mixture is forced upwards by the head of ground water.

Airline correction: A correction necessary in the measurement of water depth in order to determine true depth.

Apparent velocity of ground water: The apparent rate of movement of ground water in the zone of saturation is expressible thus: $V = Q/A$, where Q is the volume of water passing through a cross section of area A in unit time.

Appropriated rights, water: An individual's rights to the exclusive usage of water based strictly upon priority of appropriation and the beneficial utilisation of the water without limitation of the place of usage.

Aquiclude: A stratum of low porosity absorbing water slowly and not transmitting it freely enough to comprise useful supplies for a well.

Aquifer: A permeable deposit which can yield useful quantities of water when tapped by a well.

Aquifuge: An impervious rock devoid of interconnected fissures, voids or openings which cannot either absorb or transmit water.

Artesian aquifer (confined aquifer): An aquifer in which the water is under pressure and confined beneath an impermeable deposit.

Artesian head, negative: Used in regard to a well in which the hydrostatic pressure is negative and the free water level is below the existing water table.

Artesian head, positive: Used in regard to a well in which the hydrostatic pressure is positive and the free water level is above the existing water table.

Artesian slope: This refers to an artesian aquifer dipping beneath impermeable strata, ground water being stored there under pressure.

Artesian well: A well tapping artesian water.

Artificial recharge: The augmentation of natural recharge usually by spreading of water on the surface.

Attached ground water: The part of ground water which is retained on particle surfaces against the force of gravity during pumping or drainage.

Augers: Manually operated or power driven boring tools from about $1\frac{1}{2}$ to 24 in diameter.

Average velocity of ground water: The mean distance covered by mass of ground water per unit of time (equal to total volume of ground water passing through unit cross sectional area per unit of time divided by the porosity of the medium).

Backblowing: Improving water yield from boreholes, especially in fissured rocks, by use of compressed air which is either pumped into them or employed to pump in air until maximum pressure is attained and then released.

Basin: This is topographically either a river-drained area or low lying land encircled by hills. The geological meaning is different and given to an area in which stratified rock strata dip towards a central point, these strata possessing a centroclinal dip.

Basin recharge: The difference between precipitation and runoff plus other losses, i.e. that part of the former which resides as ground water, surface storage and soil moisture.

Battery of wells: Several wells in a convenient radius which are connected to a main pump for water withdrawal.

Belt of phreatic fluctuation: That mass of rocks in the lithosphere in which the fluctuation of water table takes place.

Belt of soil water: The upper part of the zone of aeration containing soil moisture.

Bernoulli's Theorem: Relating to flow in conduits, this asserts that if a perfect, incompressible fluid is flowing in a steady stream, then, neglecting frictional and eddy current effects, the total energy is constant.

Blowing well: A water well from which is periodically blown a current of air.

Borehole: A hole drilled from the surface or from a subsurface excavation into the ground in order to obtain geological data or for the drainage or abstraction of water or for access to hydraulic works, etc. In the UK, depths for tapping water may reach 600 ft or more. Diameters vary up to 40 in.

Borehole casing: A plain or perforated pipe of steel or some other material which is inserted into a borehole, often in loose ground.

Borehole log: A record, principally of the rock strata penetrated during the drilling of a borehole.

Bourdon pressure gauge: An instrument for measuring water pressure and pore water pressure.

Brackish: A word applied to water ranging from 1000 ppm up to the dissolved salt content of sea water.

Breathing well: A water well in which air is alternately blown out and sucked in, a phenomenon apparently related to barometric pressure.

Brine: A water having a dissolved salt content exceeding that of sea water.

Cable tool: A sharp chisel-edged bit utilised in drilling a deep well by lifting and dropping so as to break rock by impact, the fragments being removed by a bailer (a section of pipe with a foot-valve through which the cuttings enter).

Capillary action: A term applied to the movement of liquids due to capillary forces.

Capillary fringe: The belt of ground immediately above the water table, i.e. at the bottom of the zone of aeration and containing capillary water.

Carbonate hardness: Temporary hardness.

Catchment area: A land area from which precipitation drains into a reservoir, pond, lake or stream.

Cavitation: The formation of cavities during high speed pumping, resulting in corrosion of metal parts because of the liberation of oxygen from the water.

Cavity well: Sometimes termed a boulder well, a water well drilled into a thick aquifer comprising sand, gravel and boulders.

Chalk: The SE England Chalk is the most famous and largest aquifer in the UK. Interestingly, the rock itself is impermeable, but water can flow along fissures and wells put down in fissured regions give high yields.

Chezy Formula: An empirical formula relating mean flow velocity, V, hydraulic mean depth, R, hydraulic gradient, S, and coefficient, C, thus: $V = C\sqrt{(RS)}$.

Coefficient of permeability: The rate of flow of water through unit cross section of a medium under a hydraulic gradient of unity and at a specified temperature. Also known as coefficient of conductivity and coefficient of transmission.

Coefficient of viscosity: A quantitative expression of the friction between the molecules of a fluid when in motion. The capacity of a rock or soil to transmit water varies inversely with the coefficient of viscosity of the water.

Compensation water: Water which legally must be released from a reservoir in order to meet the needs of downstream users who received a water supply before a dam was constructed.

Cone of depression: This is the inverted conical depression in the water table round a well or borehole in which pumping is going on. Also known as cone of exhaustion and cone of influence.

Confined water: This is a term for artesian water used in the USA.

Connate water: Original water in the interstices of a sedimentary rock which was not expelled during consolidation. Also known as fossil water.

Darcy's law: This is used to determine the velocity of percolation of water through natural materials of granular type.

Deep well: One exceeding 100 ft in depth.

Depletion: Exhaustion of a water well caused by (a) excessive pumping by neighbouring wells, (b) pumping in excess of replenishment, (c) defective casing allowing leakage.

Dip: Maximum angle of inclination of any surface which may be natural or artificial.

Drawdown: The lowering of the water table in and around a well or borehole by pumping.

Dug well: One which is excavated by manual labour.

Effective porosity: The ratio of the volume of water in a pervious mass previously saturated with water which can be drained by the force of gravity to the total volume of the mass.

Effective velocity of ground water: The volume of ground water passing through unit cross sectional area divided by effective porosity of the material. Also known as field, true or actual velocity.

Effluent: Flowing out, flow of sewage from a process plant.

Electro-osmosis: A method of lowering ground water and especially applicable to silts. It accelerates natural drainage away from surface works and excavations.

Evapotranspiration: Loss of moisture from a soil by evaporation and plant transpiration.

Fault: A break in rock strata along which displacement of one side relative to the other has occurred parallel to the fracture.

Fault trap: A geological structure in which water in a porous deposit has been trapped by an impervious deposit thrown opposite it by a fault.

Field capacity: The maximal amount of water which can be held by a soil against free drainage.

Field coefficient of permeability: The coefficient of permeability at temperature of the water.

Field moisture: Term used for adhesive water (pellicular water, *q.v.*) found above the water table.

Fixed ground water: Water stored in rocks with fine voids.

Flow: The amount of water flowing in a pipe, aquifer, etc., expressed as volume per unit time.

Flowing well: A well in which the hydrostatic pressure of the water is sufficient to cause it to rise and flow out at the surface.

Flow line: Line shown in a flow net.

Flow net: A net of equipotential lines and flow lines intersecting at right angles.

Fluctuation of water table: The alternate upward and downward movements of the water table due to periods of intake and discharge of water in the zone of saturation.

Free ground water: Ground water which is not trapped or confined by an overlying impervious rock.

Fresh water: Water containing less than 1000 dissolved parts of salt per million parts of water.

Froude number: A dimensionless number expressing the ratio between influence of inertia and gravity in a fluid. It is the velocity squared divided by length times the acceleration due to gravity. In analysis of hydraulic models, the ratio should be similar in both model and full scale plant.

Gravitational water: Water in soils and rocks above the water table.

Gravity ground water: That water which would drain out of a rock in the zone of saturation assuming the zone and the capillary fringe moved downwards for a period, no water entered the area and none was lost except through the force of gravity. Water discharged from springs and that withdrawn from wells is gravity ground water.

Gravity spring: Water discharged at the surface from permeable beds under the influence of gravity.

Ground water: Water in the zone of saturation.

Ground water basin: A basin-shaped group of rocks containing ground water and with geologic/hydraulic boundaries suitable for investigation and description. A basin of this type normally includes both the recharge and the discharge areas.

Ground water budget: An estimate of water resources usually applied to a ground water basin or province. Recharge, storage and discharge are important factors in it. Also known as ground water balance.

Ground water dam: A subterranean impervious mass or a fault which prevents or at least impedes the lateral movement of ground water.

Ground water decrement: A decrease in ground water storage by withdrawal from wells, spring flows, infiltration tunnels, etc.

Ground water discharge: Discharge of water from the zone of saturation into bodies of surface water or on land.

Ground water divide: The line of maximal elevation along a ground water ridge where the water table slopes downwards in opposite directions.

Ground water equation: The balance between water supplied to a basin and the quantity leaving the basin.

Ground water flow: Part of stream flow derived from the zone of saturation through seepage or springs. Also the movement of ground water in the aquifer.

Ground water increment: The replenishment of water in the zone of saturation. Also known as ground water recharge.

Ground water inventory: An estimate of amounts of water forming ground water increment balanced against estimates of amounts forming ground water decrement for a particular area or basin.

Ground water lowering: Localised lowering of the water table so that excavations can be made in relatively dry conditions. It may be effected by wellpoints, *q.v.*

Ground water mound: An elevation formed in a ground water body by influent seepage.

Ground water province: Any area wherein the ground water conditions are everywhere similar.

Ground water recession: Lowering of the water table in a basin or area.

Ground water runoff: Runoff which existed partly or wholly as ground water since its last precipitation.

Ground water storage: Estimate of the amount of water in the zone of saturation. That stage of the hydrologic cycle when water is leaving and entering ground water storage.

Ground water storage curve: A curve which shows the quantity of ground water available for runoff at given rates of ground water flow.

Ground water tracers: These are chemical dyes or salts or compounds incorporating radioactive isotopes used to trace the source of water seeping into wells, shafts, tunnels or deep excavations. Radiotracers (as the last category is usually termed) are especially practical because they can be detected in very minute quantities.

Ground water trench: A rather narrow depression in the water table and resulting from effluent seepage into a stream, channel or drainage ditch.

Head: The potential energy of water arising from its height above a given datum.

Headings (wells): Small adits or tunnels excavated into the water-bearing rock formations in order to increase the yield of a well.

Held water: Capillary water, water retained in the ground above the standing water level.

Hook gauge: A piece of equipment designed to measure the elevation of the free surface of a liquid and comprising a pointed hook attached to a vernier which slides along a graduated staff. The hook is lowered into, say, water and then raised until the upward point just cuts the water surface. It is capable of measuring water level with considerable accuracy.

Hydraulic: Refers to the flow of liquids, particularly water, through pipes or channels.

Hydraulic conductivity: A term occasionally used for coefficient of permeability.

Hydraulic discharge: Loss of ground water by discharge through springs.

Hydraulic gradient: In a closed conduit, this is an imaginary line connecting the points to which water will rise in vertical open pipes extending upwards from the conduit. In an open channel, it is the free surface of flowing water.

Hydraulic models: A scale representation of a hydraulic structure which is geometrically similar at all solid–liquid boundaries. A resemblance to a prototype is desirable. The type of flow in both must also be similar.

Hydraulic permeability: The capacity of a rock or soil for transmitting water under pressure.

Hydraulic profile (aquifer): A vertical section of the piezometric surface from any given aquifer.

Hydrograph: A graph which shows level, velocity or discharge of water in a channel or conduit plotted against time.

Hydrograph, recession (normal recession curve): The curve obtained from specified lengths of hydrograph that represent discharge from channel storage or a natural valley after deducting base flow; the curve illustrating the decreasing rate of flow in a stream channel.

Hydrologic cycle: That series of transformations occurring in the circulation of surface waters to atmosphere, to ground as precipitation and back to surface and subsurface waters (see Fig. 1.1).

Hydrostatic pressure: The pressure at any given point in a liquid at rest; equals its density multiplied by the depth.

Impermeability factor (runoff coefficient): A factor enabling runoff to be calculated; the ratio of the direct runoff to the average rainfall over the entire drainage area for any storm.

Impermeable (impervious): Word used to describe a soil, rock or other substance permitting the passage of water at an extremely slow rate.

Induced recharge (aquifer): Recharge of an aquifer by inflow of stream water.

Infiltration: Slow movement of water through or into the interstices of a soil (see Figs. 1.1, 1.2).

Infiltration area (well): That area of water-bearing rocks penetrated in a well and which discharge water into it.

Infiltration capacity: The maximum infiltration rate of a soil or other porous material.

Infiltration coefficient: The ratio of infiltration to precipitation for a soil under specified conditions.

Infiltration rate: The rate at which water is absorbed by a soil or other porous material; varies with the infiltration capacity.

Influence basin (well): The basin-shaped depression in the water table around a well due to withdrawal of water by pumping.

Initial detention: That portion of rainfall not appearing as surface runoff or as infiltration during period of precipitation; it includes evaporation, interception by vegetation and depression storage (this last refers to the volume of water needed to fill all natural depressions in an area to their overflow levels).

Intake (well): Voids in a water-bearing rock through which water passes into a well.

Intake area (aquifer): The area of outcropping permeable rocks from which an aquifer is fed with surface waters.

Interception: That process by which precipitation is retained by foliage and vegetation prior to reaching the ground.

Intermediate belt: That portion of the zone of aeration lying between the capillary fringe and the belt of soil water, *q.v.*

Internal water: Subterranean water below the zone of saturation.

Interrupted water table: A water table with a difference in level near a fault or other obstruction to the lateral flow of water.

Interstices: Voids, *q.v.*

Interstitial water: Water contained within voids of a rock or soil.

Inverted capacity: The maximum rate at which an inverted well, *q.v.*, can remove surface or near-surface water by discharge through openings into deposits at its lower end.

Inverted well: A well in which the water flow is downwards; a recharge well.

Isobath (water table): A line on a plan connecting points at the same height or elevation above an aquifer or water table.

Isopiestic line: An imaginary line connecting points possessing the same static level; a contour of the piezometric surface of an aquifer.

Jetting: A hydraulic method of inserting wellpoints, *q.v.*, or piles into sandy material and utilised in situations in which a pile hammer could damage structure in the neighbourhood.

Juvenile water: Magmatic water or plutonic water, i.e. water derived from magmas or molten masses of igneous rock during their crystallisation or from lava flows as steam.

Lysimeter: An instrument for measuring percolation of water through soils and determining soluble constituents removed.

Magmatic water: Juvenile water, *q.v.*

Main water table: The surface of the zone of saturation, *q.v.* Also termed the phreatic surface.

Maximum capacity (well): The maximum rate at which water can be withdrawn from a well. Expressed in various ways, e.g. gallons per minute.

Menard Pressure Permeameter: An instrument for measuring directly the permeability of rock in a borehole.

Meteoric water: Water falling as rain or derived from snow, hail or dew.

Micropores: Rock voids smaller than 0·005 mm. If porosity in a rock is mostly microporous, the passage of water through it is inhibited.

Net intake: The quantity of water reaching the zone of saturation.

Non-flowing artesian well: A well which has tapped water with sufficient pressure to cause it to rise in the well but not enough to reach and overflow at the surface.

Normal depletion curve: A curve showing the normal loss of water from ground water storage.

Observation well: A well sunk to aid ground water investigations.

Open-end well: A well with a pipe form of lining where the water enters near the bottom through a screen or other arrangement within the lining.

Outcrop: That part of a rock appearing at the surface.

Overdraft: Any draft from an aquifer in excess of safe yield.

Overpumping: That situation in a well when the water pumped out exceeds the rate of replenishment from outcropping parts of an aquifer.

Pellicular water: Sometimes called adhesive water, this comprises water which is retained in a mass of soil as a result of molecular attraction, coating the soil particles and occasionally migrating from one to another.

Pellicular zone: The portion of the ground below the surface to which evaporative effects can penetrate.

Perched water table: The upper surface of a small water body above a main water table and retained in its elevated position by an impervious stratum.

Permeability: Capacity of a rock or soil or other substance to transmit water.

Pervious rock: One permitting the easy passage of water.

pH: An expression for the acidity or alkalinity of a solution, actually the logarithm of the reciprocal of the hydrogen ion concentration. A one unit change in pH value equals a tenfold change in the hydrogen ion concentration; 7 is the neutral point. Values above this indicate alkalis and values below it indicate acids.

Phreatic: A word applied to ground water and its concomitants. Thus, ground water may be referred to as phreatic water.

Phreatic wave: An undulation in the water table which moves laterally away from a zone where a large intake of water occurs in the zone of saturation.

Piestic interval: The vertical distance between two isopiestic lines on a map.

Piezometer: An instrument for measuring pressure head; normally a small pipe tapped into the side of a closed or open conduit and connected to a gauge.

Piezometric surface (potentiometric surface): The imaginary surface to which water will rise under its full head from any given ground water aquifer.

Plane of saturation: The water table.

Plutonic water: Juvenile water, magmatic water.

Pore pressure: The pressure of water and air in the interstices between the grains of a rock or soil mass.

Pores: Voids.

Pore water: Water occupying the interstices of rocks or soils.

Pore water pressure: The pressure of water in a saturated soil.

Porosity: The percentage ratio of the volume of voids to the total volume of a rock or soil sample. Thus

$$P = 100\frac{W - D}{W - S}$$

where P is the per cent porosity, W is the saturated weight, D is the dry weight, S is the weight of saturated sample when suspended in water.

Potential gradient (ground water): The rate of change in potential in a mass of ground water. Where no direction is specified, that of maximum gradient is taken.

Potential yield: The maximum rate at which water may be extracted from an aquifer throughout the foreseeable future, ignoring recovery cost.

Precipitation: Total quantity of water falling as rain, hail, snow and expressed as millimetres or inches of rainfall over a specified period. Moisture deposited as dew.

Prescribed rights (water): Legal title to the use of water acquired by possession and use over a long period without any protest from other parties.

Pressure head: Describes the water pressure in a system, expressible as N/mm^2 or psi or as metres or feet head.

Primitive water: Water trapped in the interior of the Earth since its formation.

Pumping level (well): That level from which water has to be pumped after the cone of depression has been established in the local water table.

Pumping test: (1) Water yield: quantities and water levels are recorded during the test period. The test pumping rate is usually greater than that at which water will be needed and covers a period long enough to show whether the yield can be maintained. (2) Water quality: taking samples of water during the test to determine by chemical analysis the major constituents and organic purity. Such tests may extend over 2 weeks.

Radial well: A well in which a number of strainer pipes are driven laterally into a water-bearing deposit in radial fashion from a main sump.

Radius of influence (water well): The radius of the circular base of the cone of depression formed in the ground water around a well when pumping is in progress.

Recharge of aquifer, induced: Flow of stream water into an aquifer.

Recharge well: An inverted well, i.e. one which conducts surficial water into an aquifer at shallow or moderate depth.

Rejuvenated water: Water of compaction and water released during metamorphism.

Resistivity method: A method of geophysical prospection in which direct measurements are made of the ratio of voltage to current when a current is forced to flow through the ground to be tested. The conductivity of a rock is governed by its water content and its salinity; where these values are high, conductivity is high and resistivity is low, and vice versa.

Reynolds number: A dimensionless number symbolised by R applied to fluid flow in a tube:

$$R = \frac{\text{mean velocity of flow} \times \text{pipe diameter}}{\text{kinematic viscosity}}$$

Riparian: Situated on or pertaining to the banks of a river or other water body.

Riparian rights: The right of a riparian owner to the use of a stream or other water bordering or flowing through his land.

Runoff: That part of precipitation flowing from a catchment area and finding its way into streams, lakes, etc. Includes direct runoff and ground water runoff.

Salinity (ground water): The content of totally dissolved solids (TDS) in the water; measured using the electrical conductivity method. For sea water, the content is approximately 3.5% (35 000 ppm).

Screened well: A cased well in which water enters through one or more screens and not through holes in the casing.

Seasonal recovery (*ground water*): The replenishment of water in the zone of saturation during and following a wet season with rise in level of water table.

Seismic method: A method of geophysical prospection in which the velocities of transmission of shock waves through the ground under test are utilised. A shock wave is initiated by the firing of an explosive charge at a known point or sometimes by impacting a sledge hammer on a metal plate, the shot. Thereafter, the travel time for selected waves to arrive at receivers (geophones) is recorded. Wave velocities can vary from 600 m/s for loose sediments to 6000 m/s for granite.

Shallow well: A well less than 100 ft deep.

Shot firing: Augmenting the supply of water in boreholes put down in deposits such as sandstone, chalk or limestone by detonating small charges of gelignite or dynamite in order to shatter and enlarge the fissures. Water increases of up to 300 % are feasible with optimal siting of the explosives.

Soil: The upper layer of earth on which rain falls and in which plants grow. Composed of mineral particles, some organic material and water and ranging from fine clay to gravel or boulders. The normal classification is into:

Grade	Dominant grain size (mm)
Gravel	2 and above
Very coarse sand	2–1
Coarse sand	1–0·5
Medium sand	0·5–0·25
Fine sand	0·25–0·1
Silt	0·1–0·01
Clay	Less than 0·01

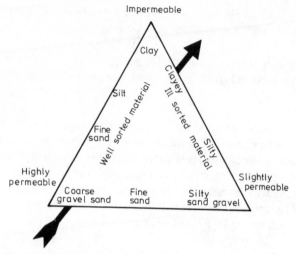

FIG. A.1. Classification of soils with respect to permeability. Arrow indicates direction of decrease in K.

In Europe, a category intermediate between fine sand and silt is recognised, namely schluff (German) or mo (Scandinavian). However, a classification based upon permeability is shown in the accompanying Fig. A.1.

Specific capacity (of a well): This is the rate at which water can be pumped from a well per unit of drawdown, *q.v.*

Specific retention: The ratio of the weight or volume of water which a soil will retain against the force of gravity to its own weight or volume. It can be determined after soil has once been saturated.

Specific yield: The quantity of water which a unit volume of soil or rock will yield after being saturated and allowed to drain under specified conditions. Expressed as a percentage of volume.

Storage: The impounding of water in an aquifer or in a surface reservoir.

Storage coefficient (aquifer): The ratio of (a) the volume of water taken into or released from storage in a prism of aquifer of unit surface area and the total thickness of the aquifer to (b) the volume of the prism of aquifer per unit change in the component of pressure head normal to that surface.

Storage of aquifer: The amount of water released from storage in an aquifer with a given lowering of head.

Strike: A line on a rock stratum at right angles to the full dip of that stratum.

Structure contours: Contours drawn on the upper surface of an aquifer and used in order to depict its form and depth.

Sub-artesian water: Artesian water which the pressure makes rise in a well, but not to overflow at the surface.

Submersible pump: Usually an electrical centrifugal pump capable of operating entirely submerged under water.

Subnormal pressure (water): A pressure converse to that in artesian water, i.e. related to confining beds in which water is being pressed downwards.

Subsurface water: All water which is subterranean, whether solid, liquid or gaseous.

Synthetic unit hydrograph: A unit hydrograph, *q.v.*, prepared for a drainage basin which is ungauged; its basis is the basin's known physical characteristics.

Tested capacity (well): The maximum rate of yield by pumping from a well without depleting its water supply. The capacity is determined by tests over a specified period.

Thermal spring: A spring which is fed by hot ground water, usually mineralised.

Total head (pump): The sum of the delivery pressure head, static pressure head and friction head.

Total porosity: This term includes capillary porosity, i.e. the small voids holding water by capillarity, and non-capillary porosity, i.e. the large voids which will not hold water by capillarity.

Total runoff: Includes both surface runoff and shallow percolation.

Tracer: A dye or a salt or another substance such as radioactive chemical compound which is employed to track the movement of water.

Transmissibility, transmissibility coefficient: The product of thickness of saturated portion of aquifer and the field coefficient of permeability.

Transmission coefficient: See coefficient of permeability.

Transmissivity: See transmissibility coefficient.

Transpiration: The emission of water vapour by living plants into the atmosphere, almost always in daylight.

Unconfined ground water: Ground water which is not restrained in its movement by an impervious or confining bed above or below.

Underground water: Ground water.

Unit hydrograph: In reference to a river, this is that hydrograph produced by an isolated storm of a given duration and of uniform intensity over the entire drainage area, which had an equivalent runoff of precisely 1 in (25·4 mm) of rain.

Unit weight of water: The weight of water per unit volume of water. Normally taken as 1 g/cm^3 or $62·4 \text{ lb/ft}^3$.

Vadose water: Water held in the zone of aeration.

Void: A pore or cavity between particles in a rock or soil mass which may be filled by air or water or both or by some other substance. An interstice.

Voids ratio: The ratio of the volume of voids to the volume of solids in a soil sample.

Water balance: The accounting for all water inputs and all water outputs within a system.

Water of capillarity: Pore water in rocks or soils above the water table.

Water table: The surface of the zone of saturation. Subject to fluctuation, it follows in a flatter form the profile of the land surface.

Water table contour plan: This shows contour lines on the water table.

Water table gradient: The inclination of the water table.

Water table level: That level at which the water table is encountered in borehole or well.

Water table profile: A vertical section of the water table in a specified direction constructed from a water table contour plan or from levels in wells or boreholes.

Water well: A well put down to provide a supply of water.

Wave of the water table: See phreatic wave.

Well: An excavation from the surface to obtain water ranging from shallow level to about 400 ft.

Well hydrograph: A graph showing fluctuations of water level in a well.

Well interference: That condition arising when the cone of depression of a well is affected by that of an adjacent well, resulting in a decrease in its yield of water. Such a diminution can be expressed as a lowering of the water table in feet or metres or alternatively as a reduction in yield.

Well log: A description of the rocks passed through in a well.

Wellpoint: A shallow well with a pump to drain a water-bearing soil around or along an excavation. A wellpoint strengthens ground and reduces the pumping necessary inside the excavation. Essentially, it comprises a tube of about 2 in (50 mm) diameter which is driven into the ground by jetting, *q.v.* The tube is fitted with a close mesh screen at the bottom and connected through a header pipe to a suction pump at the surface. On a major project, several wellpoints are sunk and connected to a common header pipe. Fine sands, of course, cannot be drained by wellpoints.

Well screen: A strainer inserted in a well when pumping water from a loose and gravelly deposit, functioning to exclude solid particles over a certain size but permitting fine sand to enter with the water and be removed.

Yield: Usually the economic yield of a well. Probable yield can be estimated if the permeability of the strata is known and a short pumping test is effected in order to give the different values of drawdown for successive increases in rate of pumping.

Zone of aeration: The ground above the main water table and extending to the surface. Comprising in ascending order the capillary fringe, *q.v.*, an intermediate belt, *q.v.* and the belt of soil water, *q.v.* Obviously variable in thickness.

Zone of capillarity: The ground above the water table containing water of capillarity, *q.v.*

Zone of saturation: The mass of water-bearing ground below the main water table and comprising solid rocks and incoherent materials.

2. Analysis of Water Quality with Reference to its Chemistry[a]

Chemical property	Usual water content	Effects (biological)	Effects (industrial)	General characteristics
Silica	<30 ppm	Nil	Nil	In waters with pH 6–8·5, insoluble
Calcium	10–100 ppm	Essential	Sometimes necessary	Loosens soils, maintains pH above 6
Iron	<1 ppm	Essential	Some industries have low iron tolerance	Solubility greater in water of pH 4·0
Magnesium		Essential	Sometimes necessary	Buffers undesirable toxics and loosens soils
Manganese		Traces are essential; larger amounts are toxic	Some industries have low Mn tolerance	Imparts objectionable taste to potable water
Aluminium	<0·1 ppm	Harmful to eyes at stated concn.	Nil	Insoluble below pH of 9·0
Sodium, potassium		Essential	Nil	Very soluble, packs soils thereby preventing aeration and nitrogenation
Chlorine		Traces are essential	Bad for the dairy, ice and sugar industries	Corrosive
Fluorine	0–4 ppm	Traces are essential	Nil	Corrosive and toxic as a gas

217

Chemical property	Usual water content	Effects (biological)	Effects (industrial)	General characteristics
Sulphate		Traces are essential	Bad for the dairy, ice and sugar industries	Very soluble, usually a pollution measure in rain and forms strong acid
Nitrate		Carcinogenic	Bad in dyeing and fermenting industries	Reacts with organic compounds and promotes excess plant growth when in excess; excess reduces permeability of soils
Alkalinity	Optimal range pH 5–8·5	Nil	Only of the individual constituents	Produced normally by hydroxides and buffers harmful pH changes
Hardness		Nil	Undesirable	Ca and Mg are the main constituents
pH DS (dissolved solids)	50–3 000 ppm	Not important More than 1 000 ppm bad for humans	Industry normally needs less than 1 000 ppm	Measure of acidity More than 2 000 ppm are bad for irrigation
DO (dissolved oxygen)	4–8 ppm	Aquatic fauna need specific quantities	Insignificant	Measure of pollution—the lower the DO, the greater the pollution Fish are normally adapted to specific free CO_2 ranges
Free CO_2		Small	Small	
Turbidity		5 ppm or less are recommended for human consumption		Normal quantities do not affect stream life

Temperature	Each life form has a specific range		Increase causes increase in organic growth and reduces palatability, i.e. warmer irrigation water promotes plant growth
Radioactivity— the relevant public water supply standards are: gross beta 1 000 pc/litre; radium 226 3 pc/litre; strontium 90 10 pc/litre; measurements are in picocuries per litre[b] for each radionuclide	Variable	Damage to photographic processes	Excess radiation is deleterious to biological systems

[a] Data derived from: SKINNER, BRIAN J., 1969. *Earth Resources*. Prentice-Hall, Englewood Cliffs, N.J.

[b] One curie is defined as that quantity of a radioactive isotope which decays at the rate of $3 \cdot 7 \times 10^{10}$ disintegrations per second. A picocurie is one million millionth of this amount.

3. Index of Relevant Organisations

Advisory Commission of Inter-Government Relations, 1701 Pennsylvania Avenue, NW, Washington DC, 20575.

American Public Power Association, Suite 830, 919 18th Street, NW, Washington DC, 20006.

American Society of Civil Engineers, United Engineering Center, 345 East 47th Street, New York, N.Y. 10017.

American Society of Limnology and Oceanography, Dep't of Oceanography, Oregon State University, Corvallis, Oregon, 97331.

American Water Resources Association, 103 North Race Street, P.O. Box 434, Urbana, Illinois, 61801.

American Water Works Association, 2 Park Avenue, New York, N.Y. 10016.

Australian Water Resources Council, Dep't of National Development, Canberra, Australia.

British Non-ferrous Metals Research Association, Euston Street, London NW1.

British Waterworks Association, 34 Park Street, London W1.

Federal Power Commission, 414 G Street, NW, Washington DC, 20426.

Food and Agriculture Organisation of the United Nations, Land and Water Development Division, Via delle Terme di Caracalla, Rome.

Geological Society of London, Burlington House, London W1.

Institution of Civil Engineers, Great George Street, London SW1.

Institution of Water Engineers, 11 Pall Mall, London SW1.

International Atomic Energy Agency, Section of Isotope Hydrology, Kärntnerring, Vienna, Austria.

International Water Supply Association, 34 Park Street, London W1.

National Water Well Association, 1201 Waukegan Road, Glenview, Illinois, 60025.

UNESCO, Place de Fontenoy, Paris, 7e.
United Nations, New York, N.Y. 10017.
US Geological Survey, Reston, Va 22092.
US Water Resources Council, 1205 Vermont Avenue, NW, Washington DC, 20005.
Water Research Association, Ferry Lane, Medmenham, Marlow, Bucks.
Water Research Foundation of Australia.

4. Some Representative Porosities and Permeabilities for Various Geologic Materials[a]

Material	Representative porosities (% void space)	Approximate range of permeability (gal/day/ft²; hydraulic gradient = 1)
Loose		
Clay	50–60	0·000 01–0·001
Silt and glacial till	20–40	0·001–10
Alluvial sands	30–40	10–10 000
Alluvial gravels	25–35	10 000–10⁶
Indurated		
Sedimentary		
Shale	5–15	0·000 000 1–0·000 1
Siltstone	5–20	0·000 01–0·1
Sandstone	5–25	0·001–100
Conglomerate	5–25	0·001–100
Limestone	0·1–10	0·000 1–10
Igneous and metamorphic		
Volcanic (basalt)	0·001–50	0·000 1–1
Weathered granite	0·001–10	0·000 01–0·01
Fresh granite	0·000 1–1	0·000 000 1–0·000 01
Slate	0·001–1	0·000 000 1–0·000 1
Schist	0·001–1	0·000 001–0·001
Gneiss	0·000 1–1	0·000 000 1–0·000 1
Tuff	10–80	0·000 01–1

[a] Data from: WALTZ, J. P., 1976. Ground water. In *Introduction to Physical Hydrology*, ed. Richard J. Chorley. Methuen, pp. 122–130.

Author Index

223

Subject Index

(This refers to the text only, not to the dictionary of water terms.)